DECADENT DIVORCE

Also by Ruth Derham

Bertrand's Brother: The Marriages, Morals and Misdemeanours of Frank, 2nd Earl Russell

To Be Frank: The Politics and Polemics of a Radical Russell

The Complete Winchester Letters of Lionel Johnson
(with Sarah Green)

DECADENT DIVORCE

SCANDAL AND SENSATION IN VICTORIAN BRITAIN

RUTH DERHAM

AMBERLEY

First published 2024

Amberley Publishing
The Hill, Stroud
Gloucestershire, GL5 4EP

www.amberley-books.com

Copyright © Ruth Derham, 2024

The right of Ruth Derham to be identified as the Author of this work has been asserted in accordance with the Copyright, Designs and Patents Act 1988.

All rights reserved. No part of this book may be reprinted or reproduced or utilised in any form or by any electronic, mechanical or other means, now known or hereafter invented, including photocopying and recording, or in any information storage or retrieval system, without the permission in writing from the Publishers.

British Library Cataloguing in Publication Data.
A catalogue record for this book is available from the British Library.

ISBN 978 1 3981 0894 3 (hardback)
ISBN 978 1 3981 0895 0 (ebook)

1 2 3 4 5 6 7 8 9 10

Typesetting by SJmagic DESIGN SERVICES, India.
Printed in the UK.

To Ian, and our present and perfect consent.

And gradually the secret imperious attraction of the Divorce Court grew clearer ... Here it was frankly admitted that a man is always 'after' some woman, and that a woman is always running away while looking behind her, until she stumbles and is caught. Here the moves of the great universal, splendid, odious game had to be described without reservation... The animal in every individual could lick its chops and thrill with pleasure... And the supreme satisfaction for the males was that the females were present, the females who had tempted and who had yielded and who had rolled voluptuously in the very mud. And they were obliged to listen, in their prim tight frocks, to the things which they had done dishevelled, and they were obliged to answer and to confess and to blush, and to utter dreadful things with a simper... As an entertainment it was unique... And only the superhuman and commanding mien of the judge, who was capable of discussing the foulest embroidery of fornication as though it were the integral calculus, saved the scene from developing into something indescribable.

Arnold Bennett, *Whom God Hath Joined* (1906)

The Macaulay of the future will find more valuable material for painting his picture of English society at the close of the Victorian era in the reports of the Dilke and Colin Campbell divorce cases than in any of the publications of recent years, and that altogether irrespective of the question of immorality.

W. T. Stead, Pall *Mall Gazette*, 4 February 1887

Contents

List of Illustrations	10
Introduction	12
Summary of the Matrimonial Causes Acts Governing Victorian Divorce	18
1 The Doors Open	20
2 Marry in Haste… (The Problem of Unsuitable Wives)	36
3 … Repent at Leisure (The Problem of Unsuitable Husbands)	60
4 Sex Crimes	85
5 Occupational Hazards	113
6 Working the System (Pt 1): Dodgy Detectives	142
7 Working the System (Pt 2): Scheming Solicitors	157
8 Working the System (Pt 3): 'Clean Hands', Collusion and the Queen's Proctor	171
9 Nullity Suits: The Letter of the Law	196
10 Issues of Access	220
11 The Doors Widen	245
Notes	259
Bibliography	273
Index	281

List of Illustrations

1. The New Royal Courts of Justice, *The Graphic*, 2 December 1882.
2. Central Hall of the Royal Courts of Justice, *Illustrated London News*, 9 December 1882.
3. 'Bench and Bar', supplement to *Vanity Fair*, 5 December 1891.
4. 'The Great Unmarrier' – Sir James Hannen, *Vanity Fair*, 21 April 1888.
5. 'Divorce' – Sir Charles Parker Butt, *Vanity Fair*, 12 February 1887.
6. 'An Astute Lawyer' – Sir George Lewis, *Vanity Fair*, 2 September 1876.
7. Sir Francis Henry Jeune, *The Sketch*, 12 November 1902.
8. Sir John Gorell Barnes, 1913 postcard by J. Beagles & Co., London.
9. W. T. Stead (undated photograph). (Library of Congress)
10. Marie Tempest photographed by Bassano in 1886 as the eponymous heroin 'Dorothy'.
11. Miss Edith Chester, *Illustrated Sporting & Dramatic News*, 16 October 1886.
12. Belle Bilton *c.* 1890, issued by the Kinney Brothers to promote Sporting Extra Cigarettes. (Metropolitan Museum of Art, New York)
13. The Howard de Walden Divorce Case, *The Sketch*, 15 March 1893.
14. *Ally Sloper's Half Holiday* cover, 19 March 1898. (Collection of Jason Lineham)
15. Virginia Mary Crawford, *The Sketch*, 15 January 1896.

List of Illustrations

16. Sir Charles & Lady Dilke *c.* 1884, *The Cabinet Portrait Gallery* (1894). (Rijksmuseum, Amsterdam)
17. Lord Colin Campbell, MP for Argyllshire 1878–1885, *carte de visite*.
18. Lady Colin Campbell *c.* 1883, *The Cabinet Portrait Gallery* (1893). (Rijksmuseum, Amsterdam)
19. 'The Divorce Shop', *Punch*, 11 January 1890.
20. Winnifrith family photograph, 22 December 1913. (Courtesy of Tom Winnifrith)

All images are from the author's own collection unless otherwise stated.

Introduction

On 1 May 1902, the 2nd Earl Russell rose in the House of Lords to propose that divorce by mutual consent be introduced into British law. Divorce for adultery had been on the statute books since 1857, but this new proposal so incensed the Lord Chancellor, Lord Halsbury, that he dismissed it out of hand, calling it 'an outrage' to the House and 'an insult' to their lordships personally. Such offence is unimaginable today, not least because divorce by mutual consent has now been the right of all British subjects for fifty years. And once divorce was accepted as a fact of life, it naturally led to calls to make the process as easy and painless as possible, resulting in the passing of the 2020 Divorce, Dissolution and Separation Act which took effect in April 2022. This Act, the last in a long line of reforms, did away with all fault in divorce and enables divorcing couples to end their marriages in a joint online application, without the need of a solicitor, in a vastly simplified process that at its least complicated takes six months to complete and for which a flat fee of £593 is charged. In its permissiveness, it is the absolute antithesis of Victorian divorce. The sentiments expressed by Lord Halsbury in 1902 were those of lawmakers who had begun debating whether or not and how divorce ought to be formally legalised fifty years earlier; and the Act they finally passed in 1857 was so controversial that the social stigma that clung to divorce well into the twentieth century was more-or-less written into it.

Understanding this helps us to appreciate both the level of scandal that unhappily married Victorians brought upon themselves and their families by choosing to divorce and the sensation caused

Introduction

by widespread press reporting of their suits. Critics of the 2020 Act have argued that it has been passed without principle or forethought, 'trivialising marriage' and reducing its status 'to that of a tenancy contract'.[1] One critic even suggested that it made the marriage contract 'less binding than a car lease'.[2] The same cannot be said of the 1857 Act. Strong religious principles lay at the heart of the 1850s divorce debates, which were heated and uncomfortable. Many officials of both Church and State then still believed that marriage was a sacrament or rite ordained by God and therefore indissoluble by man (a position still held by the Catholic Church today); and even those who did not were wary that legislating any divorce would ultimately lead to calls for its grounds to be widened; that it would become 'popular' and would thereby undermine the institution of marriage and destabilise the very fabric of the society built upon it.

The procedural changes introduced in 2020 were beyond Victorian lawmakers' imaginations, but its terms, it seems, were less so and as a consequence, to deter applicants, they created the least permissive law possible. They would only allow divorce for the most heinous of matrimonial offences – the sin of adultery – and put many bars in place to ensure that only those who approached the court with 'clean hands' could apply. Lesser marital crimes – cruelty or desertion, for example – were to be relieved with a judicial separation or the legal sanction to live apart without actually dissolving the marriage. But even these remedies were to be discouraged. Reconciliation at any point in the process – even at the eleventh hour and even to the point of a private arrangement between parties to live separately but remain married – was always preferable.

Neither were husbands and wives to be treated equally. A married woman had no legal identity in 1857 and in the patriarchal Victorian society were not considered the equals of men. Yet the 'double standard' created by the Act requiring women to prove offences additional to adultery in order to divorce their husbands, while husbands could divorce their wives for one single lapse, quickly became a bone of contention; as did the effective open invitation to the press to report cases heard by the court, which was tacitly encouraged in the belief that public exposure would deter other potential divorcees and keep the divorce rate low. Once the Act took effect, it horrified the establishment that, despite these restrictive measures, petitions 'flooded' into the court at a rate just shy of 300 a year in its first decade and that more than half of these were filed by women.

These are some of the tensions surrounding divorce that interested me when I began researching the life of Lord Russell for the biography *Bertrand's Brother* (2021). Russell was the grandson and heir of former British prime minister Lord John Russell and elder brother to the philosopher Bertrand Russell. Little known today, he was once notorious. It was his personal experience of the court – his involvement in one of the most scandalous divorce suits of the Victorian era – that led him to seek to reform the 'draconian' law that bound ill-suited people together for life. His suggestions were by no means unique. In 1643, Milton had expressed the opinion that it was 'a heinous barbarism both against the honour of marriage, the dignity of man and his soul, the goodness of Christianity, and all human respects of civility' to force two people to live together who could not be each other's helpmeet as God intended. His words and his appeal that 'some conscionable and tender pity' should be shown to those who had made a mistake in their choice of life partner were often repeated by reformers.[3]

But Russell's attempts – the first to be presented to the Lords – were easy to dismiss because of his history. Instead of giving credence to his suggestions, he was treated like the proverbial fox who had lost his tail; as a man who sought to make divorcees of everyone to lessen the shame of his own failure in marriage. The severity of this reaction led me to wonder what other individuals' experiences of the court had been like; to want to know more about the people whose unhappiness in marriage was strong enough to make them risk social ostracism, loss of financial security and permanent damage to their personal and professional reputations to achieve freedom from the marital bond; and to understand, where possible, the long-term impact of a brush with the court on their lives. To understand, moreover, the obstacles they confronted due to the manner in which the law was written and the methods employed by legal practitioners working within (and sometimes without) its limits. To peep, as it were, through the keyhole of the courtroom to see not just 'what the butler saw' but what the world was invited to see of the court's practice and to set this into context with the world outside it.

Introduction

The results of my investigations can be found in this book. The two dozen cases it features have been chosen, not for their legal significance, but for their social historical interest. Details of each have largely been taken from court files alongside a wide selection of newspaper reports and, where available, family correspondence. Underpinning this is an analysis of a systematic sample of suits filed with the court between 1881 and 1900. The featured cases were all considered press sensations at the time and all came before the court in the last twenty years of the Victorian era – a period of particular interest to me, when the opposing forces of decadence on the one hand and puritanism on the other flavoured tensions within society. It is a period that saw a shift in the general status quo exemplified by such phenomena as the changing status of women and by challenges to the authority of the aristocracy through the rising expectations of the professional and working classes, all of which affected and were reflected in the microcosm of society that found its way into the divorce court. Their stories were reported to the world outside by a national press that was itself then undergoing something of a revolution.

Coincidentally, the period also corresponds with the opening of the Royal Courts of Justice after a long and bitter campaign worthy of the feuds that would subsequently take place within its walls. There had been disagreements about the style in which the Courts should be built, the architect who should be given the honour of designing it and even its location. In the end, after the demolition of 450 houses and businesses, involving many evictions and relocations; after strikes and disputes within the workforce resulting in the importing of German stonemasons who had to be housed within the incomplete structure for their own safety, the monumental Gothic cathedral to civil law was erected at the juncture of the Strand, Fleet Street and the Inns of Court and was inaugurated by Queen Victoria in a lavish ceremony in December 1882.

The divorce court took up residence in January 1883. There, it was ordered, all divorce cases should be heard, no matter who the parties were or where they lived in England and Wales. For many potential divorcees, this stipulation became a physical bar to divorce. For us, it provides a relatable scene that retrospectively might be viewed as symbolic: a place where in a period of stable legal practice its permanent judges became the arbiters of

Victorian morality; where its barristers found a certain celebrity status providing an interesting cast of characters who will become familiar and where our imaginations might grasp something of the fascination our Victorian counterparts felt in reading about the great *causes célèbres* with their stories of decadence and disregard, arrogance and entitlement, in which the faults and foibles of the aristocracy were exposed to a growing and increasingly scathing middle- and lower-class readership; of the sagas of those of the professional classes who tasted the downside of celebrity for the first time; of the actions of less scrupulous and downright dubious characters drawn to the court for their own gain; and the pathos of working-class litigants able to scrape together enough money to extricate themselves from abusive, deserting or unfaithful spouses and the tragedy of those that could not.

Lord Russell once said that it was easy to legislate for human nature but hard to control it afterwards. Victorian legislators believed they had done their duty: that, by the law they had created, marital offences would be dealt with judiciously, divorce and separation rates kept low, public morality protected, and the interests of society and the state duly met. This book demonstrates that this was far from the case. It begins with the divorce court's first day of business in its new home at the Royal Courts and ends with an exploration of the complex and painful journey towards reform. But before our first litigant is introduced, a few words must be said about names and titles used throughout. It quickly became apparent that to avoid the excessive use of 'Mrs' this or 'Lady' that; or the confusion caused by name changes with marriage and title; or to avoid ending up with a glut of Williams, Fredericks and Henrys, etc., I must break with Victorian convention to find a means of referring to a diverse range of individuals whose stories are followed sometimes over a period of many years that was both consistent and readable. Therefore, after initial introductions are made giving full name and title, the women in this book are referred to by their given names, the men by their surname or the placename attached to their title at the point at which their petitions were filed and by which they were commonly known – 'Durham', for example, for the Earl of Durham whose actual surname was Lambton. No offense is meant by this decision and hopefully none taken.

Introduction

I must also express my gratitude to the staff of the various institutions visited in researching this book – in particular those at the British Library (London and Boston Spa), UCL and the Hertfordshire and National Archives; to Gail Savage, for answering various questions and recommending articles; to the current Earl of Durham for permission to view private family papers at Lambton Castle, Tom Richardson for a warm reception and Hester Borron for selecting appropriate material and discussing it with me; and to the various relatives of people featured in this book who gave up their time to share information about their ancestors: Tom Winnifrith; April Hoefner Orgren and David Banks (Harrison family); Darla Jean Couts (Josefa Rhodes); and to Chris Goddard for background information on Norfolk Bernard Megone and Jason Lineham for educating me about Ally Sloper and sharing images from his collection. Thanks are also due to commissioning editor Connor Stait and my copy-editor Alex Bennett and the team at Amberley Publishing for a sterling job; to William Bruneau for general encouragement and thoughtful conversation; and to Richard Williams LLP whose legal assistance with *Bertrand's Brother* remained invaluable.

Summary of the Matrimonial Causes Acts Governing Victorian Divorce

Annulment:
- A marriage could be annulled for being illegally or fraudulently contracted; or if the court ruled that one party was incapable of contracting the marriage (i.e. through imbecility or insanity) or was incapable of consummating it (i.e. through impotence).
- Any children of an annulled marriage would automatically be rendered illegitimate.

Divorce:
- A husband could petition to divorce his wife for one simple act of adultery.
- A wife could divorce her husband for *aggravated* adultery – that is adultery compounded by cruelty, desertion of 2+ years, bigamy or incest – or for the more heinous crimes of bestiality, sodomy or rape. By definition, rape was always that of another woman: a husband taking his wife by force was *not* considered rape.
- In all but exceptional circumstances, the husband must name the man who had 'defiled' his wife and make him co-respondent in the suit. He could elect to claim damages from the co-respondent for the pecuniary loss of his wife and injury to his feelings, reputation and family life. A jury decided the size of the award and the judge could make an order as to their use.
- A wife could not make her husband's alleged mistress a co-respondent and had no similar recourse to damages.

Summary of the Matrimonial Causes Acts

- These points collectively are commonly known as the *double standard*.
- A husband was not legally bound to financially support his divorced wife.
- An absolute divorce enabled both parties to remarry.

Judicial separation:
- Either party could petition the court for a judicial separation (legal sanction to live apart) for one or more of the following: adultery, cruelty, desertion of 2+ years.
- A judicial separation entitled a wife to alimony for life, but neither party could remarry during the lifetime of the other.

General terms:
- All cases were heard by a High Court judge in London.
- Either party could request a trial by jury. All jurors were men. For an additional fee, either party could request a 'special jury' made up of professional men in place of a common jury.
- The judge could make a custody order for any children of the marriage and an order for payment of costs. Usual practice was for custody to be granted to the innocent party and for the guilty party to be condemned to costs.
- Neither party must condone or connive in the marital offences of the other. The parties must not collude in the suit. There must be no undue delay in bringing suit. The party filing the petition must come with 'clean hands' – i.e. must not him-or-herself be guilty of a marital offence. Connivance, condonation and collusion were absolute bars to divorce; others were discretionary.
- Any divorce decree granted (decree *nisi*) could be made absolute on application to the court after six months, during which time the Queen's Proctor could investigate to ensure no rules had been broken. If he found evidence of wrongdoing he could file a plea with the court to have the decree rescinded.

Amendments:
- In response to a petition for restitution of conjugal rights, the court could order an absent spouse to return to the marital home. Until 1884, noncompliance was punishable by a prison sentence; after 1884, noncompliance within two weeks became legal desertion for which further relief could be sought.

1

The Doors Open

On the overcast morning of Thursday 11 January 1883, Mrs Ellen Elizabeth Gilder entered the Royal Courts of Justice. Was the thirty-four-year-old grocer's wife daunted to be leaving the relative safety of the Strand's busy thoroughfare to step into that brand-new Gothic palace of English law? The central hall of finished Portland stone that confronted her resembled a cathedral. Its vaulted ceiling towered some 82 feet overhead; its tessellated floor might have taken a hundred of her reluctant steps to cross; and, without any sunlight streaming through its lancet windows to brighten and encourage her, it must have seemed particularly cold and uninviting on that winter's morning, the court's first day of business. Strangers – mostly gentlemen and bewigged professionals in their sweeping black robes – huddled in tight groups conferring, or disappeared up shadowy stairways to first-floor galleries teeming with people none too certain as to where they should be. To compound matters, behind its highly polished façade much of the building was still unfinished and many courtrooms were therefore unusable. Misdirected litigants hurried along crowded unfamiliar passages to temporary chambers, adding to the confusion. To the uninitiated, nothing about the scene was welcoming. Frederick Inderwick QC – stalwart of the divorce court, whose name will often be repeated in these pages – later commented that the 'dignified and symmetrical' outward appearance of the building and the 'lordly proportions' of its hall which led apparently nowhere, with only wooden signboards pointing the way, produced, though unintentionally, an effect of 'great similarity to the system of judicature for which it provides a home': one of 'external beauty and internal confusion'.[1] Thus, whether Ellen had come alone or with some good friend, she may well have felt uncertain, anxious – emotions entirely understandable when one considers that her momentous purpose was to end her marriage contracted nearly seventeen years previously when she was but that age herself.

The Matrimonial Causes Act (1857), which governed her capacity to do this, was equally as hostile. Though its name might suggest otherwise, the Victorian divorce court dissolved marriages most unwillingly. Looking back at the situation that preceded it, while remembering that marriage, and therefore divorce, had always been the province of the Church, amply explains why.

Briefly then, from the Norman invasion onwards ecclesiastical courts had increasingly gained jurisdiction over family law. From the sixteenth century they'd practised largely in accordance with canon laws rewritten at the time of the Counter-Reformation when the Roman Catholic Church re-exerted its hold over Western Europe in the face of rising Protestantism. Marriage, as defined by the Catholic Church, was a sacred institution and therefore indissoluble – even by adultery, that worst of marital crimes, so severe as to have been literally written in stone. To Catholics, the Mosaic Law that stated that if a man found an 'uncleanness' in his wife he could write her 'a bill of divorcement' and send her away was overruled by Christ's teaching that this should not be regarded as a general principle. They held fast to the notion that marriage could not be dissolved without offending God.

In England and Wales (unlike Scotland) there was only one single attempt to overturn this with an impressively named document of 1552, the *Reformatio Legum Ecclesiasticarum*, which not only proposed legislating divorce, but endorsed widening its grounds to include cruelty and desertion. The untimely death of kings, however, and corresponding shifts from Protestantism to Catholicism and back again meant that it came to nothing.

Hence it was not until the late seventeenth century that a complicated, costly and time-consuming system gradually came into being that acknowledged the gravity of adultery but, in deference to the Anglican Church, necessarily and intentionally made divorce a legal but rare occurrence. By this system – henceforth referred to as the 'old system' – if a cuckolded husband wished to dispense with his wife he had first to prove her guilt in a common-law action known as *criminal conversation*. From this, he would be awarded damages payable by his wife's paramour. He could then apply to the ecclesiastical court for a divorce *a mensa et thoro* (literally, from bed and board), otherwise known as a judicial separation, which would allow him to live apart from her with the court's sanction. Only when both were granted could he apply for an Act of Parliament to terminate his marriage. Unsurprisingly, between the first parliamentary divorce in 1670 and the last in 1857, only 324 were granted, each taking anything up to three years to finalise at a cost of £1,000 to £5,000 depending on how vigorously they were defended. Wives had no comparable recourse. With no legal identity of her own, a wife could not claim damages for her husband's wrongdoing and could only approach Parliament if her husband committed the more serious offence of either incestuous or bigamous adultery. In the same period, only eight parliamentary divorces were requested by women (the first not until 1800) and only four were granted.[2]

The 1857 Act came about as part of a general overhaul of England's chaotic court system. It followed a royal commission proposed by Prime Minister Lord John Russell to enquire into the old system. The commission, headed by Lord Chief Justice John Campbell, sat between 1852 and 1853 and concluded that Parliament had stepped in often enough to set a precedent for divorce and recommended the establishing of a civil divorce court. The issue was hotly debated in Parliament and the resultant Act never intended to make divorce anything other than procedurally easier and therefore more affordable. It bound the new court to operate on terms 'as nearly as may be conformable to the principles and rules on which the Ecclesiastical Courts have heretofore acted'.[3]

Adultery, therefore, continued to be the only crime of sufficient gravity to sever the sacred matrimonial tie, and only then if perpetrated against a wholly innocent spouse. Any evidence to suggest that *both* parties might wish for a divorce or that *both* parties might have been unfaithful, or that one had in any way condoned the adultery of the other, immediately barred them both from any remedy. The Act also continued the unequal treatment of husband and wife but did give women greater access to divorce. This was considered a 'great concession' yet it came with strings.

The Doors Open

To pacify those who thought allowing women to divorce amounted to the opening of Pandora's box, it was decreed that a wife must prove *aggravated* adultery to secure her divorce – that is, adultery compounded by another crime, such as cruelty or desertion – while a husband continued to be able to divorce his wife for one single adulterous act. By the time of Ellen Gilder's appearance in court this 'double standard' had become a source of bitter contention. Those who justified it (not all of them men) did so in their belief that a wife's adultery was worse than a husband's. This was ostensibly because of the likelihood of her foisting spurious offspring on him, but equally it was considered unreasonable to expect a man to tolerate the thought of his wife having been possessed by another. 'No greater insult was ever offered to women,' wrote an incensed feminist in 1881, that the reverse was not given equal consideration.[4]

Ellen's legal position, then – like that of many women – was not strong. In 1866, when she was a seventeen-year-old tailoress working in a small family business in Norwich, she had married the grocer William Gilder, a thirty-nine-year-old childless widower. Shortly afterwards he had brought her to London, where he did well. By 1881 he had retired and the Gilders had moved from living above the shop in Marylebone to a smart villa in St John's Wood. Theirs was an apparently respectable middle-class existence, yet the marriage was childless and unhappy and William was allegedly abusive. There is no evidence, however, that he was also unfaithful. As such, Ellen's only legal option if she wished to escape him was to petition for a judicial separation on the ground of his cruelty. This would allow her to live apart from him with the court's sanction and receive alimony for life at a rate set by the court. It would not, however, give either of them the freedom to remarry during the other's lifetime. Ellen embarked on this path, but there was just one problem: how exactly does one prove cruelty when almost all such treatment goes on behind closed doors?

In the twenty-five years since the passing of the Act, in its former home at Westminster Hall, the court had heard roughly 300 causes a year from across the whole of England and Wales. Some 70 per cent of those that reached court were successful, and more than half of them were brought by women, who more often than not alleged cruelty or desertion or both. It was clearly doable, then. But given that judicial separations, for reasons that will become clear, were only half as likely to succeed, it cannot have been easy. Add the fact that each action, though considerably cheaper than under the old system, still came with a hefty price tag of anything from £50 escalating rapidly into the hundreds or thousands if defended, and it is probably safe to assume that Ellen would not have known anyone personally who had been through the process and could help her. She was, however, at perfect liberty, whenever mood and means took her, to attend court as a spectator – a popular Victorian pastime from which it was acknowledged she could have learnt much. Within three years of the 1857 Act, suspicions had been raised in the Commons that many court spectators were in fact unhappy spouses eager to learn how it operated, making it as much a 'school of divorce' as it was an arbiter of marital woes.[5]

The spectator's galleries of the two divorce courtrooms had limited capacity. One estimate suggests that each could seat only thirty comfortably. Still, almost every morning, senior court reporter Henry Edwin Fenn recalled, fifty or sixty people waited outside for the court to open. When high-profile cases were heard, so extensive were the crowds that it was not uncommon for the judge to order the expulsion of any but those with business there. In the body of the court, the majority of spectators were legal students, but in the gallery they were, to Fenn's mind, 'loafers' with nothing better to do than enjoy 'the free but morbid form of entertainment provided by the law for the amusement and diversion of gossips'.[6] Though tolerated rather than encouraged, their right to be there was upheld by the long tradition that all aspects of British justice must be seen to be done. For this reason too, court reporters were kept busy feeding courtroom fodder to Fleet Street. So, if the court's capacity or Ellen's dignity would not allow her to attend court to learn the ropes, extensive press coverage of the most remarkable cases was readily available.

The scope and style of reporting varied significantly. Establishment papers like *The Times* offered comprehensive accounts of remarkable cases as they unfolded with little or no comment.[7] 'Remarkable', in this context, meant cases of social prominence or legal significance. Cases involving the lower orders, who increasingly (though in very small numbers) petitioned the court, barely got a mention. Nevertheless, quite rightly, *The Times* is still regarded by historians as offering the 'fullest transcripts' of the largest number of cases.[8] Intentionally dry, they sought to inform but not entertain. Euphemisms were used to express the 'filthier' points of a case and anything prurient or offensive that was not essential to understanding was omitted completely. It was not uncommon to read in its reports statements like 'Medical Evidence was then heard' without any elaboration. Moreover, *The Times* held an undisguised attitude of disdain towards the court. Cases were reported because it was necessary but not commented upon because it was not: because cases 'bear on their face their moral or lesson'.[9] In this, *The Times* stood alone. Other 'serious' papers, like the conservative *Morning Post* and *The Telegraph*, had no problem passing moral judgement on cases but still produced colourless reports. It was their 'public duty to give a fair account of such public proceedings' but their 'equal duty to render reports as little offensive as circumstances permit'.[10] So much so that a hundred years later a descendent of *The Telegraph*'s then proprietor commented, 'Some of the unpleasant evidence is reported with such reticence as to be incomprehensible to the reader today.'[11]

Here, again, Fenn's memoirs give valuable insight into how this transpired:

> The public should know that what is published in the leading papers regarding unsavoury matter is the merest bagatelle compared with the details which were eliminated ... Every case is and has to be edited at the fountain source before leaving the hands of skilled reporters.[12]

A double layer of self-censoring was practised, therefore: first by the court reporter and then by each individual editor, all in the name of decency. However, the second half of the century saw something of a revolution in journalism that threatened to upset the status quo. The removal of newspaper stamp duty in 1855 and paper duty in 1861 resulted in a significant increase in obscure titles. Those like *The Divorce News and Police Reporter* (1861) were credited with increasing 'the flood of impurity' that poured into the public mind in the wake of the 1857 Act.[13] Their influence is hard to measure. Easier is that of the popular press which emerged with weekly papers such as *Lloyds's* (1842), *The News of the World* (1843) and *Reynolds's Newspaper* (1850) aimed at an increasingly literate working-class readership and priced accordingly. They quickly took a substantial share of the market, with mid-century circulation figures of around 50,000 as compared with 120,000 and 40,000 for the *Times* and *Telegraph* respectively.[14] The *News of the World* had the broadest ambition, to 'tell the truth to all and of all', while *Reynolds's* set itself apart from the rest through its republicanism.[15] By the 1860s its circulation reached 300,000. Then in 1896 *Lloyds's* became the first paper to sell a million copies. All these titles in varying degrees realised that sensational material – violent death, crime and 'aristocratic sexual misdeeds' – sold papers. For some, sensationalism also suited their political agenda. In *Reynolds's*, for example, it blended with 'radical socialism'.[16] When a divorce case involved aristocracy, the opportunity was never lost to take a swipe at the decadence of privilege.

Between the serious and popular ends of the scale, the late 1860s saw the emergence of society journalism with a range of weekly titles filled with gossip about aristocrats, sensational stories and scandals alongside social news. The most successful of these were *Vanity Fair* (1868), which invited readers in a distinctly satirical tone to 'recognize the vanities of human existence',[17] and *Truth* (1877), which led the rest of the field in stringing together 'chatty paragraphs' of rumours and facts that more sombre individuals considered 'hardly suitable for leading articles'.[18] Their content was written by and for those 'in the know' with a strong undertone of shared secrets. In this and the many other 'smart' papers that sprang up in the 1880s, gossip surrounding impending divorce cases was for the first time reported long before they came to court, heightening anticipation. *Truth* also incorporated an element of the investigative style of 'new journalism' accredited to moral crusader W. T. Stead following his arrival in 1880 at the *Pall Mall Gazette*, or 'PMG' as it quickly became known. Described as being 'imbibed with a Puritan sense of destiny and irrepressible energy', Stead strove to turn journalism into 'a potent political and moral force' and augmented the human-interest story with American-style interviews. Society papers did not report divorce cases in full. In fact they made a point of not doing so. Still, their choice comments were often repeated across the popular and provincial press; and in the PMG moral judgements from other papers were repeated to reinforce their own, providing the modern researcher with an important resource for understanding the social mores of the *fin de siècle*, albeit filtered through the most extreme puritan lens.

Finally, with the advent of the halfpenny evening dailies – most notably the colourful 'conservatively democratic' *Evening News* (1881) and the 'animated, readable and stirring' *Star* (1888), which competed with the already-established, decidedly middle-class but still satirical and 'unscrupulous' one-penny *Globe* (1803) and the vastly more conservative *St James's Gazette* (1880) – the melting pot of the British press eventually catered for every potential reader. Most evening papers provided hot-off-the-press sensational narratives from the divorce court in multiple daily editions akin in content and style to the weekly digests of the Sunday papers. They coloured them with descriptions of litigants' attire as if the trial were a grand social occasion and described their attitudes and demeanour as if they were the stars of the latest stage production. Barristers' witticisms were quoted and audience reactions inserted at key moments as '(laughter)' or '(sensation!)'. In short, these papers offered their readers as near a full courtroom experience as possible without their actually being there. They also reported sensational cases of litigants lower down the social scale and saw no contradiction in feeding readers' greed for titillation about the well-to-do before passing damning moral judgements on them after the verdict. So popular were these papers and so fundamental had the national newspaper become to every level of society that in Benjamin Rowntree's poverty budget of 1901, going without a halfpenny Sunday paper was considered 'one indication of deprivation'.

Several attempts to curb divorce court reporting across this period failed. As early as 1859, Queen Victoria had written to Lord Campbell (by then Lord Chancellor) to see if, having pushed the Obscene Publications Act through Parliament in 1857, he couldn't do something about the 'scandalous' character of newspaper reports that fell outside it and were 'most pernicious to the public morals of the country'.[19] Campbell replied that having tried and failed to introduce such a measure in the previous parliament, he was powerless to help. Other attempts throughout the late Victorian and Edwardian eras went the same way. The predominant view remained that press reporting – of all types – acted as an effective deterrent. Social stability was believed to be founded on individual and public morality and this deterrent was considered so necessary that salacious details of the immoral acts of the few continued to appear for the moral wellbeing of the many.

The net effect of all this on potential litigants like Ellen Gilder was twofold. On the one hand, daily reporting from the divorce court made divorce 'seem more natural, if not quite normative';[20] on the other, the publicity and moral judgement of the press which told readers how they should feel about the social implications of divorce was highly intimidating. As historians Jeffrey Weeks and Trevor Fisher have argued, the battle between the opposing forces of puritanism and libertinism that played out throughout the century had, by the 1880s, swung in favour of the puritans who were increasingly sustained by a succession of causes and scandals that had started mid-century with the debate on prostitution, continued with the fight for the repeal of the Contagious Diseases Acts and would crescendo with Stead's sensational 1885 exposé of the sexual exploitation of minors in the PMG. The resultant 'heightening awareness of deviations from sexual respectability' paved the way for 'a rigorous enforcement of respectable standards' which, Fisher argues, led directly to the downfall of politicians Charles Dilke and Charles Stewart Parnell after their respective brushes with the divorce court and, ultimately, Oscar Wilde's notorious libel trial and eventual imprisonment.[21]

Into this increasingly puritanical moral atmosphere, then, the Royal Courts opened its doors and within it, the divorce court provided grist to the mill of the puritan lobby. Into it walked Ellen with the moral tide against her compounding the enormity of what she was attempting to do. By initiating a separation from Gilder she risked her reputation and the possibility that she would never again be considered respectable. These social pressures might have given her pause: that they did not deter her is testament to how unhappy her marriage must have been. Armed with whatever knowledge she had gleaned from others' experiences against the weakness of her position, she took the most sensible action open to her: she employed the services of society solicitor George Lewis.

Lewis was fast becoming the most highly regarded divorce lawyer in London. Born in 1833 of Dutch-Jewish descent, he had been articled to the family firm Lewis & Lewis in 1850, becoming a partner in 1858 and, by this time, its sole practitioner. In 1867 he had married the beautiful and lively German-born Elizabeth Eberstadt who created a salon at their Portland Place home to rival those of the most renowned society hostesses. There, the Lewises entertained such distinguished guests as artists Burne-Jones and Alma-Tadema, stage sensations Ellen Terry and Henry Irving, *Truth* proprietor Henry Labouchere and, before he found himself on the wrong side of the law, the young Oscar Wilde. Lewis also counted the Prince of Wales among his friends and had advised the prince when, in 1870, he had been implicated in the Mordaunt divorce scandal. Though equally at home in the criminal court, Lewis found himself particularly suited to divorce practice and was a familiar figure at the Royal Courts in his habitual fur coat. It says much about his work in this field that his name is attached to more cases in this book than any other individual solicitor despite his recognised speciality being his ability to keep his clients *out* of court. In his 1911 *Times* obituary Lewis is described as audacious, often playing the game in defiance of the rules, with an encyclopaedic memory such that he never made notes and could therefore say with some assurance that his famous clients' secrets would die with him. His most famous epitaph came from Wilde, who said he was 'Brilliant. Formidable. Concerned in every great case in England. Oh – he knows all about us, and he forgives us all.'[22]

It was also said of Lewis that he was more like a shrewd private inquiry agent than a lawyer. It was this skill he put to work on Ellen's behalf. In the process of getting up her case he discovered that her husband had *not* been a widower when she married him, but that his first wife, Sarah, was still living and that they had never divorced. Ellen's prospects looked instantly brighter. Sarah was located and brought to London and the two women confronted Gilder in the presence of another solicitor, a Mr Lickfold. On 22 June 1882, Ellen filed a petition with the divorce court to have her marriage annulled on the basis of its illegality; at the same time, she had her husband brought up on a charge of bigamy.

The following day Gilder appeared at Marylebone police court. There, Mr Lickfold told the magistrate that Gilder and his first wife had married in Gargrave, Yorkshire in 1845 when they were both minors; that after seven years Gilder had abandoned her; and that twenty years later he had married Ellen 200 miles away in Great Yarmouth without first obtaining a divorce. When confronted by the two women, Gilder had greeted Sarah with a handshake and said he hardly recognised her. Later, at the police station, he claimed he had not seen her for thirty years and that her brother had told him she was dead. Without hesitation, the magistrate committed Gilder for trial at the Old Bailey, but proceedings there were short-lived. When the case was called on 31 July, the prosecuting barrister – Lewis's younger brother, Frederick – admitted they had insufficient evidence to proceed. The difficulty of proving beyond doubt that it was *this* man who married *this* woman nearly forty years previously was insurmountable. Gilder was found not guilty.

What might this mean for Ellen's nullity suit? A tense six months followed before her cause appeared on the list and Lewis greeted her at the Royal Courts with the advocate he had chosen to represent her.

Lewis had the pick of the crop when it came to barristers. Over the previous twenty-five years, a wiggery of more-or-less specialists had grown up around the court – some moving seamlessly between the divorce and other civil or criminal courts, others choosing to work solely within its bounds, becoming somehow not-quite-respectable outside it in the process. Then as now, the crème-de-la-crème were the Queen's Counsel that represented approximately 8 per cent of barristers, commanded hefty fees and were nicknamed *silks* for the rare fabric of their gowns that distinguished them from juniors. Working without the modern benefits of technology and forensics, each one employed his personality in the courtroom as much as his legal acumen, leaving behind an impression as distinct as his caricature in *Vanity Fair*. There was the 'manly' Charles Russell, described by his contemporaries as 'the embodiment of grit' and 'an elemental force', who apparently feared no one, had an imperious temper and was as contemptuous of his clients as he was intolerant of stupidity, folly, verbosity and affectation in his juniors.[23] It was said he rarely referred to his notes in court but told juniors he preferred instead to watch the game unfold until it was his turn to cross-examine. Then he would know exactly where to strike and would waste no time gently manoeuvring his witness to give away what he wanted to know, but would 'take him by the throat and drag him' where he wished him to be.[24] With his haughty look, noble brow, remorseless mouth and deep-set penetrating eyes it must have been a terrible sight to behold, but no guarantee of success for all that.

Russell's antithesis in temperament, appearance and technique, who by quiet persuasion was said to have won many a case a more boisterous barrister would have lost, was the aforementioned Frederick Inderwick. 'Somewhat gaunt of figure', bland of face and saturnine, Inderwick's courtroom manner was 'all courtesy, gentleness and sympathy'.[25] He was a master of both cross-examination and examination-in-chief. One of his clients said to be questioned by him was to feel 'like a swimmer who is supported in the water by a strong hand'; and with his 'insinuating, smiling personage' it was thought that his surgical skill at cross-examination must have made it 'almost a pleasure to the victim to have his motives and his mind laid bare under the operation'.[26] Moreover, Inderwick was so persuasive in addressing the jury that it was said a lady never knew how badly she had been treated until she heard him speak on her behalf. When he and Russell worked together – which they often did when a case called for two silks – they might well have been considered the late Victorian divorce court's dream team. It took someone with the stature of a 'great Victorian' to withstand them.

Such a man was Sir Edward Clarke, who was instantly recognisable by the distinctive bushy whiskers that framed his jawline and who was earnest and sincere if somewhat unimaginative in his approach. Clarke thought it 'better to be moral than amusing, and good-hearted than either'.[27] Though he had not Russell's flare he was more eloquent and could hold the rapt attention of the jury with a 'quiet and unimpassioned' summing-up that was so masterful it was often said 'the conclusion seemed irresistible'.[28] But he, in turn, had none of the playfulness that worked so well for others: Frank Lockwood, for example, who had a 'cheery audacity and breezy wit' and brightened many a courtroom's sombre atmosphere.[29] Described as 'a big, burly, healthy, nice-complexioned man, who remained a boy long after his years of discretion', Lockwood had originally been intended for the Church but became a barrister almost by accident, entering himself as a student at Lincoln's Inn on a whim when visiting friends who had long planned such a career.[30] His ebullient energy manifested itself in the courtroom in a peculiar habit of sketching the goings-on around him. Though serious about his business, whenever a humorous moment presented itself it would be transcribed onto his brief, into his notebook, even occasionally into the woodwork (so legend has it) in a hastily sketched caricature that fell from his pen and was left wherever it landed to be gathered up and prized, often by its subject. So popular were these sketches that in 1898, the year after Lockwood's death, a selection was published as *The Frank Lockwood Sketchbook*.

Lewis, at one time or another, briefed all these men and others who will appear in due course, such as the suave yet restive Henry James; the disarming Edward Carson; the gargantuan John Patrick Murphy; and the kindly and broadminded Henry Bargrave Deane, then a rising star of the court who would take silk in 1896 and become a judge in the division in 1905. Yet each of these was beyond the means of Ellen, a mere grocer's wife. Successful silks represented aristocrats, celebrities and the well-to-do. Their names appeared repeatedly in the press attached to the latest cause célèbre. Their fees reflected their status – Charles Russell's services being among the costliest. He had achieved an income approaching £15,000 per annum by 1881 when nominal annual earnings for solicitors and barristers in public pay collectively was estimated to be less than a tenth of that. On a similar footing, Edward Clarke, following his appointment as solicitor general, refused to take a brief for less than 100 guineas when a junior barrister might be retained for thirteen. On top of which a leader charged a 'refresher' of anything up to 50 guineas for each day a case continued.[31] Even if such extravagance were necessary for Ellen's cause it would have been beyond her means. As such, the advocate waiting with Lewis outside the courtroom on the morning of 11 January 1883 was the perfectly adequate and experienced 'senior junior' Robert Bayford, who had been called to the Bar in 1863 but did not take silk until 1885, whose father had been registrar of the probate court, and whose son would follow him into the divorce court.

The courtroom itself, where Ellen's fate was to be decided, had none of the magnificence of the central hall but was rather like its diminutive distant cousin in that it had a lofty ceiling and high lancet windows but was the size of a small village chapel and decidedly Nonconformist in decor. It bore the same unfussy oak panelling as all the other courtrooms – though each varied slightly in proportion and design – and row upon row of oak 'pews' where those with court business congregated. At the front, echoing the ecclesiastic configuration of altar, pulpit and choir stalls, were the raised bench, witness and jury boxes. A row of court officials sat beneath the judge's bench as if to defend him from the onslaught of the legal opponents in the well. In the heavens, looking down on the whole affair from the spectator's gallery, those who came to be educated or entertained might have been said to have the best seats in the house on a bright day, but on gloomy days strained their eyes through inadequate gas lighting (soon to be replaced with inadequate electric lighting) and shivered despite the architects', builders' and brand-new boiler's best intentions.

Sitting in judgment was Sir James Hannen, who liked simply to be called 'The President'. The division over which he presided was comprised of three courts: Probate, Divorce and Admiralty. It was a curious amalgam that had come about with the 1873 Judicature Act and was the source of much confusion. One QC quipped that he could think of no justification for it at all until he remembered that Venus rose from the sea! More likely, it was necessitated by there being insufficient business to justify family law having a division of its own, so admiralty was added as a makeweight. The decision had consequences, not least in the difficulty of appointing judges. Hannen – then the only permanent judge in the divorce court – was given the helm but could 'hardly be considered an authority on all things maritime'.[32] By 1883, when the division had grown sufficiently to warrant two permanent judges, this deficiency was remedied by Charles Parker Butt's promotion from the admiralty bar to the bench. Yet while Butt was on solid ground in the admiralty court, where he was very much considered a specialist in the field, he was all at sea in the divorce court where his dependence on the registrar's guidance did not go unnoticed. Moreover, while Hannen was complimented for being a worldly-wise, conscientious and painstaking judge, the epitome of judicial calmness and sobriety, who jealously guarded the tone of his court with a stern and impassive countenance more reminiscent of 'an earnest metaphysician than a judge', Butt was criticised for attempting to conceal a lack of worldliness and general discomfort with humour, allowing 'jesting about sin' from counsel, cracking mother-in-law jokes himself and making 'superfluous remarks and frivolous inquiries in the midst of unpleasant evidence': in fine, for being 'free from any kind of tact'.[33] He also gained a reputation for decreeing divorce 'on the most flimsy evidence', but whether one condemned or applauded this depended very much on one's moral perspective or where one sat in the courtroom.

At 11 a.m., with everyone in place, the court settled. Conspicuous by his absence was William Gilder, who had been subpoenaed but had not appeared. His absence was taken as an admission of guilt. Bayford rose and outlined the history of Ellen's marriage for the judge. Presumably Ellen gave evidence but the papers reported nothing of it, concentrating instead on Sarah's appearance. The stickler Hannen demanded proof beyond testimony that Sarah's prior claim had taken place as stated. Gilder's sister-in-law had attended the wedding, it was said, and would willingly sign an affidavit to the effect. On the strength of which Hannen decreed that Ellen's marriage was annulled and the whole business was dispatched before luncheon, leaving the president sufficient time to decree another in the afternoon.

For all the anticipation, for all the anxiety on Ellen's part, all the public fascination with the court and the numerous column inches dedicated to it in the press, this was representative of its normal business. Nearly half the cases due to be heard that session were on the undefended list – a figure that would rise to nearly 80 per cent by 1907 – by which time nearly 800 petitions a year would be filed and, it was estimated, an undefended case could be dispatched in fifteen minutes. For the most part these are not the cases written about, here or elsewhere. They are unremarkable in law and not newsworthy. Doubtless it was only the accident of Ellen's having been first on the list of 112 causes to be heard that session that we know about it at all. Yet such cases provide a necessary background to the working of the court and raise questions concerning behind-the-scenes practice. We might wonder what went on in Ellen's case. Gilder had been found not guilty of the criminal charge of bigamy yet his marriage with Ellen was found unlawful on this very ground. How had this happened? Was it simply that the substantiating evidence of Gilder's sister-in-law which clinched Ellen's annulment was insufficient to meet the higher standard of proof required by the criminal court? Or was it that the shrewd Lewis, acting in defiance of the rules, only brought the criminal action against Gilder in the first place as leverage to persuade him not to defend the divorce suit? The state of English law was then such that Lewis could well have ensured his brother was advocate for the Crown at the Old Bailey and the case allowed to fail – there being little superintendence of the majority of criminal cases.[34]

Either way, Ellen Gilder left the courtroom restored to the status of *feme sole* and the appellation 'Miss Smith', secured for the sum of £47 (payable by Gilder) and who-knows-what emotional cost. What happened to her thereafter is not known: she disappears from extant records as if into the London fog. It would be another year before Hannen would preside over a nullity suit of greater magnitude which would have scandalised the city were it not so comical. The 1884 case of Henry James FitzRoy, Earl of Euston – described by *The Times* as 'perhaps the most extraordinary case ever tried in the Divorce Court' – was such a curious puzzle, said *St James's Gazette*, that novelists like Wilkie Collins might wonder how they never came up with such a plot.

2

Marry in Haste… (The Problem of Unsuitable Wives)

> Then, the service began – rightly-considered, the most terrible surely of all mortal ceremonies – the service which binds two human beings, who know next to nothing of each other's natures, to risk the tremendous experiment of living together till death parts them …
>
> Wilkie Collins, *Man and Wife* (1870)

Victorians believed in marriage. It was the mainstay of their society and as such, it has been suggested, they had a collective moral duty to protect and preserve it 'even when the form and substance were wanting'.[1] A small minority cohabited without marriage, but as recent research by historian Ginger Frost reveals they were mostly those who were unable to marry or, like Ellen Gilder, found themselves 'accidentally' unmarried. Only very few cohabitees *chose* not to marry, either through indifference to social pressure – 'the very poor, those in "criminal" pursuits, and the parallel world of the demimonde'[2] – or as a protest against the institution. Protests were not for the fainthearted. Even H. G. Wells, who would become one of the most outspoken advocates of free love in the early twentieth century, married his second wife, Catherine, in 1895 because 'half our energy would have been frittered away' defying convention: 'We had no disposition for that kind of warfare.'[3] In 1881, a third of Britain's total enumerated population was married.

Essays on marriage and marital relations that appeared in the influential journal *Fortnightly Review* in the 1880s and 1890s demonstrate high aspirations for the institution. In 1881, feminist and educationalist Maria Georgina Grey recognised three types: marriage in which a man possessed a woman as his 'passive chattel'; marriage as a legal contract for perpetuating family where the wife was only the necessary instrument for this to be realised; and marriage as free choice, where husband and wife were bound together in 'the closest union possible to humanity'.[4] In England, she wrote, we aspire to the third and regard the first as savage. It was an opinion largely upheld by others – even the individualist anarchist Wordsworth Donisthorpe, who wrote in 1892 that the natural state of man is monogamous and that those partnerships that are based on love and respect will work and those that aren't won't. All these writers sought to improve the institution: the question was, how?

Some advocated making divorce easier so that early mistakes could be rectified and 'real' marriages entered into. Others thought this was not the answer. Author Sarah Grand thought increasing socialisation between boys and girls with 'honesty and honour' while simultaneously upholding society's disapproval of promiscuity would make the sexes more tolerant of each other.[5] Marxist and trade unionist Clementina Black suggested a higher standard of education for young women would make marriages more equal, raise their standard and diminish the probability of unsuitable matches – a view shared by George Gissing, author of an 1893 novel illustrating the hardships of spinsters aptly entitled *The Odd Women*, who complained that 'more than half the misery of life is due to the ignorance of women' as a result of their poor education.[6] All three of the female writers in *Fortnightly Review* agreed with earlier advocates like John Stuart Mill that equity in marriage was essential. Only the extreme feminist Monica Caird dared suggest dispensing with the institution altogether, while Donisthorpe put forward a radical proposal for year-long partnership contracts as a precursor or alternative to marriage. But in one opinion at least there was consensus: that divorce might be difficult, but contracting marriage in the first place was not. It was easy. Too easy. And parents and relatives who imposed little restraint on young lovers' propensity to marry in haste without due consideration, or forced them into socially advantageous marriages where there was little affection, were as much to blame when things went wrong as the law that frankly encouraged them.

Some of the reasons behind hasty marriages become apparent when they ended in divorce. Boredom, a desire to escape parental authority, money, status, familial pressure, societal expectation, necessity, lust, romantic love: all these are admitted. The law governing marriage was, and to a large extent still is, the 1753 Clandestine Marriages Act. It regulated a chaotic system in which makeshift marriages sometimes made it difficult to determine conclusively who was married to whom. It made no attempt, however, to lessen the scope of marriage, leaving large loopholes to enable the more determined to marry whomever they chose. By its terms, for a marriage to be legal, either a licence must be obtained from an authorised person or (by far the more popular route) banns must be read on three consecutive Sundays prior to a ceremony in an Anglican church in the parish where at least one of the couple lived and where they planned to wed. Minors – those under the age of twenty-one – officially needed parental consent, but because the Act didn't allow parents to impugn a marriage after the event if their objection had not been raised beforehand and didn't specify how long the betrothed couple need live in the parish before requesting banns, effectively 'a marriage by banns would be legal even if celebrated without parental consent and in a place where the parties were not known'.[7]

Historian Rebecca Probert has pointed out that where couples married on the Monday immediately following the reading of the banns their residency could be as short as sixteen days, making it almost as expedient (if not so romantic) as a flit across the border to Gretna Green to take advantage of even laxer Scottish laws.[8] This loophole helped Ellen Gilder marry at seventeen (nineteen, according to her marriage certificate) a so-called 'widower' twenty-three years her senior in Great Yarmouth, 22 miles away from her family home in Norwich, witnessed by her sister, who was only a year older than herself. The record of Gilder's request for banns shows they had both been lodging in Yarmouth for only three weeks before they married. The absence of Ellen's parents on the marriage certificate does not conclusively prove she married without their consent but the removal to Yarmouth is certainly suspicious. Furthermore, for the clergyman solemnising their marriage there was no risk. He could only be prosecuted for an offence if he 'knowingly and wilfully' married a couple despite parental opposition or solemnised it in any place other than where banns were read.

The subsequent 1836 Marriage Act, which legalised marriage in Nonconformist and Catholic churches and introduced civil ceremonies, did nothing to address this. All Church ceremonies were henceforth conducted by the same rules governing Anglican marriages and for civil ceremonies only a seven-day residency was necessary. Notice of the intended wedding was read out at three consecutive weekly meetings of the Poor Law Guardians in place of banns unless the sum of £3 were paid to negate it. No further legislation concerning marriage was passed until 1929 when Parliament raised the marriageable age from fourteen for males and twelve for females to sixteen for both.

Hence, when Henry James FitzRoy – grandson of the 5th Duke of Grafton, eldest son of the then Earl of Euston and ensign in the Rifle Brigade at Woolwich barracks – decided at age twenty-two to marry a well-known twenty-nine-year-old courtesan named Kate Cooke there was little his friends could do about it. At first, the couple had thought to marry in London and FitzRoy secured a licence accordingly. It seems they then thought better of it and eloped instead to Worcester where, on 29 May 1871, they married by banns in the parish church in the presence of the bride's solicitor, Edward Froggatt, and a church official.

Kate's past was decidedly colourful and known to FitzRoy when they married. She had been born in Ireland in 1842 in Portlaoise, County Kildare. Her father, John Walsh, she variously described as an editor and a gentleman but there is no evidence he was either. Little is known of her early years, but her life in the public eye began after she emigrated to Scotland where she joined Cooke's Royal Circus as an equestrian performer. For a while, she was the mistress of equestrian juggler and soon-to-be proprietor, John Henry Cooke. In 1863, complaining of Cooke's maltreatment, she absconded with commercial traveller George Manley Smith, whom she married on 6 July in Glasgow before returning with him to Birmingham, where he was based. The relationship was short-lived. In April 1864, Smith abandoned Kate. She took to the stage, becoming a dancer in the Midlands music halls before eventually making her way to London. There, she moved into a house in Pimlico notorious as a 'house for gay women'. She became friendly with a Madam Rosalie Bernstein who supplied her with quality clothes and took her to venues such as the Holborn Casino and the Argyll Rooms in Haymarket where she introduced Kate to gentlemen. Kate was not short of admirers. Between 1866 and 1869 she was 'kept' by several – one of whom took a house for her at 14 Victoria Grove, Kensington. When she heard she had been widowed – that George Smith had died on the SS *London*, which sank off the Bay of Biscay en route to Australia on 11 January 1866 – she thought of marrying a colonel, and perhaps would have were it not for FitzRoy, whom she met in 1870, entertained at her home and married the following year.

By this time she had moved from Victoria Grove to Montpelier Square – a move necessitated by the death of her former patron and, to some degree, by a high-profile court case early that year. In January 1870, Kate had been sued by a Mr Charles Ochse for non-payment of an account totalling £665 12s 4d and had appeared before Mr Justice Blackburn at Westminster County Court. Ochse, it transpired, was the husband of Madam Bernstein and a dealer in 'fancy articles' from a premises at 166 Piccadilly, where Kate had been his customer since 1865. The bill was for clothing, accessories and items purchased to furnish her Kensington home, all supplied on credit on the understanding that she was a widow with an annual income of £1,000. Despite having been told her husband was dead, Kate defended the action by claiming coverture – i.e. that she was a married woman and her husband was therefore responsible for the debt (a perfectly legal consequence of a wife becoming a husband's chattel on marriage which was done away with by the Married Women's Property Act, 1882). She also contended that the goods were supplied for 'immoral purposes' at inflated prices.

This bold defence meant Kate had to admit earning her living as a prostitute. This she did in open court, before judge and jury, without shame or apology. Her frank responses in the witness box – that Ochse had accompanied her and Madam Bernstein to the Argyll Rooms and seen her leave with men; that he had seen her with men in her house; that the gentleman who had taken the Kensington house for her had been into Ochse's shop and paid £200 cash down for furnishings for her; that she used to meet gentlemen at the plaintiff's house 'almost daily' – along with her indignant complaints at Ochse's exploitation in overcharging her for such items as two chemises (£5 12s), a velvet jacket trimmed with chinchilla (£35), a silk quilt (£7 7s), six French underpetticoats (34s 6d each – twice the amount she could get them for elsewhere), to say nothing of the £25 she was charged for a velvet mantle she could have bought at Swan and Edgar's for £7, and £6 10s for an ivory-handled parasol (which, the judge himself commented, was costly indeed if there was nothing remarkable about it) – all earned her the admiration and sympathy of the patriarchal press. The real scoundrels, said *The Telegraph*, were those who made their living 'on the ruin of the bodies and souls of the fallen' by inflating prices of goods she was 'compelled to buy to traffic her beauty'.[9] Frankness also won her the case. The law would not help anyone recover a debt for items knowingly supplied for immoral purposes; and letters produced by Kate and written by Madam Bernstein proved to the jury's satisfaction that Ochse knew.

That FitzRoy lost caste by marrying such a woman goes without saying. Had he kept her for pleasure, nothing would have been said. Her enchantments, as with many of those who inhabited the demimonde, were obvious: she was medium height, with fair, almost golden hair; she dressed well and with good taste and was said to have the most agreeable manners. Seven years older than FitzRoy and considerably more worldly, the *Western Mail* condescendingly suggested that she had ensnared him and he had married her from a mistaken sense of honour. His father's opinion can best be understood by his actions. The earl, realising that for Kate to have claimed coverture her former husband must still be alive, threatened to prosecute for bigamy. Investigations, however, all pointed to Smith's demise aboard the *London*, so, instead, Euston took advantage of the tempestuous nature of his son's marriage to encourage him to take a government position in Australia. The FitzRoys continued to live together unhappily on-and-off for four years before Henry took his father's advice and in 1875 set sail. There he remained until 1881, rising through the ranks of the Adelaide Rifles to become lieutenant-colonel. To all appearances, Kate was left to fend for herself.

Appearances, however, can be deceptive. At the time of their marriage FitzRoy had settled £10,000 on her, which paid dividends on which she could live. Marriage settlements among the well-to-do were then customary. Usually they would be negotiated between the fathers and direct the manner in which the young couple's portion of the family fortune could be spent. In this instance, the document was drawn up to Kate's advantage by her solicitor, Froggatt, and a local Worcester official named Mears. It was unfortunate for Kate that Froggatt turned out to be untrustworthy. As soon as Mears died in 1877, he began syphoning money from the fund to the tune of £8,000 before he was caught. Kate's notoriety increased further when she was forced to prosecute and her whole sorry story was repeated again at the Old Bailey in December 1879. Froggatt tried to claim he was acting on FitzRoy's orders but was disbelieved. He had a history of deception and was found guilty and sentenced to seven years' penal servitude.

Throughout this, Kate was supported by her next-but-one paramour. She had taken up with notorious nightclub owner Jack Coney after FitzRoy left, but since 1879 had been with successful racehorse owner and bookmaker George Haughton. Their liaison was no secret: Haughton had an extravagant lifestyle, counting many celebrities among his friends, including the stage sensation Florence St John and her producer husband Marius Duplany, with whom he and Kate socialised in London and holidayed in Monaco. As such, FitzRoy might easily have divorced her had his own hands been clean. As they were not (and Kate knew it) the family was forced to negotiate with her. It was rumoured among FitzRoy's Australian friends and confirmed by Kate in an 1884 press interview that FitzRoy's uncle – the 6th Duke of Grafton – offered her a further £15,000 to not defend a divorce suit. But money interested Kate less than status. The duke was childless and in fragile health. When on 21 May 1882 he passed away, FitzRoy's father acceded to the title and FitzRoy, as eldest son, inherited the courtesy title Earl of Euston. Kate became his countess. Immediately, a sense of urgency around their marital status grew. Bad enough a courtesan should become a countess; God forbid she should ever become a duchess! The family needed a plan. They instructed George Lewis who put his investigative powers at their disposal and once again came up with the solution.

Lewis discovered that the duke had been right: Kate's former husband was still living. George Manley Smith *had* emigrated to Australia, and a Mr G. M. Smith *had* gone down on the *London*, but it was not he. It was a George *Maslin* Smith – a brewer from Sheffield – who had left his wife, Sarah, at their Bedford home on 1 January 1866 and never returned. Sarah was located and agreed to testify. George *Manley* Smith was also discovered – a far harder task – living in Wellington, New Zealand, where (for reasons best known to himself) he passed as 'George Johnstone' and worked as an accountant to a firm of auctioneers. He was enticed to return to England in exchange for payment of his fare and on 31 January 1883, Lewis filed the petition *Euston v. Euston orse Smith*[10] for annulment of the marriage on the ground of it being bigamous, just as he had for Ellen Gilder.

The case came before President Hannen on 4 April 1884. In the interim it had been eagerly anticipated in society journals. *Modern Society* had caught wind of it in January. 'There is nothing in the wildest romance ever written to exceed the wonders of the case,' it claimed, adding rather cattily that Euston had had plenty of time to repent ever marrying 'Kate Cook, *alias* Mrs Fitzroy, *alias* Lady Euston, more familiarly known in London as Lady Euston Square'.[11] In March, *Life* perpetuated the hype: 'Surely nothing more intensely dramatic has ever been reported in the law books,' they suggested. The prospect of a commoner coming forward to stake his prior claim to a countess was mouth-watering. With superabundant anticipation they questioned what Smith had been doing all these years and why he had not claimed her before; and asked how the whole affair was viewed by the Palace given that the duke had been equerry to the queen for many years?[12] How scandalous! How marvellous!

By 11 a.m. the courtroom was packed. Hearing the case alongside the president was a 'special' jury of professional gentlemen whose services had been secured for a guinea each a day at Euston's instance – the theory being that men of this class would be more understanding of his situation than those of a broad-spectrum 'common' jury. When the formidable Charles Russell QC rose to give his opening address on Euston's behalf, he did not mince his words. The lady, he told the court, was a courtesan (sensation!). She had been a courtesan when Euston married her and she had returned to that notorious lifestyle, living with divers men since he separated from her. She was now living with a betting man whom it was not necessary to name.

If those assembled were shocked to hear a QC call a countess a courtesan in open court it was nothing to their surprise when Russell then announced in mocking disbelief that he understood her defence would be, not only that she did not know the man who would take the stand and swear he was her true husband, but that if indeed he proved to be so it was of little consequence because *he too* had been married at the time he had made her his 'wife' (more sensation!). It was, in fact, a double suggestion of nullity of marriage.

Could such an incredible state of affairs really be believed? Moreover, could it be proved? Russell was convinced it could not. He called Euston to testify as to his marriage, followed by George Manley Smith to swear to his prior claim. Smith identified Kate in court as his wife. Russell then called Mrs George *Maslin* Smith to testify as to her husband's demise and closed for the prosecution confident that his case was made and was watertight. During Manley Smith's cross-examination, Kate's counsel – Mr Inderwick, again – tried and failed to discredit him by drawing attention to the fact that he had deserted his first wife, Mary Ann, before marrying Kate and then had abandoned Kate to elope to Australia with another woman, travelling under his deceased wife's maiden name of Johnstone. To Russell, such information was irrelevant and not this, nor even the admission forced from Manley Smith that the only evidence he'd had that he was a widower before he'd married Kate came from the verbal communication of a friend of Mary Ann's that she had died three weeks earlier, dented Russell's confidence. Mary Ann Smith was dead, and nothing the defence could do would resurrect her.

As such, when Inderwick rose and announced that he would open the case for Kate by saying that she had seen Smith in court and heard his evidence and was now convinced that this *was* the man she had married, and that her defence, therefore, would rest solely on their proving that Manley Smith was already a married man when he went through the marriage ceremony with her, Russell interjected that such evidence, if they could produce it, would take him completely by surprise. Surprised, therefore, he must have been. Inderwick produced in succession first Manley Smith's eighty-three-year-old mother to identify her son and prove he had written to her from Australia as 'George Johnstone', followed by Mary

Marry in Haste... (The Problem of Unsuitable Wives)

Ann's siblings, both of whom testified to being at her bedside when she died on 9 June 1867, four years *after* Kate married Smith. With that, Euston's case collapsed. The jury annulled Kate's marriage to Smith, making her legally single when she and Euston had married. Euston's petition was dismissed with costs.

No wonder the press described the story as stranger than fiction. Correspondents around the world treated their readers to jocular accounts of the hearing, passed moral judgements of their own and with bated breath speculated as to what would happen next. *The Globe* wrote that it seemed as if the whole case had been brought without the least notion that it might fail. If so, then Kate's solicitor, Thomas Duerdin Dutton, had for once 'out-Lewised' George Lewis! Yet Lewis had another card to play. That very day he filed a second petition, this time for divorce on the ground of Kate's adultery with George Haughton. Kate hit back with a page-one interview in the *Evening News* in which she slammed the family's 'inhuman' treatment of her, claiming Euston had left her penniless and that she had subsisted on the late duke's charitable offerings of poultry and vegetables which ceased entirely when Euston emigrated. Such treatment, she said, was making her 'spiteful' and, she claimed, she held a trump card. A fortnight later, she played it. Her answer to Euston's petition was a counterclaim that he had deserted her without cause, thereby conducing her adultery (if any); and further, that he had committed adultery with Mrs Georgina Sheridan, a 'singularly beautiful' specimen of the demimonde, once known as 'Baby' Thornhill, and a particular friend of Kate's.[13] With that, the Eustons' cause was stalemated – at least as far as the court system was concerned. If further negotiations followed, it was strictly behind closed doors.

And that, roared the 'Thunderer', was as it should be. Would that it had never darkened the doors of the divorce court in the first place. In a very rare instance, this case moved *The Times* to issue a harsh warning to the establishment: that the increasing fashion for the aristocracy to wash their dirty linen in public – especially in an arena *The Times* considered largely the province of the lower-middle class – would be their undoing:

> In these democratic days ... nothing certainly would sap more swiftly the authority and the influence of the English aristocracy

and all connected with it than the notion that its tone of morality had lowered ... What [the average Englishman] cannot tolerate is the sight of names which they have been accustomed to regard with respect surrounded with low and contaminating associations.

This extraordinary statement was more than a comment on aristocratic involvement in scandal: it reveals the wider level of ruling-class anxiety caused by the rising influence of the professional class and the expectations of the the working classes. But it was interpreted by more democratically minded papers, not as censure of the behaviour itself, but as a warning to them not to be caught out. Wrote the *Western Mail*, if Euston had been *more* immoral and not married Kate, but kept her as his mistress and cast her off when he was sick of her, he could have become 'the respectable and respected head of a virtuous household, instead of having the finger of scorn pointed at him by all the journalists in the kingdom'. It was one of a raft of similar opinions voiced about the decadence of the aristocracy excited by the case. The republican *Reynolds's Newspaper* said Euston's escapades were unlikely to inspire the populace with 'profound feelings of reverence for inherited titles'; the radical *Referee* went further, speaking of the public's 'growing impatience' with the 'gross and flaunting immorality' pervading society. In the face of so much criticism, the society paper *The Graphic* did its best to reassure its readers that Euston's unfortunate mésalliance did not spell the end of the class system as they knew it: 'Some great noblemen,' they declared, 'have taken wives much below them in station, and have done very well for themselves.'

Euston would never be one of them. Kate died in 1903 and in the nine years left to him thereafter he would not remarry nor produce a legitimate heir. In fact, his notoriety would only increase when in summer 1889 he wandered – unwittingly, he claimed – right into the middle of the Cleveland Street Scandal. This scandal centred around a male brothel which Euston said he had only been enticed to enter after being handed a card advertising '*Poses Plastique*', which he thought would be a live tableau of female nudes. What he actually saw, he claimed, appalled him and he left immediately. Still, a rent boy named him as a habitué of the brothel – a fact reported in the *North London Press* in a pivotal exposé. Euston sued the editor for libel to clear his name, but fears that the government was behind a cover-up to protect the identity of others involved did nothing to allay public perception that decadence was rampant throughout the establishment – a perception that only increased when news broke that another 'fast' young aristocratic would soon be dragging his family's name and reputation through the divorce court in a suit that would outstrip even Euston's for sensationalism.

William Frederick Le Poer Trench, Viscount Dunlo, aged twenty, had on 10 July 1889 secretly married a young lady he first met at the Corinthian Club at the end of April. The club, situated just off St James's Square, offered its clientele 'fun in the early hours' and 'a delightful absence of ceremony with respect to both sexes'.[14] Like The Gardenia and the Lyric Club it was the sort of place where a gentleman could rub shoulders with sportsmen, theatre impresarios and minor actresses. In that free-and-easy environment it was a high crime to call anyone by his patronymic. Dunlo was therefore known there as 'Fred', and gambling, dancing and dinner were the order of the day. Dunlo's father – the 4th Earl of Clancarty – disapproved. He suspected his son was falling into bad company. The first he knew it was anything more serious than that was when he opened the PMG on 16 July. In the bottom-right corner of page four – unmissable in following news of the dramatic scenes at the Parnell Commission that day – ran the announcement 'Lord Dunlo marries Miss Belle Bilton'. Belle – or Miss Isabel Maude Penrice Bilton, as the faithfully reproduced copy of the marriage certificate identified her – was no courtesan, but neither was she respectable. She was 'the much-photographed music-hall artiste': one half of the Sisters Bilton – beautiful, wistful and with a cultivated innocence which found expression in such choruses as 'We're fresh, fresh as the morning, sweeter than new mown hay'.[15] The younger sister, Flo, might have been: a horrified Clancarty would discover that Belle was not.

Dunlo was immediately summoned home. He went at a time when his father was absent, treated it all as a jolly good joke with his mother, then returned to his hotel, thought better of it and wrote a full confession to Clancarty which, far from proclaiming his love for Belle and his determination to stick by her, abandoned her to her fate. 'Tell me all you wish me to do,' he wrote, 'and I will faithfully do it.'¹⁶ What his father wished was to separate him from the clutches of an adventuress who had obviously beguiled him beyond reason. He hastened plans he had been hatching for Dunlo to see out his minority on the other side of the world and demanded he embark forthwith for Australia with a companion named Robinson. He further instructed George Lewis to have Belle watched. By autumn, Clancarty was convinced he had all the evidence necessary for his son's divorce. He had Lewis draw up a petition and send it to Dunlo in Sydney for signing. In an accompanying letter Lewis wrote that they had no doubt Belle had committed adultery with a Mr Isidor Emanuel Wertheimer 'who has been daily in her company since you left'. He asked Dunlo to consider Belle's 'previous history' and do justice to himself and his family by signing the petition.¹⁷ On 17 December, Dunlo did as requested and on 4 March 1890 – only six weeks after Euston's libel hearing – it was filed with the court.

Within days, news of the impending trial was reported and some intriguing titbits appeared in the relatively new 'smart' paper *Hawk*, which had begun as *The Bat* in 1885 and been rebranded by Augustus Moore (brother of writer and critic George Moore) in February 1888. Moore claimed that after signing the petition Dunlo had written to Belle saying he had no intention of parting with her and that he had signed the paper 'when in a state in which he was not responsible for his acts'. It might seem folly, wrote Moore, but was not at all unlike Dunlo who had formerly told friends he had been drunk when he proposed to Belle, had asked them to retrieve an incriminating letter and when they had done so, married her anyway! 'As I have always contended,' continued Moore, 'he is a nice boy, but what can you do with an irresponsible creature who has been tied to his mother's apron strings all his life, and suddenly finds himself "alone in London"?' Moore then wrote that while Wertheimer claimed his innocence and many might hope he was, Moore himself did not: he thought Belle better suited to Wertheimer whose 'devotion should really be rewarded'. In such a manner Moore established himself as 'one who knows' and concluded enticingly, 'There is sure to be lots of fun.'¹⁸

Much of that fun was generated by Moore himself. The following month, he revealed he had received a letter from Dunlo written on his way home from the antipodes disputing Moore's previous assertions. Moore published a lengthy extract from it which earned him a strongly worded reprimand from Belle's solicitor questioning both his right to do so and the letter's veracity. Moore published that too and followed both with a piece suggesting the unfortunate Wertheimer had since been made co-respondent in *another* divorce suit. As such, when the case finally came before the president and a special jury on 23 July 1890, anticipation was high and the courtroom so crowded that at the end of the second day the president ordered that for the remainder of the trial there was to be no further admittance once seats were filled unless the latecomer could prove he had business there.

Leading for the prosecution once again was Charles Russell, this time with Inderwick supporting. For the defence, Belle's solicitors – Messrs Wontner and sons, who had made their name as solicitors to the Metropolitan Police and the Treasury but had expanded into divorce litigation and in this instance also represented Wertheimer – had instructed the ebullient Frank Lockwood for Belle and senior-junior Charles Frederick Gill for her supposed lover. After relaying the circumstances of the Dunlos' meeting and marriage, Russell's opening speech was largely taken up with impugning Belle's character and establishing a long entanglement with Wertheimer that preceded her marriage to Dunlo.

Belle was the daughter of a former staff sergeant in the Royal Engineers who had been pensioned in 1880 and subsequently worked as a clerk at the Greenwich Telegraph Works. She had taken to the stage at fourteen and had worked more-or-less consistently in London and the provinces since. Early in 1887, when she was not yet twenty-one, she had met a twenty-nine-year-old married man named Alden Carter Weston. Weston had told her he was an army officer and seemed financially flush. He'd set Belle up in a house in Victoria Street. But in February 1888, Weston and four others were arrested for misappropriating £50,000, tried at the Old Bailey, found guilty and sentenced to eighteen months' imprisonment. It was while Weston was in prison that Belle met Wertheimer at The Trocadero. Within a fortnight she had confided in Wertheimer that she was pregnant by Weston. Wertheimer chivalrously took a house for her – Farleigh Lodge in Maidenhead – and there she lived under his protection until after her confinement on 29 July 1888. The son she gave birth to was registered as Weston's child and named 'Isidor' for Wertheimer. Following her confinement Belle's health was poor and Wertheimer took her and the child to France where they stayed in the same hotels in Trouville and Paris. When they returned to London, Wertheimer took an apartment for Belle in Hanover Square and a large villa for himself at 63 Avenue Road, Primrose Hill. In February 1889, the child's health became a concern and Wertheimer offered his villa to Belle. She lived there under his protection until she married Dunlo.

In spring 1889, Wertheimer argued with his family and on 19 April was sent by them to New York. Russell described Wertheimer's father as a well-known Bond Street bric-a-brac dealer. It was a rather disparaging depiction. Isidor's grandfather Samson had arrived in London in 1830 'a ragged, barefooted Jewish boy, penniless, unable to speak English, and alone' but had become wealthy, first by making and selling knick-knacks, then by dealing in quality curios known as *objets de vertu* and, ultimately, antiques and fine art.[19] By 1890, the standing of Messrs Wertheimer – which by then included Isidor's father and uncle – was such that they were able to purchase £50,000 worth of paintings from Lord Sackville; and when Samson died in 1892 he left an estate worth nearly £400,000. Russell was equally disparaging concerning Wertheimer's argument with his family, claiming Belle was its cause: Isidor, he claimed, had been sent to New York by his father who disapproved of their growing attachment. Isidor said he was sent on business and that he'd argued with his family because they thought he was unfairly favoured in his grandfather's will. Either way, he was in America at the time when Belle and Dunlo met and returned on 18 July 1889 to find her married, soon to be abandoned. He continued to assist Belle as she moved from one apartment to another in the months that followed, was constantly in her company, and eventually, in September 1889, moved her back into his Avenue Road villa.

No one disputed that Wertheimer was in love with Belle or that she had lived in comfort at his expense in a well-furnished house, with servants and a carriage-and-four at her disposal. No one disputed either that she seemed to have inducements that made men rather foolish over her. Wertheimer said in evidence that he had greatly admired her from the moment they met and had asked her to marry him on several occasions, the last of which was in a telegram from New York. Belle, in her evidence, said she'd shown this to Dunlo who had dramatically announced, 'You are not going to marry him; you are going to marry me' and may well have secured the licence as a result. And several of Dunlo's love letters, couched in the most affectionate terms, were read to the court; as was his confession to his father in which he said he had not been drunk when he proposed to Belle but had been 'rather off my head during the last few months' – a condition for which Belle was in no way responsible. Even Wertheimer's coachman, called to give evidence as to whether he had ever seen his master's arm around Belle's waist in the carriage, replied (to everyone but the judge's amusement), 'Yes, what I should have done myself!' The only thing that was disputed was whether Wertheimer had always acted as respectfully towards her as he claimed. With her history, the naming of her child and her acceptance of Wertheimer's patronage speaking against her, it must have been with a confidence akin to that in Euston's cause that Russell called his first witness.

That witness was Dunlo, described by *The Star* as tall, slim, beardless and elegantly attired in the latest fashion in frock-coats which only enhanced his awkward gait. In the witness box he admitted he had married Belle without parental consent even though he was financially dependent on his father and had then returned to his father's house as if nothing had happened. He had then spent three nights with Belle at the Victoria Hotel the week after they married during which time he'd promised he would take her to Australia with him even though he knew his father would never allow it. On the last night he'd told her he would be leaving without her. He claimed he thought she commanded an income of £1,000 a year and could manage, therefore, quite well without him, but was forced to admit the information came from gossip. Further, he admitted he had signed Lewis's petition and an affidavit swearing to its veracity while not believing a word of it and had written to Belle to tell her so. He claimed he had assumed the petition would not be used straightaway and had therefore returned it signed to a solicitor named Robinson, the brother of his companion, with the instruction that further evidence must be forthcoming before it should be filed. He had then written again to Belle, not mentioning the petition but saying all would be well and expressing relief that his father had now begun to pay his debts which were 'as innumerable as the hairs on his head' (laughter). In such a manner, Dunlo appeared weak-willed (or as Russell would later concede, not 'endowed with high intellectual attainments') and to have completely underestimated his father's wrath.

Such impressions were magnified by his father's appearance the following day. Clancarty – proud, dark-haired and 'utterly devoid of sympathy' – answered questions put to him under cross-examination with devastating candour. Asked whether he had told Dunlo that if Belle went abroad with him he would utterly refuse to have any more to do with him, he replied, 'Oh, yes.' Asked if he thought leaving Belle without her husband's protection would increase the likelihood of her falling into immorality, he said that now Lockwood mentioned it he thought it 'extremely probable' (laughter). Asked if he did not care, he answered, 'No.' Asked if it was not the case that Belle had written to him asking if she might see him to clear herself of these unfounded charges, he did not respond. Asked if he ever gave her the chance to meet the charges, he said, 'I had nothing at all to do with her.' Instead, he chose to interpret Dunlo's confession as an expression of regret and instructed Lewis to get Dunlo out of the marriage 'in any way he could'. Asked by Mr Gill if he knew that this meant Belle was shadowed by detectives continually for three months, he coolly replied that he did not know what Gill meant by 'shadowed'; and when Gill clarified that it meant having her every action watched every day without relent, Clancarty answered that he did know: he had authorised it and informed Dunlo of it and the responsibility for it was therefore his son's.

This admission, Gill later told the court, indicated that the Clancarty family had done all they could to hound Belle into temptation to perform the single act of adultery Dunlo needed to rid himself of her. Their ability to prove she had succumbed depended on the credibility of the private inquiry agents chosen by Lewis to watch her. Here too, Lewis had his pick of a growing number of keyhole detectives, many of whom were down-at-heel characters employed to dig up dirt by any means. In this instance (and many others) Lewis's choice was a still semi-respectable former detective inspector with the Metropolitan Police named George Clarke, whose private inquiry agency kept three generations of the family busy. The youngest, George's grandson Granville Clarke, aged nineteen, entered the witness box first. Granville opened his notebook and proudly reported that he had watched Belle every day between 20 July and 17 October 1889. He recalled dates on which he had seen her dine with Wertheimer at the Savoy and Bristol Hotels; the numerous occasions on which he had seen them alone together in the public dining room at the Café Royal; the one occasion on which he followed them from the Empire Theatre to the Café Royal, which they did not leave until midnight; the innumerable times he had seen Wertheimer's carriage outside Belle's apartment in Conduit Street, and afterwards in Bennett Street when she removed there, and how they frequently travelled together in Wertheimer's carriage to Avenue Road. It would have been a damning indictment had not Lockwood, when he rose to cross-examine, asked to see Granville's notebook and after thumbing through it asked, was it original? No, replied Clarke: he had copied the entries from his original book into this one about a fortnight previously and had then destroyed the original. His reason for so doing was that there were other cases in the book that he wished not to be seen. Lockwood objected to the evidence being used; the president sustained the objection.

Next up was the young detective's father, Henry John Clarke, forty-three, who had been given the responsibility of following Belle by Clarke senior and who had shared the task with his son. The most important thing Henry had seen was a 'tussle' at the window of 63 Avenue Road when Belle had leaned out to call a cabman and Wertheimer had pulled her back. They had struggled for a few minutes, apparently larking, and Wertheimer had 'caressed' her and then kissed her. Lockwood asked to see Henry's notebook too, only to discover that this was not original either. The original was at home. The president, somewhat irritated, sent him to get it. When Henry returned, the judge, by now thoroughly exasperated, discovered that what he called 'the original' was no better: Henry was in the habit of jotting down what he had seen on scraps of paper and transferring them at a later date to save him having to carry the book around. When Lockwood pointed out that he could see nothing about a kiss in the book anyway, Henry replied that that was something he carried in his memory (laughter).

Lewis and Russell must have despaired at the ineptitude – more so because their troubles were not over. The discrediting of the detectives meant they were forced to allow Dunlo's friend,

Marmaduke 'Marmy' Wood, to take the stand. Wood had only come forward on the third day of the hearing after reading reports of the trial – something that was not uncommon and sometimes, court reporter Fenn observed, 'altered the entire complexion of the case'.[20] Whether for better or worse, in this instance, remained to be seen. At first, it seemed Wood's evidence favoured the prosecution. He had seen Belle at Plumpton Races with Wertheimer. She had led Marmy to believe she was fond of the man and had told him Dunlo would win his case easily if it came to court. Surely, Belle would only speak to Wood in such a manner if she had something to hide? Russell must have congratulated himself on the good fortune of Wood's appearance. But Lockwood had the means of his undoing. In cross-examination he asked if Wood had not been at the Lyric Club the evening before he came forward, bragging that he too had been unduly intimate with Belle before her marriage? Moreover, that his friend Lord Osborne had too? And that Osborne and Dunlo had tossed a coin for Belle and Dunlo had won? Wood, who had strutted into court the previous day full of 'theatrical mannerisms', quailed under a tirade of questions, first denying he had said such things, then admitting he could remember saying one thing but not the other. When it was put to him that he had either lied in a public club or was now lying in the witness box, Marmy (said the PMG) simply smiled vacuously, 'aimlessly stroking the place where beard and moustaches ought to have grown', and cut so sorry a figure that Lockwood declared himself done with him and the 'miserable creature' left the box and almost immediately the court.

It was a weak point for the prosecution to end on; and when Lockwood rose to address the court on Belle's behalf he led with a damning attack on Wood and the breed of young gentlemen who hung about nightclubs and thought it amusing to toss a coin for a woman, thinking nothing of her reputation. It was an attack continued by Gill who produced a letter from Belle to Dunlo which revealed that Wood had pursued Belle even in Dunlo's absence, inviting her to sup with him and saying he knew Dunlo would not mind. Gill followed it with an assault on Clancarty's tactics and Dunlo's acquiescence, saying if chastity was the duty of the wife, protection and moral support was that of the husband. The family had done worse than leave her with neither: Wertheimer's character was purer than either of theirs. Such posturing was all very well, countered Russell in his closing address, but rather neglected the real substance of the case. In emptying 'their vials of wrath ... over the devoted head of Lord Clancarty' the defence had missed the point that Clancarty had acted as any responsible father would and ignored the fact that Belle and Wertheimer had acted in a way that could not reasonably be explained except with the hypothesis of an improper connection, which was all the law required. It was a valiant attempt to justify Clancarty's conduct which, after the event, was almost universally condemned: by *The Times* at one end of the scale as 'a piece of sharp practice' and by *Reynolds's* at the other as 'sheer unadulterated blackguardism'. Between counsels' opposing addresses the jury had heard from Belle and Wertheimer themselves and, as a consequence, any ambiguity in their relationship was quickly dispelled.

Belle spent the greater part of the fourth day and the morning of the fifth in the witness box. Her charm on the stage she demonstrated to the court. For this performance the popular press marvelled at her pretty gown of French grey cloth 'with a lot of corrugated flummery on the arms, a cross-over arrangement from the right shoulder to the waist and a lot of silver embroidery'. From a pink-flowered black hat, a thin veil fell lightly over her face which she removed when she entered the box to reveal her ashen beauty. Altogether, said *The Star*, it was a nice, artistic costume, prettily and becomingly set off by her denial in toto. The quiet, dignified manner in which she responded frankly to Lockwood's examination and the pleading tone adopted in response to Russell's persistent enquiry as to why she had suffered Wertheimer to 'dangle' at her heels – 'My husband did not look after me, so what was I to do?' – won her the understanding of the court.

But the real star was Wertheimer, who convinced court and press alike that his actions throughout had been motivated by chivalry and sentiment in equal measure but not lust. He had willingly provided for Belle and allowed her to name her child 'Isidor' in recognition of what she called 'his kindness' without interpreting it as encouragement or ever overstepping the bounds. Only once before her marriage had he put his arm around her waist 'much to her annoyance'; afterwards, he would never have insulted her in such a manner. It is possible to imagine from the evidence of Belle's sister Flo and her husband, and their older sister Violet, who followed Wertheimer into the witness box and all spoke of being frequent guests at Avenue Road, of trying to prevent Belle's marriage to Dunlo and in acknowledgement of Wertheimer's devotion and forbearance, that Wertheimer might have hoped that, despite protestations to the contrary, Belle might one day relent and consent to be his wife. If so, his performance in court was doubly magnanimous: he had nothing to gain by her winning but potentially much to lose.

After a six-day trial, it took the jury only fifteen minutes to find Belle and Wertheimer not guilty. The spontaneous applause that greeted the verdict was suppressed by the president who dismissed the petition with costs. On the Strand, traffic came to a standstill as hundreds of people gathered to see Belle leave court. Men clambered onto omnibuses to catch a glimpse of the star. Hats and handkerchiefs were waved and cheers of 'Bravo, Lady Dunlo!' went up all around. The following evening, Flo performed at the Trocadero a chaste ballad containing the refrain 'he lost it' and referring to a man 'sorry he got married' with a subtlety of suggestion that was not lost on its audience and was greeted with rapturous applause.

In the days that followed, the press dissected the case and speculated on the Dunlos' futures. The barristers were praised for their performances. Said the PMG, Lockwood's cross-examination of 'Marmy' Wood was excellent at short notice; Gill had fought like a man determined to win and Russell had made the best of a bad case, considerably weakened by Wood (to whom Russell actually referred in his closing address – and *The Times* reported it – as one of those 'unhealthy fungi' that sprang up around music halls and suchlike). On Sunday 5 August, the *Irish Times* published an interview with Belle given at a Dublin hotel. Their readers no doubt rejoiced to hear that she and Dunlo had reconciled and Dunlo had shaken hands with Wertheimer. Belle's career was also advantaged: the Trocadero, London Pavilion and Royal Theatre all sought to sign her at £100 a night if she would leave her current engagement that would see her tour Belfast, Edinburgh and Newcastle before returning to Drury Lane for the Pantomime Season.

And Clancarty? How was he? Said the *Dundee Courier*, it must have stuck in his craw to have to pick up the bill for the trial 'only to behold his hopeful heir rushing to congratulate his spouse'.

Marry in Haste... (The Problem of Unsuitable Wives)

And so it must. The 'roaring success' of Belle's tour and reports of Dunlo's frequent presence in various theatre boxes 'beaming at all and sundry' as his wife delighted fans from the stage contrasted sharply with personal attacks on Clancarty in the press. Only Augustus Moore defended him, saying he had done his duty as a father and anyone who said they would not do likewise was either 'a drivelling idiot or a liar'.[21] Once again, Clancarty's actions best betrayed his feelings. On 12 August 1890 – less than two weeks after the verdict – he rewrote his will. On 29 May 1891, he died. Though there was nothing he could have done to prevent Dunlo inheriting his title and the settled Irish estate of some 27,000 acres in east Galway and south Roscommon, he had cut him completely from inheriting anything from his personal estate, valued at £53,823.

Most modern accounts prefer to leave the story there: a fairy-tale ending in which the hard-hearted earl dies, his wronged son takes his place and his beautiful leading lady, from humble origins, leaves behind an adoring crowd to become Countess Clancarty, mistress of Garbally Court, afterwards often to be seen in her carriage in nearby Ballinasloe where she would 'dazzle the inhabitants with the extravagance of her turnout'.[22] 'I am home,' sighs Belle in the closing words of Nuala O'Connor's fictional adaptation of the story, *Becoming Belle* (2018). Such an ending obscures the fact that the Dunlos' married life was not without difficulties. The estate Dunlo inherited was nearly bankrupt. He was forced to contest Clancarty's will and in 1893 was awarded £6,000 and some of his father's belongings, but he would be plagued by financial difficulties and bankrupted on several occasions. Belle allegedly struggled to adapt to her new role. Her trips to Ballinasloe have been interpreted as attempts to relieve the tedium of their austere Galway lifestyle and a means of consoling herself from the inescapable truth that she was 'never really accepted by the Ascendancy world'.[23] Children were born – three sons and a daughter – but what became of Belle's first – young Isidor – between the hearing and his emigration to Canada in 1914 is unclear. His namesake – the chivalrous Wertheimer – was dropped by the Clancarties a year after the trial when his fortunes changed and Belle was named principle creditor in his bankruptcy proceedings. When she died from cancer in 1906, aged forty, a sympathetic press expressed the hope that her later years out of the public eye and in the 'affectionate and tender comradeship' of her marriage had finally brought her some peace.[24]

The flavour of press reporting in both these cases was typical. Atypical was *The Times* choosing to comment in both instances. Its criticism of Clancarty was no less a warning to the aristocracy than its observations made in relation to Euston. A father had an 'honourable obligation' towards his son's wife, it said, 'however mortifying the alliance may be to his family pride'. That the commoner Wertheimer had proved more chivalrous than Clancarty or his son was an embarrassment. That Belle's popular appeal was heightened by Clancarty endeavouring to make himself an accessory *before* the fact was even worse. Disapproval and disgust at Clancarty's behaviour and Euston's and Dunlo's decadent lifestyles heightened sympathy for a courtesan and an actress to an unprecedented degree and enabled both women to make full use of the relatively new phenomenon of the American-style interview to further their own ends: Kate to play on growing prejudice against the aristocracy to manipulate her private negotiations with Euston's family and Belle to garner popular support for a career that would be brought to a sudden end with Clancarty's death. Whether they achieved their respective aims is a moot point, but a sense of the upsetting of the usual order can be seen in a post-Euston-trial comment by the *Aberdeen Evening Express* that Kate was 'more of an ornament to the peerage than her husband' and in the post-Dunlo-trial observation by the PMG that sales of Belle's photo by Bassano had seen a 'rapid upsurge'. A certain temperance of 'Belle fever' was called for as a result. *Lloyd's Weekly*, for example, commented that while her triumph was a cause for celebration, 'the observer may not unnaturally see elements of danger to Society and the State in the utter immoral conditions of life disclosed at the trial'. Augustus Moore was quick to reinforce that this referred as much to Belle as Dunlo. She was, after all, the mother of an illegitimate child fathered by a convict. If she had been born 'in the purple', Moore wrote, instead of being poor, she would have been outcast for behaving as she had done, whether she had been found guilty or not.[25]

The essayists quoted at the beginning of this chapter with their high aspirations for marriage would doubtless have concluded that both these cases demonstrate perfectly the consequences of ill-assorted unions engaged in without due consideration of their relative positions in society or respect for the institution of marriage. They might also have been tempted to offer some late-in-the-day advice to the parents, perhaps akin to that proffered by *The Observer* in the wake of the Dunlo case: that because getting rid of clubs like *The Corinthian* was probably an infringement of personal liberty, parents would be well advised to drop in occasionally to ascertain the exact moment at which it became desirable to send their young charges around the world to spare themselves 'the subsequent sorrow of wringing their hands over their unavailing efforts for the reparation of the irreparable'. Would those who worried about public morals and disapproved of divorce and its reporting ever have come to the conclusion of historian Anne Humpherys, made with the benefit of hindsight, that 'newspaper press reports from the Divorce Court ironically played a role in the idealization of marriage' by lessening tolerance for violence in marriage and promoting the notion of marriage as 'an equal companionate relationship'?[26] They knew that parental diligence on its own was no guarantee of success. As the cases in the next chapter will show, a 'good catch' did not necessarily become an admirable husband.

3

... Repent at Leisure (The Problem of Unsuitable Husbands)

> My own impression is that among marriages which are actual shipwrecks of happiness, the greater number have been wrecked by the faults of wives, but that, of the more numerous marriages which drag on, not altogether intolerable, but very uncomfortable, the greater number are made unhappy by the faults of husbands...
> Clementina Black, 'On Marriage: A Criticism' (1890)

Though rather a broad generalisation, the view above is underpinned by, and the inevitable consequence of, the double standard written into the divorce law. The fact that for a divorce or judicial separation most women had to prove either desertion (of a minimum of two years' duration[1]) or cruelty (which was harder to prove if short-lived) necessarily meant they were more likely to suffer longer in unhappy marriages than men. Compounding matters was another clause from the 1857 Act which stated that a petition must be brought without undue delay. It affected both parties but not necessarily equally. For a husband, the clock started ticking as soon as he became aware of his wife's infidelity. He was expected to immediately cease marital relations with her (otherwise he would be said to have condoned the adultery) and instigate proceedings soon after. But when the issue was a husband's cruelty, it took until the wife's health broke down – potentially years after her ill-treatment began – before relief was sought. Gladstone had recognised this and in debates before the law was passed had repeatedly urged that 'cruelty practiced in a house by the husband

... *Repent at Leisure (The Problem of Unsuitable Husbands)*

on his wife might be a more aggravating evil than repeated acts of transient adultery' and should, therefore, be a ground for divorce in its own right if divorce was to be enacted at all. George Lewis, repeating this in an 1885 article, suggested that the double standard displayed 'a blind ignorance of domestic tragedies';[2] and Clementina Black defined the predominant fault of husbands who mistreated their wives as 'a tendency to domineer, to tyrannize, to enforce a surrender more or less complete of the wife's will and individuality', which, to overcome, required a change of attitude on both their parts.[3] Where this statement applied to marriages that ended in divorce, the wife's change in attitude was often her breaking point, her hopes and expectations for her married life long shattered.

Two ladies who married apparently respectable gentlemen with parental approval but who claimed to fit this description were Blanche Holden, who married at age twenty-one, and Martha Mary Spain, who was seventeen.

Blanche's intended was Frederick George Ellis, 7th Baron Howard de Walden, to whom she was introduced at the home of a family friend in early January 1876. Blanche's father was long dead, so her mother and stepfather – a Liverpool solicitor named Powles – gave their consent. Initially they had concerns that the forty-five-year-old grandee was perhaps rather too entrenched in 'bachelor habits' to make a good husband, but Howard's easy assurances to the contrary quickly pacified them and the couple married on 27 April that year. At their divorce hearing seventeen years later, Blanche's barrister portrayed her as young and innocent at the time of her engagement and awed by her intended's status, which was vastly superior to her own. His maternal grandfather was the 4th Duke of Portland and Howard was third in line after his mother and aunt to inherit the Portlands' vast Marylebone estate and lands in Ayrshire. Already, he had an annual allowance of £3,000 compared to the £180 Blanche had from her father's will.

Martha and her fiancé, Joseph Charles Tasker, were more evenly matched. Martha's father was a retired butcher and Tasker's had been an accountant. Tasker had been orphaned at age seven and his paternal uncle, a dentist, was his guardian. The families knew each other well. Martha's brother Lewis married Tasker's sister Annie in 1884; Martha was friendly with Tasker's other sister, Sarah; and

Tasker used to go about with her brother Arthur. But by the time Martha and Joseph married on 28 November 1888 at the Roman Catholic Church of the Sacred Heart of Jesus in Hampstead, his situation had dramatically changed. A distant cousin had died on 3 January 1888 leaving him a fortune that would be his without restriction when he came of age, along with a large residence, Middleton Hall in Brentwood. The cousin, Helen Tasker, who had been made a countess by Pope Pius IX in 1870, had been a major benefactress of the Southend Catholic mission. The fortune, in which she'd had a life interest, had been amassed by her father through investment in the United Mexican Mining Association and valued by probate in 1861 at nearly £500,000. It passed to Joseph for lack of any other male heir. Thus on 30 October 1899, less than a year after he and Martha married, he became unexpectedly extravagantly rich. By careful investment the fortune had grown to nearer £800,000, giving him a £30,000 annual income: a situation that Martha's barrister described as 'unfortunate' when their case came to trial in 1894.

In both cases, the wives instigated proceedings alleging cruelty. Blanche sued for judicial separation on that single ground and Martha sued for divorce claiming cruelty compounded her husband's adultery. Both husbands denied the charges and countersued for divorce.

Women in general charged their husbands with cruelty more frequently than any other offence. The 1881–1900 sample of wives' petitions shows cruelty charged in nearly three-quarters of those for divorce and two-thirds for judicial separation – figures that are largely consistent with earlier periods.[4] For most of the eighteenth century 'cruelty' had meant either extreme physical violence or the wilful communication of a venereal disease. Why sexually transmitted diseases should have ranked alongside violence is uncertain, though it has been suggested that a wife's refusal to have sex with her infected husband carried with it a potential for assault which qualified her for the law's protection.[5] Either way, in 1790 the position changed with a series of comments on the general nature of legal cruelty by High Court judge Lord Stowell which were considered profound enough to take on the force of a statute. Stowell's view was that the court need not wait until violence had occurred before acting to protect a petitioner: the *apprehension* of violence or bodily harm was sufficient to justify their intervention *if* it rendered cohabitation unsafe or was shown to have impacted on the petitioner's health. The primary consideration was the protection of the innocent spouse.

Stowell's interpretation marked a significant shift of focus away from the conduct itself (usually, the husband's) to its consequences (on the wife) and undoubtedly benefited aggrieved wives following the 1857 Act. Immediately wives began filing petitions for divorce or separation in equal if not greater numbers than men. Still, by Stowell's definition, the threat must be real, not 'arising merely from an exquisite and diseased sensibility of mind': 'What merely wounds the mental feelings is in few cases to be admitted where they are not accompanied with bodily injury, either actual or menaced', for only the duty of self-preservation came before the duties of marriage.[6] It was also necessary for the injured party to show that any grievous conduct or its consequences were sufficiently 'grave and weighty' as to render the continuation of married life impossible. A single reprehensible act was not deemed cruel if there was no likelihood it would be repeated (unless it was particularly vicious) and it was not until 1870 that mental abuse was considered cruel, and then only if it impaired the health of the spouse. A general atmosphere of marital thunder, though unpleasant, was insufficient. Swearing and blasphemy in themselves were not cruel (even if aimed at a wife) though as a background to violent conduct they might indicate a general savage temperament from which she needed protecting and their inclusion in petitions was therefore permitted.

The relaxing of the interpretation of 'cruelty' over time was made possible by the fact that there was no statute that specifically defined it. When extreme violence was the benchmark a close definition was unnecessary and after 1790, the persistent refusal of judges to provide one demonstrated an awareness that there was such a thing as *relative* cruelty and that each case needed to be decided on its own merits. A loose definition also accommodated judicial discretion which was amenable to social change. As such, some of the petitions filed by late Victorians were mild by comparison with those filed earlier in the century. Mid-Victorians would no doubt have considered some of them as stretching the definition. In 1861, for example, in *Smallwood* v. *Smallwood* it was held that 'viciously shaking a wife by her throat' and 'throwing her violently to the ground' was insufficiently serious to be cruel.[7] Whereas, in 1892, the president found enough in the fact that Emily Latham Curling's husband 'on one occasion became angry and struck her three times on the head' in conjunction with his single act of adultery to grant a degree for divorce.[8] By 1910, Mr Barnard QC observed, judges and juries always tried to find cruelty in wives' cases where adultery was clear and grant a decree even if the cruelty was 'borderline'.[9] This, he said, had been the case throughout his thirty-year career.

Nevertheless, many petitions filed in this period still make horrific reading. The 1895 petition of Johanna Vaughan of Brecon, for example, alleges that her husband of ten years – a coachman – 'frequently and habitually assaulted and beat and pinched and kicked her' and used 'violent, offensive and threatening language' towards her so as to greatly impair her health. In specific, that three days after the birth of their first child, he threw a lighted candle at her when she was in bed with the baby, took hold of the child by its gown and hung it upside-down, ejected the midwife and 'forcibly and against the will of your petitioner had carnal connection with her'. Then when their second child was an infant, in a violent rage he smashed pictures and threw the cradle in which the infant was then lying on the fire, struck Johanna violently upon the face and took up two large stones and threatened to smash her brains out with them. Finally, in 1892 (when the children were aged six and seven respectively), he dragged her from the bed in which she and the children were lying to his bed and forced his hand into her private parts with such violence that she was in great pain, fainted and became ill. Numerous other points in the seven-page document speak of occasions when he beat and kicked her and when she had to seek the refuge of friends. In August 1893 she left him, and in December he committed adultery. The petition went undefended and Johanna was granted a divorce and awarded custody and costs of £94.[10]

Such extreme acts of violence would never had been reported in graphic detail in the press – they were deemed unpalatable for a civilised reader – but nonetheless, the reporting of high-profile cases, such as those of the Taskers and the Howard de Waldens, brought into sharp focus the fact that gentlemen – both those born-and-bred and those educated as such – were just as capable of abusing their wives as were working-class men. Though the civilising effect of wealth and position and the restraining effect of the continuous presence of servants and visitors in their houses might, to some degree, have stayed their hands, their wives still suffered the pain, indignity and fear of assault, particularly when whatever restraint a gentleman acquired from his surroundings was countered by the pernicious effects of alcohol.

Blanche's petition, filed with the court on 14 December 1891, alleged that Howard de Walden was a man 'of gross and confirmed intemperate habits' who failed to provide for her, neglected her and treated her with 'systematic insult and contempt'. It specified three occasions in 1877 and 1878 when he was physically violent towards her. On the first, he violently twisted her arm, causing her great pain; on the second, he punched her in the head, raising a bruise; and on the third, he struck her with a brush on the shoulder and drew blood. On a fourth occasion, he had thrown a heavy atlas at her that would have hit her had it not been caught by a gentleman staying in their house. The other seventeen allegations collectively illustrate the erratic, alarming and sometimes frankly odd behaviour of a man so afflicted by drink that he was, as Blanche's barrister put it, 'scarcely responsible for his actions'. Blanche alleged that Howard habitually fired his revolver in the house and out the window. He ranted and raved, accused Blanche of stealing, ordered servants to ignore her and called her opprobrious names. On one occasion in 1878 he came into her bedroom at night and pulled off all the bedcovers and her nightdress (for no specified reason); and in 1880, when she was pregnant, in the early morning he came in ranting, smashed furniture and set fire to the window shutters.

Blanche was so terrified by Howard's behaviour that after her confinement she took their son and would not return until he agreed to reform. In May 1881 she returned, but his behaviour was no better. He refused to take her into society, banned her relatives from the house and when on several occasions she went out with friends, he locked her out so that she had to use the servants' entrance. He frequently shook and shouted at their son and, when she remonstrated, swore at her and threatened her. He habitually sat up all night drinking and his personal habits were so filthy and disgusting as to greatly annoy and distress her. In the further and better particulars requested by Howard's solicitor this was enlarged upon to reveal that Howard constantly soiled the bed, often vomited at the dining table and used the fireplace in the dining room as a urinal. His clothes were consequently always soiled and he was in the habit of removing them and standing naked at the window in full view of the houses opposite (much to the embarrassment of the female servants who worked there). Blanche claimed that his behaviour retarded her recovery after her confinement; and when in 1888 she fell dangerously ill with peritonitis, he was so noisy and violent that Blanche was removed from the house by medical attendants who feared for her life and had never since returned. As a consequence, Howard subsequently gradually deprived her of the society of their son and, from May 1891, ceased to make her an allowance.[11]

Martha Tasker's petition of 24 May 1894, by comparison, alleged her husband's continuous cruelty and habitual neglect since their marriage nearly six years previously. The neglect, enumerated in her particulars, consisted of ten specified occasions when Tasker abandoned her for as little as a fortnight and as long as three months to go travelling. It listed eleven occasions on which he threatened her or called her opprobrious names. 'Opprobrious' often meant calling someone 'brute', 'devil' or occasionally 'whore'; and swearing meant 'go to hell', which was considered highly offensive and appeared in newspapers as 'go to H—', if at all. Martha's allegations were rather stronger. She alleged that Tasker had called her a 'bloody fucking bitch', a 'Goddamned son of a whore's dropping hatched in the sun' (whatever that may be) and claimed he expressed the desire that 'God fuck your bloody soul to hell'.[12] None of these expressions were repeated in court: Martha couldn't bring herself to voice them but swore in the witness box they were true; the particulars were shown to the jury to read for themselves; none found their way into the papers.

On nine of these occasions, Martha alleged that the verbal abuse became physical. On six of them Tasker allegedly struck her on the breast and arms; on another, he rushed at her with a knife, threw her to the ground and seized her by the throat until she choked; on another, he came home late, attempted to gain entry to her bedroom with a hatchet and, when she opened the door in fear, threatened to kill her with it; on the last, he struck her while she was in bed, threatened to shoot her and so aggrieved her that she took poison in his presence. She also alleged that when Tasker was on his travels he slept with divers women from whom he contracted gonorrhoea which he recklessly and wilfully communicated to her. She supplemented her petition two weeks before their hearing with another alleging adultery with a 'Mrs Rhodes' in June and November 1894.

By the time these suits came to court Hannen had left to join the appeal bench and had been replaced as president of the division by his second, Charles Butt. The man chosen to fill Butt's seat was the hitherto largely unknown Sir Francis Henry Jeune. Jeune had spent most of his legal career in various ecclesiastical courts, becoming chancellor in seven dioceses before his elevation to the Bench. He knew nothing of the business of the court and there were doubts he had 'ever addressed a jury in his life'.[13] With his long experience, Inderwick had been considered the obvious candidate. Yet Jeune was a diligent, studious man who went on to perform the difficult duties of the court with 'infinite tact and discretion'. He was always courteous, could be strong when necessary, was considered handsome – reminiscent of Charles I in his grooming, apparently – wore 'a large eyeglass and an apologetic manner' and was possessed of so sympathetic a voice that 'many a fair lady, blushing in the witness box, had fallen straightaway in love with'.[14] When in May 1892 Justice Butt's heart gave way following a lengthy battle with influenza, Jeune was considered fortunate to find himself president after only fourteen months on the Bench.

The vacancy left by Butt's death still did not favour Inderwick. An admiralty specialist was called for and Inderwick's vast experience was predominantly in the divorce court. The position went instead to Sir John Gorell Barnes who, ironically, is not remembered for his admiralty work but as a great champion of divorce law reform. At the time of his appointment, however, he was the youngest man on the Bench and 'the most rapidly-successful commercial and Admiralty lawyer of modern times'.[15] He was a quiet judge, not prone to putting in his own questions – unlike Jeune who, in the Howard de Walden trial, interposed so frequently during Howard's questioning that it was 'almost an evenly shared examination'.[16] Barnes was more patient. He had 'a good presence, a pleasing voice, a well-stocked and well-ordered mind, and an unruffled temper'.[17] He enjoyed grappling with the law, hated criminal work because, he said, 'there was no law in it', but found plenty in the divorce court where, according to his biographer, 'the anomalies and injustices' of the 1857 Act 'sank deeper and deeper into his heart until to remedy them ... became his fixed determination'.[18]

Jeune presided over both the Howard and Tasker hearings, and both were led by silks not yet introduced. Blanche was represented by Sir Henry James, a dark, dapper man with small features, variously described as suave and dignified, solid but not brilliant, restive and uneasy and with a reputation for throwing in the towel sooner than was necessary, but also shrewd, with a propensity for biting questions. Sir Edward Carson, the proud Irishman who represented Martha, had been solicitor general in Ireland before joining the English bar in 1893 and was considered a disinterested man of honour, praised by his biographer for 'his virulent invective, his uncanny skill in laying traps for unwary feet, his power of making witnesses say ridiculous things by an almost diabolical mastery of cross-examination' and for giving 'strange weight' to everything he said with his 'great personality and expressive voice'.[19] The substance of his opponent in the Tasker trial was equally self-evident. John Patrick Murphy, who weighed in at 20 stone, was a large presence both physically and professionally. The weapons in his armoury were tact, resourcefulness and the 'infinite capacity for presenting commonplace arguments in an attractive form'.[20] A good-humoured man, he was kind to juniors and for all his forensic vigour was said to 'roar as gently as a sucking-dove', enabling him almost to draw tears from a jury.[21]

Whether he succeeded in drawing any for Martha is not recorded but from the extent of suffering expressed in both hers and Blanche's petitions, the potential was there. The difficulty was that the contents of petitions could not always be taken at face value. This, of course, was the purpose of a hearing: to ascertain not just whether the conduct alleged was severe enough to fulfil the legal requirement for divorce but whether it was truthful. Writing in 1962, legal academic John Biggs observed that throughout its 100-year history the divorce court had dealt with – and continued to deal with – the interweaving of characters, conflict of wills and general wear and tear of daily life in a manner that quite surpassed any other. A jury's task was made difficult by husband and wife pouring forth 'in alternate streams of opposite colours' a domestic history spanning

... Repent at Leisure (The Problem of Unsuitable Husbands)

years, distorted by poor memory, antagonism, exaggeration and sometimes imagination, with few supporting documents and often only their personal credibility to depend upon.[22] The collision of directly contrary testimony, alongside the shenanigans of witnesses who sometimes had their own agenda, earned the court the epithet 'The Supreme Court of Lies'. The inquisitorial system of the court inevitably made it so and it accepted and tolerated what might be considered perjury in other courts, especially from husbands and wives charged with immoral conduct ruinous to their reputations. Here more than elsewhere it was essential that individual events must not be taken out of context but set against the background of the whole married life within the bounds of permissible evidence. When both parties petitioned the courts with allegations against the other, one side was heard in its entirety before the barrister for the other had chance to speak. Customarily, the party that filed their petition first was heard first. This often meant the complexion of a case changed dramatically as it progressed. No wonder spectators sat transfixed as that which at first appeared tragic became comic, or vice-versa, as villain became good guy, as long-suffering wife became shrew, backwards and forwards until the jury gave its verdict and the audience departed to discuss whether the ending was to their satisfaction and the pressmen to report and moralise, mindful (or not) of the consequences for the parties at the heart of the drama.

In the Howard de Walden suit, James opened for Blanche on 2 March 1893. His client had much to recommend her to the court. She was described as a tall, handsome woman of thirty-seven who dressed quietly in a brown robe trimmed with dark fur and matching bonnet – an ensemble that, contrary to the unspoken rule of court attendance that 'fashionable ladies must appear in a new outfit each day', she did not change until day four of their seven-day trial. She remained elegant, dignified and self-possessed throughout. By comparison, the 'short thick-set figure' of Howard was 'barely noticeable'.[23] James spoke on her behalf for nearly an hour and a half, revealing that it took less than a year for Howard to expose himself as a drunkard and to show that he had no real affection for her and disliked her company. On their first Christmas day together he abandoned her to go to his club and often humiliated Blanche in company. On an occasion when they dined with friends at Mortlake he got so drunk that on their return journey he had to be lifted from the railway carriage by two porters and deposited in a cab. But his 'filthy and repulsive' habits meant he had long since ceased to be invited to anybody's house, family included.

James spoke of Blanche's terror when Howard's drunkenness made him abusive and erratic; of all the events described in the petition and of how Howard was also a liability to himself, falling downstairs on one occasion and breaking two ribs. He spoke of his dissolute habit of sitting up all night drinking on three nights out of every seven, and how he would go to bed at 10 a.m. and not get up until late afternoon. He spoke of the miserliness that made Howard tell his young wife when heavily pregnant with their first (and only) child that she must wait to see if the baby survives before buying it any clothes, and of his becoming angry when Blanche could not then nurse the child, forcing him to have to pay for a wetnurse. This had all been a terrible shock to the young bride. No wonder she had been forced to seek the sanctuary of friends.

James (himself a great respecter of persons) then spoke with reverence of the 'great kindness' extended to Blanche by the numerous branches of Howard's family while Howard himself alienated them. He told the special jury that Howard's maternal aunts, Lady Harriett Bentinck and Charlotte, Viscountess Ossington, received Blanche at Claridge's when she was forced to leave Howard and assisted in bringing about the reconciliation of 1881; and that Augusta, Baroness Bolsover, mistress of the magnificent Welbeck Abbey and stepmother of the current Duke of Portland, had invited Blanche to stay on numerous occasions (without her husband); and that her stepson had, as head of the family, condescended to intervene on Blanche's behalf when she was dangerously ill with peritonitis to stop a tragedy occurring of Howard's making. What message did it send to the jury that this great lady not only received Howard's ill-used wife but gave a deposition in her favour; and that a bevy of very well dressed ladies (in different gowns each day) graced the court with their presence in support of their friend, even if it was from the relative safety of the back row? Perhaps the fact that, from the second day of the trial, the 'unusually gay' gentlemen of the jury co-ordinated their buttonholes – with those in front wearing white orchids while those behind alternated between English violets and lilies one day and red hothouse carnations the next – answers that question.

Family solidarity was further emphasised when Blanche revealed in evidence that she had wanted to petition in 1881 but had not done so out of respect for Howard's aunts, who desperately desired the avoidance of scandal. In return they paid £1,500 per annum into a household account to ensure Blanche and her son, Tommy, did not go without. This was how society expected its aristocracy to behave; not in a manner 'such as scarcely a beast in a field would have resorted to'. Their subsequent coming forward to publicly support Blanche when she did finally petition the court was also just how it should be. But the coup-de-grâce from James's perspective must have been the appearance in the witness box of the 6th Duke of Portland himself, who testified that when he'd intervened on Blanche's behalf it was to ask Howard to stay away, as his presence was considered so dangerous to her welfare that she might die 'and every right thinking man would consider he had murdered her'.

Only a sterling performance from Howard could have turned the tide that was building against him after nearly all his servants had appeared as witnesses for Blanche. Sadly, it was nothing of the kind. The sixty-three-year-old baron made a sorry witness, cringing forward as a result of increasing deafness and nervously fingering his coat buttons as he gave evidence. He stammered over his answers as he admitted he had banned Blanche's mother from his house a month after their marriage because she 'made mischief'; that Blanche was a poor housekeeper who could not control the extravagances of his cook; that her mother, he suspected, had kept some of the money he had paid out for Blanche's trousseau and that he'd insisted Blanche write to ask how his money had been spent; and that he had objected to her outings with friends because they were a 'fast' set that led her into extravagance. On the occasion she claimed he had punched her (he had not, but he had 'boxed her ears'), she had been to Goodwood without his consent. He claimed to have no recollection of striking her with the brush, throwing the atlas or tearing off her nightgown, but it was not because he was drunk: he thought he never was *very* drunk. (The president retorted, a drunken man very seldom does!)

From there on, Howard's answers provoked increasing hilarity as he tried to explain that the burning of the shutters was an accident: he had been burning paper to dry wet paint from his wife's decorating (the odour of which he found offensive) and they had accidently caught fire (laughter). The shooting of his revolver in the house had been up the chimney to bring down soot to prevent a chimney fire. It was unorthodox, perhaps, but it had worked (more laughter). At the Mortlake dinner he had not drunk to excess, but the spirits had 'got into' his head when they mixed with the quinine he was taking for a medical condition (even more laughter). On the occasion of his broken ribs, he had been sitting up reading, smoking and drinking and had been going upstairs by candlelight when he 'unfortunately missed the top step' (louder laughter still). But he was not drunk. He drew a distinction between being 'drunk' and being 'worse for drink' and said he had been drunk no more than ten times in his life. Of the other charges against him (those he could recall) he was inclined to think they were jokes. When, for example, he twisted Blanche's arm, he had been trying to get money out of her hand, which was funny because he knew Blanche was only pretending to steal it. When James suggested the joke was rather one-sided Howard responded that it may have been but at least he got his money back! Finally, he denied the disgusting habits he'd been accused of, which the president said was surprising because his counsel had conducted his case as if those allegations were tacitly admitted.

It is true that Clarke offered little by way of defence for his client's behaviour. The most he did say when he addressed the jury on the fourth day was that Howard's 'bachelor habits', though 'perhaps not conducive to a happy married life', were known to Blanche when they married. From there, he quickly moved on to the counter-allegations of adultery. Doubtless he knew that Howard's behaviour was indefensible and that the only way he could protect his client was to stalemate the case by proving Blanche's guilt.

There were two charges against Blanche. The first, of adultery with family friend Captain Noel Winter, whom Blanche allegedly met daily while holidaying in Hythe in late September 1892, where they lunched together and spent several afternoons in the hotel's public lounge, was easily dismissed. Though Blanche received no other visitors and there was certainly 'the opportunity for unfaithfulness', there was no evidence of intimacy. But the other allegation extended over a fourteen-month period between

... *Repent at Leisure (The Problem of Unsuitable Husbands)*

February 1890 and April 1891 and was, said Clarke, of much graver importance. It was of adultery with a young sportsman, seven years Blanche's junior, named Count Jean de Madre, who resided in Paris and Pau and was known as an enthusiastic polo player. He had met Blanche when she went to Pau for her health in winter 1889 with her cousin, Miss Evelyn Holden. It was charged that Blanche and the count committed adultery on numerous occasions in London, Pau and Argelès and for this, said Clarke, there was plentiful evidence. Most of it was proffered by two servants: James Crocombe, the count's valet – a keen-looking, balding, middle-aged man with small moustache, who might have been thought of 'foreign extraction' but for his perfect English – and Lizzie Crook, Blanche's lady's maid, who looked uncomfortably hot in a thick coat and feather boa but answered counsel's questions with 'perfect sang-froid'.

The essence of Crocombe's testimony was that wherever the count travelled, Blanche followed, and vice-versa. Crocombe claimed to have seen the count wandering the hotel at night and that on those occasions his master's bed did not look slept in. He also claimed to have found a lady's wristwatch on the count's bedside table. It was inscribed with the monogram 'H de W'. He had presented it to the count who had quickly pocketed it. He had also found a lady's gold cuff-stud in his master's pocket. He'd put it on the dressing table, from where it vanished. This evidence sent a stir throughout the courtroom. Further sensation was caused when Crocombe stated he'd seen Blanche and the count go into the count's bedroom together one day at 4 p.m. The count had locked the door after them, which Crocombe knew because he'd tried the door (laughter). Dates for all these events he'd recorded in his Bradshaw's guide.

Crook stated that she'd been in Blanche's service since November 1890 and frequently saw the pair together. The count had visited Blanche in her bedroom when she was laid up with influenza and Blanche, she claimed, had afterwards said to her, 'For God's sake don't tell anyone he was here or people will talk like they did at the Hotel Continental in Paris.' Crook claimed she'd seen the count stoop over Blanche's bed as if to kiss her and to have spotted that her mistress was missing the cuff-stud Crocombe had found, only to notice it magically reappear three days later. When they travelled to Argelès in March 1891, the observant maid noticed her mistress's trunk in her bedroom had been moved – something she said could only have been done by a man. The enterprising maid had repositioned the trunk's strap in such a manner as to be obvious if it had been moved again. It enabled her to confirm that the man entering her mistress's bedroom was a regular guest. After which, she hid herself on the upper landing and claimed to have clearly seen the count entering Blanche's bedroom at night and leaving the following morning, thereby deducing it was he who had moved the trunk. To top it off, she claimed to have found one of the count's coat-buttons on the floor near Blanche's washstand and triumphantly produced it then and there to the sound of laughter in court. The outcome of her investigations she recorded in a notebook.

On the surface, Crocombe and Crook appeared to be a perfect pair of witnesses, until it became clear that they were also a 'pair' in every sense: lovers, conspirers and partners in crime. Under cross-examination, a letter was produced that Crocombe was forced to admit he had written Crook after they both left service:

My dearest,

You ask me if I miss you or care for you as much as ever. If that question is put to me four years hence I will be able to answer it one way. I shall never forget; it is useless trying. Oh how I wish I could command money! I would show you then I was in earnest ... I cannot give up that idea with Lord H...

The 'idea' revealed itself in another letter from Crocombe to Howard dated May 1891 and sent within days of his leaving the count's employment, asking if it would be to Howard's advantage to receive proof of his wife's adultery. Crocombe was subsequently paid £25 by Howard's solicitors, Messrs Wontners, to stay in London and a further three guineas a day for travelling with Wontner's clerk to Paris and Pau to gather evidence. There were strict rules as to how much a witness could receive in the course of legal business and this, if not exactly flouting them, was 'not ungenerous'.[24] The motivation and veracity of these witnesses was further challenged by the fact that though they claimed otherwise,

... *Repent at Leisure (The Problem of Unsuitable Husbands)*

Crook had been dismissed by Blanche after she had attended three masked balls with Crocombe and been seen leaving his room late at night and Crocombe had left the count in solidarity with Crook. Crook had told Blanche that if she was sent away, she would write to Howard and 'create a scandal'. If any further rebuttal of their evidence were necessary it was supplied by the appearance of the watchmaker to prove that Blanche's watch had not been made until December 1890, six months after it was supposedly seen in the count's bedroom.

Blanche firmly denied all charges, even to the loss of the cuff-stud and the existence of the button. Cousin Evelyn attested to never leaving Blanche's side throughout her illness and claimed equal friendship with the count. Both ladies said further that the count's English was so terrible they'd had to converse in French which neither of the servants spoke (Crocombe's 'foreign extraction' went no further than Devon) and his sole topic of conversation was horses. By day seven, even though the count had refused to come to court, claiming, as a Frenchman, it had no jurisdiction over him (something that would normally have been seen as a black mark against the wife), the jury intimated they had heard enough and, with the president's consent, dramatically brought the case to an early close. Counsel agreed to forego their addresses and the verdict was immediately returned that Howard was guilty of cruelty and Blanche not guilty of adultery. Blanche was granted a judicial separation and awarded custody of Tommy, £1,000 annual alimony and costs. *Truth* immediately began a campaign to have Crocombe and Crook prosecuted for perjury to prevent the court from becoming 'the happy hunting ground of professional spies, perjurers and blackmailers' and 'a terror to every man or woman with a character to lose'.[25] The public prosecutor declined.

Afterwards, *The Globe* commented that Howard could congratulate himself that his wife escaped his clutches without damage to her reputation but not, it must be said, without substantial humiliation at having to air her private affairs in a public courtroom, however stoically she did so. *Reynolds's* added that Howard had revealed himself to be 'a brutal and disreputable blackguard – a creature whom every honest man would be glad to thrash to within an inch of his disreputable life', not fitted for anything better than 'cleaning cesspools'. He had appeared in court a bumbling fool, but underneath was a miserly, paranoid, angry man who had alienated his whole family. Much later his son Tommy would question 'whether he had been conceived in love or spite': whether Howard's prime motivation in marrying Blanche in the first place had not been a desire to revenge himself on a mother whose bounty, he believed, extended only to her chosen charities and his younger siblings, and whether he had not been conceived simply for the purpose of producing an heir. Howard died in 1899, a 'grim fierce old man without a friend in a nursing home'.[26] Blanche afterwards married the 2nd Baron Ludlow and was remembered as 'one of the most attractive and popular figures in society'.[27] Rarely were defended cases so one-sided.

The Taskers' court experience was a very different story. They were comparatively young for petitioners – Martha being twenty-four and Joseph twenty-six – and had been married less than seven years when their trial began on 4 July 1895. For Martha's barrister, Carson, it was Tasker's 'unfortunate' inheritance that had brought them there. His annual income of £30,000 was double that of top-earning barrister Charles Russell, 100 times the nominal earnings of clerks in public pay and more than 600 times that of a lowly agricultural labourer. The Duke of Portland might have earned more than three times as much from rents, but he had his salubrious estate to maintain: Tasker had only Middleton Hall.[28] So how does 'a cheery, intelligent, good-looking, quite clever in some ways' young man with 'the keenest sense of humour' get through such a sum without gambling it away, asked Tasker's old schoolfriend, the journalist Basil Tozer, in his memoirs of their joint adventures published in 1902 under the title *Around the World with a Millionaire*? Answer: he 'bought a coach and a dozen horses, a 500-ton yacht, and one or two other things'.[29]

All these luxuries and the decadent lifestyle they betrayed delighted and horrified readers following the Tasker trial in equal and opposite measure. The yacht was an iron screw steamer – the *Zingara* – formerly the property of the Maharaja of Baroda, in which Tasker set out to circumnavigate the globe. The 'other things' were mostly pedigree diamonds, for which he had a particular weakness. To Martha he gave £500 a year pin money and various jewels; to Tozer, when they met again after he and Martha had separated in 1894, a salary of £1,500 a year to give up scribbling and become his travelling companion. Tozer's memoirs portray Tasker as a man who 'lived only for sensation and excitement', never knowing one day what he would do the next, surrounded by a clique of hangers-on – 'parasites, every one' – who gathered in his dining room to gorge themselves at his expense. Clearly Tasker did not perpetuate cousin Helen's brand of Christian charity, though, if Tozer is to be believed, he did have 'a distorted idea of philanthropy', giving away 'enormous sums' but preferring to roam the Embankment at night and slip sovereigns directly into the hands of the men sleeping rough on its benches rather than trust it to organisations 'who might squander it'.[30]

While certain of Tozer's recollections have proved unreliable – such as Tasker buying their way into the cell of condemned anarchist Émile Henri in Paris the night before his guillotining on 21 May 1894 (Tasker was actually admiring merchandise in the Bond Street establishment of eminent jeweller Edwin Streeter that day) – and others could well be apocryphal – such as the occasion on which he stopped a passing policeman to ask if he knew of any shops that sold fire engines as he'd promised to buy one for Brentwood and had decided to do it 'while I think of it' – they are stories not uncharacteristic of Tasker, who ended up suing Streeter to recover cheques and bills amounting to nearly £84,000 for the purchase of a handful of brilliant gems (including the Agra and Hope diamonds) which he said he had committed to buying when 'suffering from the effects of drink'; and who, in the divorce court, likened himself to Mr McGoosely, the drinking companion of popular late Victorian comic character Ally Sloper, whose drunken adventures openly mocked traditional Victorian aspirations of self-improvement, moderation and temperance.[31]

Perhaps, then, Carson was right and Tasker's windfall had been a curse. Certainly it is what drew the attention of the popular press. In 1893, much of it went into the pockets of various medical men as Tasker's organs struggled to keep up with his lifestyle and he eventually developed delirium tremens. From April 1894, much more was swallowed up in litigation. Not only was there the action against Streeter, but another against Martha for the return of jewels which he claimed were 'paraphernalia' and therefore reclaimable on their separation.[32] Moreover, they had been arguing through their solicitors over their divorce since May, having already failed twice to negotiate terms for a private separation. Their court file had grown to 118 pages (compared with eight-or-so for the average undefended case); and now here they were, with forty witnesses who needed to be kept in London for the duration and a mountain of evidence that took four silks ten full court days to get through – all of which Tasker had to give security for before the trial and would have to settle in full afterwards in the event that he lost. That's to say nothing of the costs of two co-respondents, each with his own barristers, defending Tasker's allegations of adultery. There was no doubting he could afford it. On day one of the trial, the *Evening Post* lead with the headline 'Mr Tasker, of Diamond Fame, Settles a Little Matter in the Divorce Court' before describing the appearance of the 'dapper little man, with a bullet head and glossy black moustache' who sat in court surrounded by a coterie of legal advisers, 'conspicuous by thickly clustered diamonds on his fingers'. Martha, by comparison, was 'more than ordinary'. She calmed her nerves with smelling-salts and was first in the box.

For each event Martha recalled, Tasker had a different version. There were so many it would be tedious to record them all, but it was immediately clear that their early globetrotting had quickly resulted in friction. In brief, then, in February 1890, Martha said Tasker left her alone in Bombay and when she remonstrated with him on his return he abused her with very bad language, seized her by the throat, threatened her with a knife and put his hand over her mouth to prevent her screaming. Carson produced the knife in question: it was 'a formidable-looking weapon'. Then, hearing someone in the passage, Tasker had fled. The following morning Martha was seen by a doctor. She had been so distressed by the incident she'd tried to poison herself with ether (sensation!). But when it was Tasker's turn in the box he countered (in a surprisingly low voice for such a small man) that Martha knew full well he was going to Baroda to buy his yacht and that she had nagged him the whole time they were away, which was 'enough to drive anyone crazy'. He denied the assault but said *she* struck him and he restrained her. She'd taunted him, calling him a coward and 'a little duffer', so he'd put his hand over her mouth and said, 'You see I could hold you if I liked' just for the fun of it. Then he'd kissed her and they went to bed. He'd never heard until that very moment in court that she tried to take her own life that night.

... Repent at Leisure (The Problem of Unsuitable Husbands)

Afterwards, they'd travelled to Ceylon in the *Zingara* and in April 1890 returned to England. Martha said Tasker was unkind to her the whole way and often drunk. At Colombo he told her he wanted to travel home alone and left her on the yacht while he took a steamer, though she begged him not to. When she arrived at Plymouth he was waiting with jewels bought as a peace offering. Said Tasker, it was Martha who wanted to travel home without him and he took the steamer instead of her because they only had a man's berth available. The jewels were not a peace offering but a gift because she loved jewels.

In the summer, they cruised the Mediterranean and sailed on to Melbourne. In both places Martha claimed he left her alone for days. They returned home via Suez, arriving in England in September 1891. She was then seen by a doctor who diagnosed gonorrhoea – or as the *Evening News* discretely put it, 'an illness that was the result of his wild conduct'. She accused Tasker of unfaithfulness, refused to cohabit with him and went to a hotel. There he wrote to her admitting fault and promising to be faithful in future. She returned to him, but on 5 October he set off on his own again to the Cape, not returning until December. Tasker refuted all of this. He *had* written to his wife 'I am no saint, and have been to blame' but this referred to drinking, not adultery. He went to the Cape alone because she'd said she was too ill to travel. When he returned, they continued to argue. Most of their arguments were alcohol fuelled.

In June 1892, Martha said that when Tasker was drunk he forced his way into her bedroom with a hatchet and threatened her with it (sensation!). Tasker claimed he had broken the door down because Martha suffered from fits and he was concerned when he'd called her and got no reply, but he did not threaten or strike her. Following this, Martha said, he went on a coach trip to Edinburgh without her. Tasker said she hadn't minded: she'd gone to Torquay. In 1893, Martha said Tasker communicated gonorrhoea to her again after he returned from France. Then on a trip in *Zingara* to Norway, he hurled abuse at her, threatened her and struck her before departing the yacht. Tasker said the episode started with him objecting to Martha spending so much time on deck after dark, after which she came into his cabin and struck *him*, blackening his eye, and so he left (laughter). In August, at the Hotel Metropole in Brighton they had a furious row (the only one they largely agreed upon) in which he accused her of being born into trade and she had called his mother a barmaid, and observed that 'as all barmaids are ———, I suppose she was one, and you, therefore, are the son of one', which is worse. Following this, Tasker wrote to her, 'I could not possibly have anything but abhorrence for a woman who would say such vile things.' He offered her separation terms of £2,000 a year and her own horses and carriage, but she declined.

Martha then said in January 1894 he left her alone again and went to America for three months. When he returned they argued bitterly. He threatened her with his revolver, knocked her about and pulled her hair. She'd said 'You wish me dead' and went and got chloroform and drank it in front of him. He made no attempt to stop her. Tasker denied her allegations and said he tried to knock the bottle from her hand when he saw what she was about to do. She became insensible and he sent for a doctor. They administered mustard and other antidotes and stayed with her until she was well. Afterwards, he and Martha separated for good.

Martha had few witnesses to support her testimony: her brother Arthur, who confirmed Tasker's drunkenness and vile language and said on one occasion he had seen him strike Martha; and one servant who said she had seen a bruise on Martha's arm after the hatchet incident. Most importantly, she had three doctors who testified to treating Tasker not only for symptoms associated with drink but also, in 1891, for gonorrhoea. Her other witnesses all spoke of Tasker's meetings with the mysterious 'Mrs Rhodes' in private lounges of hotels and the rooms she rented at Queen Anne's Mansions on various occasions since their separation.

Tasker, on the other hand, had his butler, who testified to removing the hatchet after the bedroom door was penetrated, giving him no chance to threaten Martha with it; and to hearing Tasker do no more than 'damn and blast' her, which he thought nothing of (laughter). Tasker also had the captain of the *Zingara*, who said Martha had asked him if he'd heard her screaming after Tasker supposedly attacked her, but he had not. He had noticed, however, that Tasker had a bloodshot eye following Martha's alleged attack on him. Moreover, Tasker's numerous servants testified that Martha was often visited at home by the two co-respondents, Archibald Paton and Horace Lowe, when Tasker was abroad; and various hotel staff swore to seeing her out with each of them at various seaside towns.

Collectively, the picture they painted did not look good for Martha. Their evidence revealed that from October 1891 (a month after Martha was proved to have gonorrhoea, but close enough to throw doubt on Tasker being the cause of it) until April 1894, Paton had paid regular Sunday visits to her home, sleeping there on two occasions; that they regularly went to dances together; and that Martha had been with him in Torquay when Tasker was in Edinburgh in 1892. In addition, that Paton had introduced her to Lowe and that throughout the time Tasker was in America, Lowe had visited her on separate occasions to Paton and had gone with her to the south coast where they revelled in all the delights, spending £9 on wine over five days in an Eastbourne hotel (where champagne was 11s per bottle and claret 15s) before joining friends in Bournemouth where four of them consumed thirty bottles of champagne in three days. Though nothing compared to Tasker's drinking, Martha's champagne consumption clearly exceeded respectable levels. In her boudoir, she was also forced to confess, there was a cunning little cabinet innocently disguised as a card table in which her own personal supply of wines and spirits were concealed. Collectively, this evidence destroyed the impression she'd cultivated of a dutiful abandoned wife deprived of her husband's society while he travelled unencumbered. To compound matters, Tasker's sister, Sarah, whom Martha had said was her constant companion, produced incriminating letters to show this was not always so.

Paton and Lowe, for their part, both claimed their interest in Martha was actually her penchant for matchmaking: Paton with Martha's sister Agnes (who confirmed he had once briefly courted her) and Lowe with Sarah (who was engaged to a man Martha disapproved of).

This left only Mrs Josefa Rhodes to take the stand. She was a tall, good-looking American whose husband had made his money in Californian mines before committing suicide in 1893. She was self-sufficient and claimed she had intended to come to England to have her eleven-year-old son educated here before she met Tasker in a San Francisco hotel. She admitted that she had changed her travel arrangements so they could return together. She also frankly admitted that subsequently they'd met openly in London and Antwerp and spent hours together 'reading' in her rooms and that she had known he was separated from Martha when they'd done this. Equally as frankly, she denied any romantic attachment: they had mutual business interests, enjoyed each other's company and Tasker had helped her find suitable schooling for her son, but nothing more. There was no evidence of intimacy and, in his closing address, Mr Murphy argued on Tasker's behalf that Martha had made her allegation about Josefa at the eleventh hour to prejudice the jury against her husband. Moreover, she had fabricated her allegations of cruelty only after he had heard of her behaviour in Eastbourne. On the other side, Carson argued that Tasker had fallen instantly in love with Josefa and had forced the quarrel with Martha on his return from America because he wished to replace her with the widow and in court had deliberately vilified Martha's character with the intention that she should leave court a branded perjurer and adulteress.

This was how the case stood when proceedings were adjourned at the close of day ten. When the court reconvened the following morning it was to hear that there was to be a further adjournment. Two days later it was announced that on the advice of counsel the Taskers had come to a private arrangement and signed a deed of separation. For the scandal-hungry public it was like reaching the end of a sensational novel only to find the last page missing. Without a verdict, the majority of papers fell silent. Only a handful of provincial papers commented, describing the affair as a 'tragedy of riches': a husband who could have done infinite good but had chosen instead a path of 'undiluted self-indulgence' and a wife whose 'little pleasure trips with other girls' lovers involved hotel bills of the most roystering and Bacchanalian description'. Like a pair of naughty children, said *The Hampshire Advertiser*, they were 'in need of a good whipping'.

For the Taskers it was a resolution of sorts: a financial one, at least. Money more than reputation, wrote court reporter Fenn, was 'the motive which keeps litigation moving in the Divorce Court' and in this case it appears he was right.[33] Martha had quite frankly told the court that she'd rejected Tasker's earlier offer of £2,000 because it was insufficient. Doubtless when their case gridlocked he offered more. The president approved this course, saying neither had sufficiently proved their case. In fact, their respective lifestyles made it impossible for the jury to identify an innocent party in need of relief. The judge concluded proceedings by expressing the hope that their differences were not irreconcilable. Well might he have added the words of Lord Stowell from 1790: that, so far as the law is concerned, when misconduct that falls short of cruelty exists on one side or the other (or both) 'the suffering party must bear in some degree the consequences of an injudicious connection' and 'both must suffer in silence'.[34]

It was this apparent unwillingness to offer relief to an obviously ill-matched couple that made the court appear hard to the few reform advocates then vocal. But the outcome was as the law had intended: a punishment for their mutual wrongdoing. By contrast, Blanche Howard de Walden is an obvious example of the tyrannised wife the court was established to protect and in her case it quite rightly did; though even her relief came at a price. The Howard family might have been kind to her but it is difficult not to sympathise with Blanche for the many years spent caught between their desire to avoid scandal and her callous husband. Martha was young and frivolous by comparison, but was her situation any less tragic? Both Taskers clearly made a mistake in their choice of spouse, yet establishment fear of the impact on the institution of marriage and common decency if the grounds for divorce were widened kept them bound for life; and for Martha, as a middle-class woman, the matrimonial solace that the same orthodoxy upheld was thereby denied her.

To a few more openminded souls this was wrongheaded thinking. As George Bernard Shaw later argued in the long preface to his 1908 play *Getting Married*, divorce 'is not the destruction of marriage, but the first condition of its maintenance': the open door that removes its sense of bondage and makes 'prudent people' treat each other with greater respect. With a growing number of divorcees choosing to remarry at a faster rate than people chose to divorce, Shaw asserted: 'Divorce only re-assorts the couples: a very desirable thing when they are ill-assorted.'[35] The Taskers could only have concurred. Following the trial Joseph Tasker changed his name to James Cleveland Thomas to avoid further press attention and steamed around the world for another year or two with Tozer, overspending until it became problematic. In 1897 he sold

Middleton Hall and his yacht. Tozer's memoirs were published in 1902, serialised in *To-Day* in 1903 and republished in 1923 and 1945, demonstrating the longevity of public fascination with the extravagances of the *fin de siècle*. He never reflected on whether either he or Tasker found anything like happiness or contentment thereby. If Martha found any, perhaps it was through the daughter she adopted two months after the trial and baptised Jessie Maria Ivy Tasker. Unsurprisingly, the Taskers never reconciled. Martha died on 13 November 1906 when her daughter was just ten. Four weeks later Tasker married Josefa Rhodes.

4

Sex Crimes

O year of filth, O year of mighty bawd!
Armstrongs and Campbells bear thy banner, Dilke
Thy crown, and Fanny of ambitious ilk
Thy leaflets sibylline. The idle gaud,
The tumbled hair, the keyholes, May and Maud,
Heard of when waking, their mouths pressed for milk:
Of rapes in rags, of adulteries in silk
They learn the tale, and parents smile unawed.
And bookstalls groan beneath great quires of lust,
Of perjury, of virgins certified,
Until it seems as if the Pig had thrust
Its snout through all and tossed the world aside.
O year of filth! the filthiest that may be—
Be it my fame that I was scorned of thee.

                       George Moore, 'A Farewell to 1886'[1]

Contrary to popular perception, sex was at the heart of Victorian social discourse. Quite apart from whether people talked about sex or did not, or had sex or did not, the classification of sexual practices, the development of the language of sex, its social implications in terms of birth rate, death rate, birth control and prostitution, its relation to married love as defined by the Church and the seemingly endless debates concerning its destabilising influence on social morality all belong to this era. 'What seems to be happening in the nineteenth century,' wrote historian Jeffrey Weeks, 'is a continuous battle over the definition of acceptable sexual behaviour within the context of changing class and power relations', particularly with the middle class attempting to impose its sexual morality on the classes above and beneath it. With interest, Weeks notes that the earliest critiques of 'Victorianism' stem from the 1880s when 'social purity' first gained major legislative purchase.[2]

The role of the divorce court in this discourse stems from the need to prove adultery for divorce, which necessarily put sex on its agenda. Paradoxically, it was the Church that put it there – erroneously, in the view of John Milton who over 200 years earlier claimed that the Church's insistence that only adultery could dissolve a marriage was based on a misreading of scripture. In *The Doctrine and Discipline of Divorce* (1643), Milton argued that the Hebrew word *ervah*, translated as 'nakedness' in Genesis, had been mistranslated as 'indecency' or 'uncleanness' in Deuteronomy, giving rise to the notion that a husband could only write his wife 'a bill of divorcement' for adultery. By implication, this suggested there was nothing more important in marriage than 'the prescribed satisfaction of an irrational heat' – something Milton considered ignominious to the sacred institution and dishonourable both to 'the undervalued soul of man' and to the doctrine itself. Instead, Milton argued that 'nakedness of anything' was a more accurate interpretation, which might also signify 'unfitness of mind' and therefore a wife's incapacity to fulfil the role of helpmeet that God intended for her.[3] His views would be reiterated time and again by reformers in the early twentieth century, but in the meantime the stigma attached to the divorce court in the sexual discourse of the 1880s stemmed from the necessary public expounding of how, when and where adulterers conducted their illicit liaisons – their very illicitness suggesting something more depraved than anything performed in the marriage bed.

Human nature being what it is, in the majority of cases it was probably nothing of the kind. Moreover, proving adultery meant little more than proving guilty intention and opportunity. Though the Campbell commission had originally intended that proof of adultery must be 'strict, satisfactory and conclusive', by the 1880s 'fair suspicion' seems to have been sufficient, such as might lead 'the guarded discretion of a reasonable and just man' to the conclusion adultery had taken place.[4] In practice this meant producing witnesses to the kind of intimate moments that were lacking in the Dunlo and Tasker suits: a furtive arm about a waist, a secret correspondence or rendezvous; a maid, perhaps, coming upon her mistress sitting on a gentleman's knee or her master guiding a stray hair away from a young lady's face. Though the language of some petitions might suggest otherwise, this was largely the sort of detail the court heard – or at least, the sort of detail reported in the press.

As a case in point we might take the 1893 petition of Harding Edward de Fonblanque Cox. Cox alleged his wife committed adultery on the 3.46 from Winchester to Basingstoke. He probably didn't mean to imply she had been caught *in flagrante* in broad daylight on public transport, her multiple layers of skirt and petticoats discarded or awkwardly thrust aside while one Mr Dyball satisfied his wanton lust (though such things were entirely possible given that private compartments and lack of internals corridors then made few places as private as a first- or second-class railway carriage between stations) but that witnesses on the platform had seen Dyball stealing a kiss and Mrs Cox not objecting, which, Cox hoped, when added to other similar evidence, might convince the jury that in the balance of probability, either in the railway carriage or at a more discreet location, the lovers had indeed broken the seventh commandment. In court, the newspapers would report, Mrs Cox blushed at the suggestion and in a quiet, shaky voice denied the scandalous charge; Dyball, on his honour (and to protect hers), emphatically did so; their advocates painted the picture as advantageously as possible for their own client while blackening the reputations of others; the judge made some strong comments on sin; and the jury drew its conclusion. Editors and correspondents then wrote some choice words of their own in judgement before moving on to the next case. Thus adultery was dealt with in as civilised a manner as possible and, for all but the guilty parties, a veneer of respectability was maintained. But if this was the norm, the question then follows, why did the divorce court become such a pariah and, more specifically, how does one account for Moore's poem directly referencing two divorce cases and bidding a less than fond farewell to 1886? Clearly, something exceptional happened that year.

Moore was not the only writer to think so. Looking back on this era from the 1900s, John Galsworthy chose 1886 as the year in which his anti-hero, Soames Forsyte – his passion aroused by an evening stroll through Hyde Park where countless lovers expressed their 'myriad passions' under cover of darkness – re-exerted his conjugal rights over his increasingly cold and distant wife, Irene, taking her by force in an act that triggered their separation and ultimately their divorce. Galsworthy dubbed it the year 'when extravagance was fashionable': when the veil of Victorian respectability decidedly slipped.[5] Two great causes célèbres famed (to quote Moore again) for their 'animal uncleanness, foul and sardonic vice, or stupendous revelations of mean hatred and meaner vanities' were the cause.[6] They involved aristocrats, the nouveau riche, professionals and politicians in the most compromising of positions. They revealed a depravity that was the absolute antithesis of Victorian sexual ideals. Even worse, at the heart of the first was an apparently respectable woman and the particular depravity she admitted, decorously described as

Vices Française.

The twenty-three-year-old's name was Virginia. At the tender age of eighteen she had married Donald Crawford, the forty-four-year-old secretary to the Scottish Lord Advocate and soon-to-be MP for Lanarkshire North-East. Virginia never loved him. The match had been more-or-less arranged by her parents, who considered Virginia wilful and in need of a firm hand. Virginia's father, Thomas Eustace Smith, was a wealthy shipbuilder from North Shields and MP for Tyneside; her mother, Martha, a patron of the arts and society hostess. Virginia and her sisters had been educated principally by governesses at the family's London home in Prince's Gate with a year at finishing school in Lausanne; following which they entered society and were expected to marry well. The eldest, Maye, fell for editor Ashton Wentworth Dilke, a man of good stamp and brother to rising star of the Liberal government, the MP for Chelsea, Sir Charles Wentworth Dilke. Maye married Ashton in 1876 and was widowed in 1883. The next eldest, Helen, accepted stockbroker Robert Harrison in 1877; and the youngest-but-one, Ida, was eventually (though begrudgingly) allowed to marry a doctor in 1884. While Maye was desperately happy, Ida seemed so and Helen's happiness is obscured by events and a lack of surviving documentation, Virginia was, by her own admission, desperately unhappy. In London during the parliamentary season she spent as much time as possible away from home, either out with her sisters or in the East End doing socially acceptable charitable work. A highly intelligent, strong-willed and robust young woman, the restrictions society and married life imposed upon her were a constant frustration. Very soon she began to develop decidedly 'inappropriate' interests.

The first suggestion that Virginia was going wrong came in an anonymous letter to Crawford in April 1882 – nine months into their marriage. 'Beware the member for Chelsea,' it warned, and watch out for a female relative who, with Virginia, has been seen flirting with male students at St George's Hospital. Crawford confronted Virginia. She denied the charges and he burned the letter. Then at Whitsun 1884, Crawford discovered that Virginia was corresponding with a Captain Forster when a letter addressed to her at the Whitechapel Mission was forwarded to him by its founder, Canon Barnett. Virginia admitted the correspondence but claimed it was nothing improper. Crawford insisted it cease or he would speak to her father about it. Virginia's sister, Maye, stepped in and smoothed matters over. In March 1885, a second anonymous letter arrived. 'The first person who ruined your wife was Sir Charles Dilke,' it read – Maye's brother-in-law. 'She has passed nights in his house, and is well known to his servants.' Crawford showed the letter to Virginia. She read it quietly and then dismissed it as the jealous and bitter invention of her mother, who at one time *had* been Dilke's mistress and with whom Virginia was on less-than-good terms. Crawford accepted her answer and threw the letter on the fire but was disquieted by Virginia's growing excitement when talking about her mother and her insistence that Dilke must be warned. On 10 June, a third letter arrived: 'Your wife was seen at the Metropole on Monday with Captain Forster. Are you a fool?' it asked. This time, Crawford was not satisfied with Virginia's denial and started to question her movements and inspect her correspondence. Finally, on 17 July he came home late from the Commons to find a fourth letter awaiting him on the hall table:

Fool! looking for the cuckoo when he has flown, having defiled your nest. You have been foully deceived, but dare not touch the real traitor.

Crawford took the letter to Virginia in her bedroom and on her request read her its contents. Calmly, she got out of bed, lit the gas lamp and stood looking at her husband. Once again, Crawford demanded to know if the allegations were true. 'Yes,' she replied. She had known she would have to tell him sometime and now he had a right to know. Crawford's mind immediately sprang to Forster, but this was wrong, she said: 'The real man with whom I have been guilty, the only man with whom I have been guilty, is Charles Dilke.'[7]

It is no exaggeration to say this confession marked the beginning of what would become one of the most scandalous and mysterious news events of the whole Victorian era. Unlike Crawford, Dilke was no mere Liberal backbencher, but had been Under-Secretary of State for Foreign Affairs from 1880 to 1882 and had subsequently entered cabinet as President of the Local Government Board. Backed by his close friend Joseph Chamberlain, he was hotly tipped to take over the leadership from Gladstone with all likelihood that he would become the next Liberal prime minister. Yet here was Virginia presenting Dilke as a Lothario. Her confession, as Crawford later remembered it, continued thus:

Dilke had visited her six months after she and Crawford married, spoken seductively to her and kissed her. When they all came to London for the next parliamentary session in February 1882, he'd called on her again and told her to meet him later that day at a house off Tottenham Court Road. There, he'd successfully seduced her. They'd subsequently returned to the house on one other occasion for sex. Thereafter, they met at each other's houses whenever they were in London. In February 1883 they'd spent two whole nights together when she'd come up to town before Crawford: she'd got home just in time to bathe and dress before his arrival. She was indeed known to Dilke's staff, she said: his footmen let her into his house; his coachman drove him to hers; and his servant Sarah – who had also been Dilke's mistress – helped Virginia dress after she and Dilke had been to bed. The affair continued until August 1884 when it ceased on the entreaty of a Mrs Rogerson, a close friend of Dilke's whom Virginia had taken into her confidence. Virginia paused. There was a moment's silence. Then almost as an afterthought she suddenly blurted out, 'He made me go to bed with Fanny' – another of his mistresses:

I did not like it at first, but I did so because he wished it. I would have stood on my head in the street if he had told me to do so. He used to come to bed beside us. He taught me every French vice. He taught me all I know. He used to say that I know more than most women of thirty. He said he took me first because I was so like my mother.

Crawford spent the night in his dressing room. The following morning he asked Virginia if there had been others. 'Never,' she replied: she had been overfamiliar with other men, but they never seduced her. Forster, too, had never been her lover. Virginia then left their home and went to Maye's. On 5 August, Crawford petitioned the court naming Dilke as co-respondent. The press immediately caught wind of it, the PMG reporting events as they unfolded under the damning headline 'The Great Social Scandal'.

It was, in fact, the divorce court's first public political scandal and as such there was no precedent for Dilke's response. He immediately offered to resign, but friends rallied and talked him out of it. The press, too, seemed content to await a verdict. *Vanity Fair* wrote that such a move was unnecessary if Dilke was only guilty of 'ordinary venial indiscretions' but admitted itself confused that in his letter to the Chelsea Liberal Association Dilke complained of having already been 'condemned unheard' while in the same breath offering to resign, which 'seems unnecessary' if he was innocent.[8]

On 12 February 1886, the case came before Justice Butt. Inderwick represented Crawford, Lockwood appeared for Virginia (though she was not present and did not defend the suit) and for Dilke were the sitting attorney general, Charles Russell, and the restive Henry James. Crawford was called and plainly relayed Virginia's confession. Two servants then gave corroborative evidence concerning Dilke's visits and Virginia's movements but nothing more; and with Mrs Rogerson declared too ill to attend court, having previously been too ill even to have her evidence taken on commission, the prosecution rested.

What happened next transformed the suit from a hiccup in the career of a successful politician to the potential means of its destruction. Russell rose and declared that as the prosecution's evidence rested solely on Virginia's confession there was no case for Dilke to answer. The judge agreed that the case against Dilke had not been sufficiently made. In such a situation, normal practice was for the co-respondent to be invited to enter the box anyway to declare his innocence on oath for his reputation's sake, but in this instance – incredibly – Russell announced that Dilke would not. For a man in Dilke's position, Russell argued, it was not necessary for him to put himself in a position where he might be cross-examined about other possible 'indiscretions' in his life 'such as all men have'. This was their advice to Dilke and he accepted it. Inderwick answered that if the judge accepted Virginia's confession, what Dilke did or didn't do would make no material difference to Crawford; Lockwood made no comment. So Justice Butt declared Virginia's confession 'clear, distinct and circumstantial' but said there was no evidence against Dilke. As such, he saw no reason to deny Crawford relief while simultaneously dismissing Dilke from the case.

To say the press were astounded would be an understatement. Justice Butt had effectively ruled that Virginia had committed adultery with Dilke, but Dilke had not committed adultery with her! He was heavily criticised for it. In actual fact, it is not *quite* what he had done: in the decree *nisi* report it is stated that as Dilke had been dismissed from the case, Virginia had been found guilty of adultery but not 'with' anybody.[9] Nevertheless, the verdict caused consternation. The *Law Journal* tried to resolve the matter, stating that it was a perfectly logical and acceptable ruling, but commentators had misapprehended Butt by forgetting that the law of evidence is directed to *results*. So far as the result to Dilke was concerned (costs), he had been found innocent; but so far as the result to Mrs Crawford (decree *nisi*) he had been pronounced guilty, and if he had not been, a gross injustice would have been done to her. As a clarification it failed completely. Said *The Bat*, it looked 'uncommonly like a mock trial'.[10] The fact that Butt had been a Liberal MP before he was raised to the Bench and was 'an old friend of Dilke's' left the impression it had all been 'squared' beforehand.[11] *Vanity Fair* called for Butt's dismissal, arguing that his application of a rule of law that set technicality above reason made a mockery of the justice system and left Virginia dishonoured and degraded while Dilke left court 'untouched, uncensored and indemnified'.[12] *The Times* simply said it was 'unfortunate' the trial hadn't been delayed for Mrs Rogerson to be heard. Meanwhile,

Liberal papers such as the *Daily News* greeted Dilke's vindication with satisfaction, claiming it a monstrous thing that his career should potentially have been blasted by the 'hysterical tendencies' of his accuser.[13]

Dilke's constituency got behind him and Dilke, having been awarded costs, considered himself completely and publicly exonerated. But he had not counted on the 'atmosphere of uncertainty', as the *Morning Post* called it, that lingered around the legal ambiguity. Spurred into action by the protestations of the *Daily News*, W. T. Stead, freshly released from prison following his controversial child-sex-trafficking exposé, 'The Maiden Tribute of Modern Babylon', wrote a leader for the PMG asking how bad Dilke's other 'indiscretions' must be to have kept him out of the witness box given the 'appalling' nature of the charges actually brought against him; and castigating Russell's use of Dilke's position as reason to evade a potentially awkward cross-examination.[14] Over the coming weeks the PMG repeated everything said about the case in other major papers across the country and vice versa. Eventually, the storm stirred up by Stead wore away Dilke's confidence and he began to see he had been badly advised. But what could be done? Ironically, the answer to that question also appeared in the PMG. Three days after the hearing, its readers were reminded of the existence of a public functionary, the Queen's Proctor, who had been specially appointed to prevent miscarriages of justice in divorce suits. Surely, in this case he was duty-bound to intervene.

On 20 April 1886, the Queen's Proctor, Sir Augustus Keppel Stephenson, expressed his intention of doing just that. Later, it would transpire that Dilke (*against* the advice of many friends who told him he should just let matters lie) had been instrumental in interesting him in the case. The proctor's petition, filed on 5 May, alleged that material facts had been withheld from the court and claimed there were witnesses known to both parties but not called whose evidence was material to determining the veracity of Virginia's confession. On 16 July, the whole cast (with the single exception of Fanny) reassembled for a second trial, this time to be heard by President Hannen and a special jury.

If Dilke had imagined this was his opportunity for vindication, he was sadly mistaken. The inference of bias in interim reporting – that *all* the silks in the first hearing were either Liberals or Dilke's friends or both – perhaps influenced the choice of advocates for the second round, which raised eyebrows but proved decisive. The proctor briefed an eminent ecclesiastical lawyer, Sir Walter Phillimore, and Crawford's solicitor chose Tory MP Henry Matthews QC. Matthews ran rings around Dilke, who when he finally entered the box made a terrible witness, giving lengthy explanations instead of answering questions plainly and succinctly; and Phillimore failed to cross-examine Virginia with anything like Matthews' precision. But more importantly, because Dilke had been dismissed from the first hearing, his counsel were reduced to the role of spectators at the second. They could not cross-examine witnesses on his behalf or object to damaging questions, such as those concerning Dilke's relationship with Virginia's mother; or the one that naturally followed his affirming that he owned property in Provence: that he must therefore be familiar with 'French ways'. Moreover, at times, it wasn't clear who the proctor's witnesses actually advantaged. The proctor's function, of course, was to test the veracity of Virginia's confession, not defend Dilke. Though the one aim often aligned with the other, Phillimore did not have Dilke's reputation on his conscience. Over the course of the next seven court days the public were transfixed by the sordid nature of the allegations and the juxtaposition between the evasiveness of some witnesses and the frankness of others.

Dilke completely denied the adultery and offered evidence to prove that his political commitments and the number of people coming and going from his Sloane Street home on political business made it impossible for the adultery to have happened as and when Virginia described. His footmen denied having let her into the house; his secretaries asserted that from their office on the half-landing they saw everything that went on in the house (which in relation to this charge was nothing); and his servant Sarah denied completely the role she had been accused of playing as Dilke's mistress, as Virginia's dresser and, more importantly, as the means of getting Fanny into the house and up to Dilke's bedroom – Fanny being her younger sister and a regular visitor to the house on Sarah's days off. But another servant, Ellen, contradicted Sarah's assertion that when Fanny called she always stayed downstairs, saying she had seen Fanny upstairs 'a good many times' *with* Sarah. Moreover, Ellen stated she had seen 'a lady' in Dilke's bedroom, which was unfortunate for Dilke but inconclusive as Ellen could not identify the lady due to her 'large black hat'.

Fanny's role in the affair was key, her evidence essential; but at the time of the second trial she could not be found. Under oath, Dilke's solicitor, Humbert, was ambiguous on this point. He stated that he'd known where Fanny was before the first hearing – he'd found her a position with a good family well known to him in Essex and had paid her expenses while she was there – but had lost her by the time the case was called. He'd re-established contact afterwards, but had then lost her again just before the second. This all seemed very convenient. He swore that Dilke was not involved in these arrangements and that Fanny had secrets of her own entirely unrelated to this case that kept her on the run. Subsequently, she had married and her husband forbade her to give evidence. Mrs Ruffle, in whose house Fanny had stayed, corroborated. But these claims were somewhat undermined by the evidence of another former servant of Dilke's, Anna Dessouslavy, who received a pension from him and lived in the infamous house off Tottenham Court Road. Anna told the court that during one of Fanny's disappearances she had employed her as a companion after bumping into Fanny quite by chance. As a witness, Anna served the proctor's purposes by denying that Dilke ever brought ladies to her house but had sobbed her way through both her examination and cross-examination, making it difficult for counsel to get her evidence straight and leaving the distinct impression she was not being completely honest. Matthews certainly doubted her capacity to afford a companion without subsidy.

Then there was Mrs Rogerson. The illness that kept her from the first hearing was revealed to be temporary insanity. She had, in fact, been under restraint at her doctor's house at the time. Her role, too, was considered ambiguous and has been questioned by commentators ever since. Had she been another of Dilke's mistresses? Was she a woman scorned and author of the third anonymous letter, written for her own dubious reasons to incriminate Virginia with Forster? This she denied, but she did confirm that she had been in Virginia's confidence. She also caused great sensation in court by admitting she'd played a pivotal role in an affair between Virginia and Forster from February 1885, allowing them to meet in her house, both in her company and alone. Her maids and footman corroborated this and two officers from Forster's regiment came forward to swear that Virginia had openly visited Forster at their barracks. This all tended to prove that Crawford's early suspicions about Forster were correct and Virginia had lied to him on that score, but where did that leave the affair with Dilke? Dilke's theory and the argument Phillimore relied upon in his closing address was that Virginia, her revengeful mother and the thwarted Mrs Rogerson had conspired to blacken Dilke's name and protect Virginia's real lover, Captain Forster. Why she might do this they could not explain and from an evidential point of view they did not consider it relevant: the fact that Virginia had lied to Crawford about Forster was enough to throw doubt on her whole confession.

Perhaps if Dilke had been a better witness and Phillimore a better advocate their argument might have won over the jury, but the combination of Matthews and Virginia proved too much for them. With a coolness that has subsequently been described as heartless, Virginia recounted frankly and shamelessly every detail of her affair with Dilke and how she had been seduced. She had succumbed to whatever he asked, she stated. At Anna's house, they'd arrived separately and remained only half an hour in the bedroom while Anna was in the parlour. At Sloane Street, she'd visited Dilke in a fifteen-minute window before he left for the Foreign Office, where he was expected at midday. She described how she waited in the street until the coast was clear for the footman or Dilke himself to let her in and then tiptoed up to the first-floor bedroom, creeping past the secretary's office unnoticed, her movements muffled by the thick-pile stair carpet. She'd lied to her husband as to her whereabouts so she could spend whole nights with Dilke, she said. On one occasion, she, Dilke and Fanny had all gone to bed together and Sarah had dressed her afterwards; and, on another, a maid came into the bedroom when she was there, looked horrified and ran. And so it went on, with each admission substantiated by convincing detail.

Some of her facts differed from those recounted by Crawford at the first hearing. This, she explained, was due to errors in Crawford's understanding or resulted from information that had only recently been verified, such as the address of Anna's house which Dilke never let her write down and which she had only recently discovered by diligent searching of the area to see if she could recognise it four years after the event. What were the chances she would identify a house belonging to Dilke's pensioner? If the jury had any doubts that this incredible event occurred, Virginia answered them by offering to sketch a plan of its interior, which she did there and then in elaborate detail. She also described the layout of Dilke's bedroom in Sloane Street with perfect aplomb (but questionable accuracy) and withstood any suggestion under cross-examination that there was simply not time for the adultery to have occurred on the days specified due to both her and Dilke having other proven commitments. She emphasised the brevity of their encounters, the necessity for her to rush and, on one occasion, actually miss luncheon to catch a train she was known to be on. She was even able to explain the fact that she had lied to Crawford about Forster and then asked him to keep Forster's name out of the proceedings: at the time she was sleeping with Forster he was engaged to be married to someone else (sensation!) and, she said, she did not wish to destroy his future happiness. The fact that Forster was called to confirm that their meetings had taken place during his engagement not only at Mrs Rogerson's but at a house of ill-repute only increased the likelihood in the jury's minds that Virginia had been brazen enough to conduct the affair with Dilke as she described.

When after an hour and a half Virginia left the box, they were more-or-less convinced. Maye's appearance in the box, followed by Virginia's solicitor – George Lewis, again – cemented their opinion. Both Lewis and Maye confirmed that everything Virginia had said was consistent with what she had previously told them. Moreover, weight was added to Maye's evidence by her stating that Dilke had visited Virginia while she was staying with Maye after leaving Crawford and effectively threatened the whole family with ruin if she did not retract her confession. That Matthews then brought forward witnesses the proctor had subpoenaed but failed to call – residents of the house where Anna lodged who testified that Dilke *had* been there with at least one other unchaperoned woman (though not Virginia) – clinched him the case.

In his closing address Matthews told the jury that they must either believe that Crawford had been 'befooled and bejuggled' by his clever wife or brand Dilke a sexual deviant who, with brutal behaviour more becoming a beast than a man, had treated Virginia in a worse manner than most men would treat a French prostitute. Or they must brand him a coward for sitting mute throughout the first trial while he knew (if he was innocent) that a serious miscarriage of justice was being perpetrated and while a woman *he* now branded a liar blackened his name and triumphed. In answer, Phillimore attempted to console the jury that, if they found for the proctor, thereby confirming Dilke's innocence, Crawford would still be able to re-petition the court for a divorce on the confessed ground of Virginia's adultery with Forster. He picked at the holes in Virginia's story and questioned her motives, but the jury were not convinced. After only fifteen minutes' deliberation they upheld the verdict of the previous trial. The president granted Crawford a decree absolute and condemned the proctor to costs.

So much about this case is incredible, from Virginia's confession, to Dilke's public proclamation of innocence, to the role of the press – particularly that of Stead – in encouraging the second trial and its upholding of the equivocal verdict of the first. In its immediate aftermath, calls for Dilke's prosecution for perjury dominated press reporting. A respectable young lady would never blacken her own name with false testimony: Dilke, therefore, must be the liar. Though historians now question the stereotypical view of the innocent, passionless Victorian woman, mores, manners and medical ignorance then demanded that women were still portrayed and treated as 'timid creatures and natural invalids' incapacitated by their biological cycle and in need of masculine protection.[15] Virginia's confession may have appalled, but she was still a woman: there had to be a man to corrupt her. The manner in which she spoke of Dilke's hold over her confirmed this and Matthews' comments resonated. Virginia was to be pitied. The moral, if not the legal, guilt was Dilke's.

Dilke's friends, however, denounced this as a wave of sensationalism bordering on mass hysteria. 'What hypocrites – what hypocrites we are!' began Henry Labouchere in *Truth*, admitting he may be prejudiced but he preferred to consider his friend innocent until proven guilty. In a long article he dissected the evidence before suggesting that the all-male jury had been taken in by Virginia's beauty, soft voice and winning manner.[16] Dilke, who had lost his seat in the disastrous Liberal defeat of

July 1886, became obsessed with clearing his name. He turned to the more-than-willing popular press to promulgate his innocence. In October 1886 his 'Notes' appeared in the *Evening News*, filling ten columns over two days with his version of events. He then spent huge sums on investigators who dug into every aspect of the case and fed back to a committee of his friends established to prove his innocence. In 1891 they published their findings ahead of Dilke's anticipated return to politics as MP for the Forest of Dean. The lone voice against him by then belonged to Stead, who continued his 'relentless persecution' of Dilke on a 'solemn charge' to Cardinal Manning (then deceased) that he would keep the 'deviant' out of public office.[17] Despite Stead's best efforts, Dilke was returned to parliament in 1892 but was destined thereafter to remain a backbencher.

With so many witnesses in this case having their own agendas, it is impossible to determine exactly what happened and between whom. Increasingly, however, history has favoured Dilke's conspiracy theory, drawing heavily on the work of biographer Roy Jenkins who was first to examine Dilke's private papers after they became accessible in the late 1950s. Virginia never spoke another word about the affair. She converted to Catholicism and, with Stead's help, became a writer and social campaigner much admired within the Catholic community. The vast array of disparate facts, theories, suppositions and information about this 'Great Social Scandal' would easily fill another book. But would it come any nearer to solving the mystery?

In the wake of the case newspaper proprietors were accused like never before of cashing in on and raising the fever pitch of sensationalism. In this they were outdone by the 'great quires of lust' referenced in Moore's poem: at least three fly-by-night publishing houses produced verbatim reports of the second trial, advertising them in the popular press as containing such enticements as 'authentic portraits' of Dilke, Virginia and Fanny and detailing the whole case in 'handy volume form' – all for a penny. Their existence horrified some and delighted others but provide historians with valuable material for compiling an image of society at the *fin de siècle* – not least because, just four months after the divorce court doors closed on Dilke, their presses were at it again, churning out copious reports of the next great cause célèbre. Moore's year of filth was not yet done: December saw public fascination with the artfulness and intrigue of the Crawford case give way to utter repugnance at the allegations of Lady Colin Campbell and sheer titillation at her husband's faith in

What the Butler Saw.

One of the things master tactician George Lewis knew was the importance of invoking the court's first-come-first-served policy in suits with cross-petitions that, unless there was good reason for doing otherwise, allowed the advocate representing the leading petitioner to open the hearing and close it. It was an advantage well worth having and resulted, on the morning of 26 November 1886, in the comical sight of the juniors for both sides in the Campbell suit competing to be first on his feet to lay claim to the privilege already secured by Lewis having raced Gertrude Campbell's petition round to the court twenty-four hours before her husband's solicitor could file his. Russell, as lead counsel for Gertrude, weighed in behind his junior. Justice Butt upheld their claim; and Campbell's leader – the hard-headed, able and plain-speaking Scotsman Robert Finlay QC – was forced to concede (not for the last time) that in addition to battling Russell in court, he was up against the unrivalled legal generalship of Lewis, who also knew that attack was the best form of defence.

The first round of attack in this suit had actually happened two years previously when Gertrude sued for a judicial separation alleging the cruelty of her husband, the fifth son of the Duke of Argyll and most recent in a long line of Campbells to represent Argyllshire in Parliament. On 26 March 1884, President Hannen and a special jury had heard the case in camera following a last-minute application by Russell that the nature of the charge called for privacy. The verdict had gone in Gertrude's favour and Campbell had appealed, claiming the private hearing had thrown 'undeserved imputations' on his character. By his insistence that the appeal be heard in open court, the general public learned that the nature of Campbell's cruelty had been to wilfully and recklessly infect his wife with a venereal disease three months into their marriage. His assertions that he had followed the advice of medical men, that Gertrude had known of his condition and been in no danger at the time of their intercourse and that the president had misled the jury in suggesting otherwise were rejected, and Campbell was ordered to pay Gertrude permanent alimony of £225 a year. But he was not content to leave matters there. On 12 November, the press announced that each had sued the other for divorce. 'Happy lawyers!' wrote the *South London Chronicle*: it promised to be 'a great entanglement!'

How great was perhaps determined by Campbell's overblown sense of injustice at proceedings thus far. Historian Gail Savage has made some interesting observations about cases involving venereal disease. She suggests that women who charged their husbands with cruelty of this kind 'wielded a very powerful weapon', for while the Contagious Diseases Acts had focused on women as the reservoir of venereal infections, ignoring the role men played in spreading them, the divorce court did the opposite. A wife was assumed to be pure unless proved otherwise. It naturally followed, then, that venereal disease was most often brought into the home by a husband's sexual misconduct. Moreover, unlike acts of violence behind closed doors, the evidence held within the wife's own diseased body was difficult to argue against. Thus it could be said that infected wives 'deployed the double standard in their own defence'.[18] A husband's best course in such a situation was to overturn the assumption of her purity by destroying her reputation. This Campbell set out to do, accusing Gertrude of adultery with not one co-respondent but four: Captain Eyre Massey Shaw, Chief of the Metropolitan Fire Brigade; Brigadier General Sir William Francis Butler, then serving in the Sudan; Dr Thomas Bird, her physician and, at one time, Campbell's; and George Charles Spencer-Churchill, Marquis of Blandford at the time of the alleged adultery and Duke of Marlborough by the time it came to court. Marlborough's inclusion was most damaging: in 1877 he had been co-respondent in the highly publicised Aylesford suit, and in 1883 his own wife had successfully divorced him over the same affair. Gertrude's association with him was therefore already suspect and Lewis was 'very nervous' about his cross-examination.[19]

By comparison, the allegation in Gertrude's rushed petition was trivial: one act of adultery with a maid, Amelia Watson, in June 1882 for which there was only one witness: Gertrude's cousin Lady Frances Miles of Leigh Court near Bristol, who came forward late in the day having never previously told a soul what she had seen. Knowing how flimsy this evidence was, Russell used his opening address to regale the court with all the details of the offence for which Campbell had *already* been found guilty in what Finlay described as a blatant attempt to prejudice the jury against him.

The Campbells had met in September 1880, when he was twenty-seven and Gertrude twenty-three. They had fallen in love at first sight and become engaged three days later. The match was welcomed by her family, the Edmund Bloods of County Clare, but only reluctantly accepted by his: the Duke of Argyll wished for a more auspicious alliance for his son. At the time, Campbell suffered from a perineal fistula – an abnormal channel between the anal canal and the perineum, usually associated with chronic abscesses – that Russell described as the result of a 'youthful indiscretion' ten years earlier. It was disputed whether or not he had made the Blood family fully aware of the nature and cause of his condition but he had told Gertrude that if they became husband and wife they would not be able to consummate their marriage straightaway. They married on 21 July 1881. There was no further allusion to sex until October 1881 when, after two failed operations to repair the fistula, Campbell communicated to Gertrude via a fragment of a letter from his doctor that it was their medical opinion that sex would now be beneficial for him. According to Russell, the 'innocent' Gertrude felt revulsed at the suggestion and was shocked when, before their first intercourse, Campbell told her she must take precautions to protect herself; precautions which later evidence revealed to include douching herself with vinegar. Within weeks, she was 'suffering and in pain'. Campbell, nevertheless, insisted on intercourse again the night before a third operation on 19 December.

Thereafter, Gertrude suffered in varying degrees with little reprieve until long after their separation. Following a fourth unsuccessful operation in September and a long convalescence at Frances's home, Gertrude asked her cousin to convey to Campbell that her life had become 'revolting and unbearable' as a result of her having to submit to his embraces. She begged to be allowed to live with him henceforth as his nurse and friend only and promised to keep his secret if he would relieve her of any sexual obligation. He replied that fistula was a common complaint and he hoped she would not slander him as being 'unfit for marriage'. In April 1883, Gertrude suffered such severe pain and flooding at menstruation that Campbell verbally accused her attending physician – Dr Bird – of 'managing' a miscarriage for her (which must have been the result of adultery as they had not had intercourse since the previous June); and when following his fifth operation he propositioned Gertrude again and she told him that if he insisted on sex he would wake to find her dead in the bed beside him, according to Russell, Campbell said she must submit or leave his house. Knowing she could not do so without becoming prey to gossips herself, she warned her husband that if he made her an outcast their whole story would have to be made known.

Finlay's response was to argue that at the time of Campbell's proposal he had not been infectious for many years; that his fistula was a common complaint that might equally have been caused by external injury;[20] and that their periods of abstinence were to prevent Campbell injuring himself rather than the spread of infection to Gertrude. He also claimed their marriage had been pushed ahead by Mrs Blood, who interpreted Campbell's warning about consummation as him trying to renege on his proposal.

Really there was nothing for the silks to argue over. The question of venereal disease had already been decided. Going over it again in so much detail did nothing but cause the press great consternation. They didn't like having to report medical evidence but in this case had no choice. How it fitted into the case was not yet certain. Across the board, correspondents strained their ingenuity to avoid making any direct reference to anything so distasteful. Campbell's conversations with the Bloods were described simply as 'delicate' and his condition as 'infectious' or, at worst, a 'loathsome disease'. Still, *The Bat* accused the press collectively of disseminating 'the most revolting details' ever published purely for pecuniary gain 'within their legal rights, but without moral excuse'.[21] As the case progressed, the columns dedicated to it only increased and Stead, still smarting from accusations of excessive prurient interest in his 'Maiden Tribute' exposé, named and shamed the worst offenders in a leader entitled 'Pecksniff and Poison'. The PMG, by comparison, restricted itself to a mere selection of verbatim questions and answers, allowing Stead to claim the moral ascendancy. It was clear that this case was going to be as controversial as the Crawford's – and there was much more 'filth' to come.

Gertrude had been an inattentive nurse, said Finlay, preferring to socialise than sit with her husband whose health often confined him to bed. Her alleged adultery with Marlborough extended from Purfleet to Paris and found them inhabiting adjoining bedrooms at Leigh Court during Easter 1882. Those with Butler, Shaw and Bird took place in the drawing or dining rooms of the Campbells' Cadogan Place home while the cuckolded Campbell was confined upstairs incapacitated. Moreover, Finlay claimed, it was only *after* Campbell first voiced his suspicion to Gertrude of her infidelities that she and George Lewis first concocted the trumped-up charge of venereal infection to screen her guilt. Lewis had then written a threatening letter to Campbell demanding he sign a document to say he had deceived Gertrude as to the risk of sexual relations and promise to proposition her no more or they would expose him. Gertrude's vaginal discharge was a common complaint that preceded relations with Campbell and did not incapacitate her or prevent her committing adultery, Finlay claimed. Moreover, he would prove that the adultery with Amelia Watson could never have taken place: the *pièce de résistance* of Finlay's opening gambit was the immediate calling of a Dr Clement Godson, who announced that he had examined the maid and discovered her still to be *virgo intacta*.

'Sensation!' cried the press. But such a finding, surprisingly, did not necessarily preclude a guilty verdict if there was sufficient evidence of overfamiliarity. The evidence, in this instance, was that Lady Frances claimed to have spied on the pair one evening in June 1882 having become 'full of suspicion' after Campbell told her Amelia had 'very pretty hair' which he liked to take down and play with. So she had watched and espied Campbell 'sitting on the edge of the bed in his nightshirt with his arms around [Amelia's] neck and she leaning against his knee'. Frances did not then linger to see any more; and she did not mention the incident to anyone until Campbell told her he was going to instigate proceedings against Gertrude. Her response then was to tell Campbell what she had seen; to announce she would expose him. This she had done. But her protestations about Campbell's flirtation with Amelia were compromised by Finlay producing letters Frances had written

Campbell in 1884, in which it sounds suspiciously like she was trying to convince him to do the 'decent thing' and commit an act of adultery with a prostitute to enable Gertrude to be the one to divorce him. Why would Frances have done this, asked Finlay, if she knew that Campbell had already committed adultery with Amelia?

As to Gertrude's adultery, most of Campbell's evidence came from servants. The well-to-do were completely dependent on household staff and those who spent time 'above stairs' were often privy to much of what went on in the house. Yet they had more in common with each other than with their employers and when relationships soured were apt to be vindictive and insubordinate. One object lesson from the Campbell case is the consequence of unrestricted gossip in the servants' hall.

In the witness box, accused maid Amelia Watson said she and Gertrude's lady's maid, Rose Baer, used to watch from the upstairs windows to see gentlemen callers come to the house. She claimed they had seen Captain Shaw walking up and down outside; that Rose had shown her many letters Gertrude asked her to post to Marlborough; and that Gertrude had insisted neither Shaw nor Marlborough were to be announced in Campbell's presence. Rose Baer said that Marlborough was a frequent visitor and that she delivered letters to him from Gertrude every day. On several occasions when Gertrude had ventured out alone after dinner and returned home late, Rose noticed that her mistress's dress was disarranged at the back and the skirt open as if it had been taken off in the meantime and hastily put back on. She also claimed that when Gertrude went to Leigh Court at Easter 1882 without Campbell, she'd found a gentleman's neckerchief in Gertrude's bedroom and that one night, when she was helping Gertrude undress, she'd heard someone's footsteps on the stairs and Gertrude coughed loudly to indicate she was not alone. The person went into the next-door bedroom: Marlborough's. Every morning she could tell Gertrude's bed had been slept in by two people; and the discovery of 'some appliances' in the bedroom that Rose was surprised to find because she knew Gertrude was not sleeping with her husband led her to the conclusion Gertrude was 'bad after men'. All of her suspicions she shared with the butler, James O'Neill, on her return to London. As a consequence, she was sacked.

O'Neill corroborated Rose's evidence. He said he frequently opened the door to Marlborough and Shaw and on one occasion when he took tea up to Gertrude and Marlborough he found the drawing-room door locked. When he returned ten minutes later it was unlocked, the sofa and cushions were disarranged and Gertrude's face flushed. A similar event was witnessed by the previous butler, Albert de Roche, who remembered Gertrude once leaping up from the sofa where she had been sitting next to Marlborough when he entered. She was flurried and her skirt was raised. She shook it out as she stood up, but he was quite certain he'd seen her petticoat. O'Neill continued that on another occasion when Shaw visited he heard noises coming from the dining room when he was in the pantry below it. O'Neill went back upstairs and looked through the keyhole. There he saw Gertrude lying on the dining room floor with Shaw on top of her. He could see Gertrude's head and face but not her feet, which were pointing away towards the window. He could see Shaw as far down as his waist. The 'minute particulars' O'Neill went into were reduced in newspapers to the fact that the couple were 'in a position that would admit of but one construction'.

'Sensation!' once again. Ten years before the invention of the mutoscope that would introduce frequenters of Britain's seaside piers to primitive movie reels depicting *What the Butler Saw*, headlines proclaimed the thrill in relation to the Campbell case. Yet the evidence of former servants was never taken at face value and Russell gave all their evidence short shrift, seriously flustering Rose in his relentless cross-examination before setting about trying to undo O'Neill by questioning his ability to hold a tea-tray balanced on his knee with one hand while he opened a door with the other, and querying whether there wasn't a curtain behind the door obstructing his view that would have needed a third to sweep it aside. O'Neill haughtily responded that his evidence 'amply demonstrated' his tea-tray-juggling abilities and that the curtain was pushed back by the opening door.

Russell was less easily deflected on the issue of the keyhole in what turned out to be the most comical aspect of the case. He asked O'Neill to repeat word for word what he had seen through it, which O'Neill did with perfect aplomb. But how could he explain having seen *anything* through the aperture when there were brass drops over the escutcheon plates on both sides, asked Russell, pointing out that for these to remain up the key had to be in the lock. Sensation rapidly turned to consternation. So crucial was this point that the defence asked the judge for permission to go and inspect the lock for themselves! The judge was reluctant and one outraged juror said they could get quite sufficient keyhole practice at home. Fearing that the inspection would not come off, Gertrude's brother, Mr Neptune Blood, made a private application to the then-residents of the house for him to inspect it alone and entered the witness box several days later to advise the court that the keyhole was quite considerably smaller than many he had attempted to look through since O'Neill gave his evidence! Moreover, with the key in the lock nothing could be seen on the floor. Blood was bombarded with questions by the jury: Had he actually placed anything there to test it? Answer: No. Did the dinner-wagon he described as being behind the door disrupt the view? Answer: Not in the slightest. And so it went on until Russell announced that an architect would be called. The following morning, armed with a sketch of the lock and a plan of the house, the architect told the jury that an experiment with a coat and carpetbag had convinced him *nothing* could be seen. But his subsequent announcement that the drops, if carefully pushed, *would* stop above the keyhole, created doubt. Nothing, it seemed, would satisfy the jury but an excursion to the property, which finally took place on day sixteen. Reporting back, the foreman announced that what they had seen had thrown 'a good deal of discredit' on one of the witnesses' statements. 'O'Neill's?' asked the judge. 'No, Neptune Blood's,' replied the foreman (sensation!): the dinner-wagon obstructed the view entirely (always supposing it was there then, of course).

Only after all his servants had gone before him did Campbell, deathly pale and careworn, enter the box himself. His evidence revealed the extent to which his nurses, as much as his servants, had dripped poison into his ear. The worst culprit was Annie Duffy, who had nursed him for two years from September 1882. She had already denounced Gertrude's concern for her husband's welfare to the court ('she left everything to me'), adding that this made her suspect Gertrude's interest in medical matters (she kept a book 'of a very disgusting nature about men's and women's diseases' covered in white paper in her room) – particularly after she'd heard Gertrude talking knowledgeably about contraception with her sister-in-law. Annie had also kept a very close eye on Gertrude's dealings with Dr Bird, putting a disreputable interpretation on the length of time he spent alone with her in her room (once 'he came at 3 or 4 p.m. and stayed with her until 11 p.m.... he said he'd fallen asleep'). All this Annie fed back to Campbell. She was also the originator of the suggestion that Bird had performed an illegal abortion on Gertrude in April 1883 – which she'd deduced from the intensity of pain and haemorrhage Gertrude suffered that day – and the cause of Campbell suspecting General Butler. Gertrude had known the general since childhood. Annie alleged Gertrude had entertained him alone two weeks before the abortion and had emerged flushed and dishevelled from the drawing room to say she was 'not at home' to a visiting friend. A young housemaid afterwards claimed she'd seen the 6-foot-4-inch forty-five-year-old general tiptoeing from the house.

All this and Gertrude's comings and goings while Campbell was confined to his bed played on his 'diseased' mind, argued Russell, making him 'suspicious, morbid and jealous'. For this, he was to be pitied: for falling prey to what Edward Clarke described in Bird's defence as 'the malicious and imaginative memory of an acidulated nurse' (for there would have been more to fear from Bird's prolonged visit had the doctor remained awake!) Campbell's suspicions concerning Marlborough – which had extended from 1881 to 1885, throughout the whole time he alleged Gertrude was sleeping with the three other men – had led him to take some extreme actions. In June 1884 and again in March 1885, when Campbell suspected Gertrude was in Paris with Marlborough, he had reported her to the French authorities. By the terms of the Napoleonic Code, had she been caught in an act of fornication she could have been arrested and imprisoned at St Lazare with the prostitutes of the city. She wasn't on either occasion, but the thought that a British gentleman would attempt to instigate such a thing – twice – against his own wife, and then shamelessly admit it in court, was indefensible.

Gertrude followed her husband into the box and gave a clear and convincing account of her movements, which included a great deal of charitable work (which other witnesses verified) and produced letters to her mother that revealed she was less than happy about having to go into society alone due to her husband's poor health. She, Captain Shaw and Dr Bird answered all allegations against them. The doctor's late inclusion in Campbell's petition was put down to Campbell wishing to avoid paying his bill. Marlborough, to Lewis's great relief, admitted liaisons with two other women (one of whom accompanied him to Purfleet) in answer to the charges concerning him. Despite all this and the impassioned speeches of counsel and a lengthy afternoon's summing-up the verdict was by no means a fait accompli. The jury retired at 6.44 p.m. on the eighteenth day. Their prolonged absence led to excitement inside court and out. At 9.15 they returned to say they agreed as regards Campbell – that he was not guilty of adultery – but were in complete disagreement about Gertrude. Their job had been made harder by General Butler's point-blank refusal to return to England for the trial, which had been explained as being due to his devout Catholicism which denied the divorce court's right to exist, but which was highly suggestive of guilt. The judge impressed upon the jury the 'calamity' of their failing to agree. Perhaps, piped up a juror, if they could just have something to eat they might have another try. The judge agreed and asked them to return by 10 p.m. When they finally re-emerged at 10.13, the judge had already gone and their verdict was delivered to the registrar: not guilty on all counts. To this the foreman added that the jury wished to express their opinion that in not coming forward in the interests of justice, the general's conduct was 'unworthy of an English officer and a gentleman'.

This sentiment was echoed throughout the press as loudly as were the praises of the legal personalities involved sung, particularly those of George Lewis. 'Whitewashed All Around' ran the PMG headline – principally by Lewis's skill in representing Marlborough, Butler, Shaw and Gertrude: he had 'literally pulled the case out of the fire' to win a complete, if unexpected, victory.[22] Others disagreed. Said *Vanity Fair*, 'the obvious, the crushing, the inevitable, the only possible conclusion' was that Captain Butler was guilty; and the author Mrs Belloc Lowndes recorded in her diary that some years after the event, Lord Haldane had seen a votive offering in a church placed by General Butler on the anniversary of the verdict – something he interpreted as 'conclusive proof' of his guilt.[23]

At eighteen days, the trial was the longest in the divorce court's history. The evidence of forty-four witnesses had been heard. With three firms of solicitors briefing three silks and six juniors, it was also one of the most expensive. *Vanity Fair* had it on 'good authority' that the *real* cost (as opposed to those the court allowed) was around £18,000 – a figure more-or-less confirmed by Campbell's appearance in the bankruptcy court the following year with liabilities of over £15,000, of which a third represented costs he was condemned to pay for Gertrude and the four co-respondents. The rest was mostly unrepaid family loans. The trial ruined Campbell in every respect. While Gertrude embarked on a career as a journalist and playwright, garnered the admiration of the artistic community and literati and was declared welcome at court (the queen believing her to have been treated most shamefully by the Campbells, according to *Truth*), Campbell was barely seen in England again. He emigrated to India where he practised at the Bombay Bar until his death on 18 June 1895, aged only forty-two.

With these two high-profile suits, divorce court disapproval reached a new zenith (or perhaps, more correctly, a new depth). Never before had there been such a perfect storm of salaciousness, celebrity and intrigue. Anticipation of the Campbell suit had begun the moment the court doors closed on the Eustons, and the calling of the Crawford suit between the first and second Campbell trials was manna to scandalmongers and moralists alike. Each seemed to magnify the other and afterwards they were often recalled together. So closely were they linked that, looking back on his time at the PMG some fifty years later, journalist J. W. Robinson-Scott completely confused them, adding the Duke of Marlborough and Captain Shaw to Virginia Crawford's list of possible paramours![24] New calls to curb press reporting were heard and ironically led by Henry Matthews QC, the star of the second Crawford trial, who had afterwards been made Home Secretary by Salisbury as a reward for his performance. Matthews tried to secure the support of President Hannen for his campaign, provoking uproar among the 'new journalists' that it was nothing more than a thinly disguised attempt to protect those living the high life from scandal. Matthews' failure allowed the Dilke and Campbell suits to become a kind of shorthand for everything deemed morally abhorrent about polite society. In 1890, both cases featured heavily in an article by George

Moore entitled 'The Legal Laundry', published after the Dunlo suit and ahead of the next great political divorce scandal involving Irish nationalist Charles Stewart Parnell. In it, Moore called for all suits to be heard in camera like the French, who did this not because their cases were filthier than ours but because they knew 'that dirty linen is better washed at home'. 'Divorce Court filth is becoming the habitual colour of the Londoner's mind,' he warned.[25]

There was no shortage of it. The 1885 Bosvile case, in which Thomas Bosvile accused his wife of adultery with the Hon. Augustus William Craven and won, reared its ugly head again in 1886 when his divorced wife appealed to the court to have their son named his legitimate heir after Bosvile denounced him. Throughout the whole of 1887 this case was kept in the public eye by her failure and various unsuccessful appeals. In 1889, it was the turn of stage sensation Marie Tempest to fill the courtroom with theatrical celebrities to witness her admitting adultery with Henry John Leslie, owner-proprietor of the Lyric Theatre. The following year saw Dunlo and Parnell in court, followed by the 1891 suit of Captain Frederick Molison Burke, retired officer of the British India Steamship Company and one-time Consul General to the King of Portugal for the province of Algiers. Burke accused his wife, Lucy, of adultery with no less than six co-respondents. To the delight of court followers, Lucy was revealed to have been a frequenter of masked balls in Algiers (a highly *un*respectable pastime) and to have been arrested for soliciting in Switzerland (sensation!), but even more scandalously, one of the co-respondents – a young Frenchman named Camille Avon who had written to Lucy that he was going 'mad at the mere thought of kissing your adored lips' and that her 'possession' made him 'insatiable' – dared to admit that, though he hadn't actually managed to seduce her, he would have liked to! Lucy's guilt made the front cover of the *Illustrated Police News* under the catchy headline 'A Plethora of Co-Respondents'.

Then there was the even more scandalous suit of the Earl and Countess Russell, which extended throughout the whole of the 1890s and provided the only example of divorce litigation in this and the Edwardian eras to involve allegations of homosexual activity. In the first round, Mabel Russell alleged her husband visited the bedroom of a man named Roberts late at night after he had undressed and remained with him 'for several hours, and again in the morning'.²⁶ She failed to convince the jury. In the second round, Russell alleged that her repetition of the allegations after the hearing in an interview in *Hawk* amounted to legal cruelty. The trial took place just as Oscar Wilde's libel trial was being heard at the Old Bailey and, though again unsuccessful, led the editor of *Reynolds's*, W. M. Thompson, who had been in court for Mabel's cross-examination, to conclude in a leader entitled 'Sex-Mania' that the aristocracy was obsessed with fornication and that their idleness led to the even worse crime of sodomy. 'For a body so limited in numbers,' Thompson wrote, 'the amount and the gravity of their offences against public and private morals are astounding. By what is revealed we may guess at what is concealed.'²⁷

And this was key. It didn't matter what the more respectable factions of the press suppressed, compressed or paraphrased, the imaginative public could and did fill in the blanks. Though the lifestyle of those who could afford to make use of the divorce court in long-drawn-out battles was alien to the majority of spectators, the secret of sex was something everyone shared and there was a certain voyeuristic delight in watching the well-to-do have their private lives undressed; the unspoken things that were not respectable or of which they were ashamed revealed in a public arena. With the Obscene Publications Act (1857) controlling what could be written in fiction or shown on the stage, where else could such an experience be found, unless in the bawdy music hall? Looked at in this light, Moore's complaint against the 'complete licence of expression' given to newspapers in reporting celebrity scandals might more accurately be considered an expression of long-felt disgruntlement at the 'excessive prudery' demanded of novelists than any real offence to his moral sensibilities. Moore was not known for prudery. In his 'year of filth' he too had pushed the bounds of respectability by putting a conversation about the realities of premarital sex into the mouths of young maidens fresh out of convent school in *A Drama in Muslin* (1886); and later he emphasised the pivotal sex scene in *Esther Waters* (1894) by expressing it in ellipsis. Not until 1926 did the Regulation of Reports Act restrict press reporting of divorce cases: a restriction that still applies. Still, the divorce court continued to find its critics, its fans and its victims, willing to gamble everything for the opportunity to start life anew.

5

Occupational Hazards

CASSIO: Reputation, reputation, reputation! O, I have lost my reputation! I h' lost the immortal part of myself and what remains is bestial! My reputation, Iago, my reputation!

IAGO: ... Reputation is an idle and most false imposition, oft got without merit and lost without deserving. You have lost no reputation at all unless you repute yourself such a loser.

Othello, Act 2, sc. 3

'Reputations are mysterious things,' wrote H. G. Wells in relation to the press's capacity to make them, 'and not so easily forced.'[1] Were they, though, more easily lost once won? If there was one thing the Crawford and Campbell suits proved it was that a brush with the divorce court could change the course of a man's life whether the verdict went with or against him. Dilke's performance in court, as much as any suspicion of his guilt, unfitted him for high office; and Campbell was condemned as much for having accused his wife of multiple adulteries as for his proven cruelty. Reputing oneself a loser, whatever Iago might say, was not requisite. Dilke had, on several occasions, cried out like Cassio, but was always talked round by political allies and friends; Campbell had not, but would perhaps have spared himself much agony if he had capitulated after the first hearing. Charles Stewart Parnell, meanwhile, the enigmatic leader of the nationalist Irish Parliamentary Party, appeared decidedly unperturbed when on Christmas Eve 1889, Captain William Henry O'Shea made him co-respondent in a suit against Katharine, his wife of twenty-six years and the mother of his five children. Whatever the verdict, Parnell adjudged he could not lose. If O'Shea won, Katharine would be free to marry him; if he lost, Parnell would continue to live with her anyway, believing, as he did, that it was their destiny to be together: 'I will give my life to Ireland, but to you I give my love,' he'd apparently told her.[2]

It is possible Parnell's cavalier attitude was based on the assumption he could retain his position, secure Home Rule for Ireland *and* have Katharine. There were considerable reasons for him thinking so, wrote Stead immediately after the event, if he compared his situation with Dilke's. Dilke may have lost his seat, but he was never charged with perjury and had remained an 'honourable' and a member of her majesty's privy council. Moreover, no serious person could contend for a single second that Parnell's conduct compared with the 'infamies' of Dilke.[3] For as Parnell's biographer Paul Bew points out, rarely had an illicit amour been more domesticated or well known: it had been an open secret in the corridors of Westminster for years. Home Secretary Sir William Harcourt had in 1882 openly referred to O'Shea in a cabinet meeting as 'the husband of Parnell's mistress'.[4] In addition, the Parnell Commission had just concluded that Parnell was not responsible for writing a letter published in *The Times* connecting him unequivocally with the 1882 Phoenix Park murders. As such, when accused by O'Shea, he allowed George Lewis to put in an appearance on his behalf and then filed a denial within the requisite twenty-one days, but at some point thereafter changed his mind.

Parnell's biographers have suggested that his own straightforward view was that in all conscience he could neither deny O'Shea's charge nor be condemned for it. His first meeting with Katharine had been at a dinner party she hosted in 1890 at O'Shea's request for the express purpose of bringing him into their orbit. He had believed Katharine when she told him she was, to all intents and purposes, 'free' (her relationship with O'Shea had been platonic for years and they lived apart). Parnell had demanded and gained her fidelity: the youngest two of O'Shea's children, born in 1883 and 1884 respectively – along with a third who'd died in infancy in 1882 – were actually his. Moreover, O'Shea had not been deceived: he had tacitly approved and even gained from the arrangement. Therefore there was no shame. This did not mean Parnell assumed he would emerge from proceedings completely unscathed – there would be a howl, he told Katharine, but it would be the howl of hypocrites or the deluded who thought 'that forms and creeds can govern life and men' – but it did mean he decided, for good or ill, not to defend the suit.[5]

In many respects, the O'Shea/Parnell story is a political rather than a courtroom drama. O'Shea was MP for Clare in 1880 when he encouraged Katharine to court Parnell socially for his own advantage, little anticipating the intense attachment that would result. When he discovered their amour early in 1881 he challenged Parnell to a duel, more from a sense of outrage at Parnell encroaching on his chattel than from affection for Katharine, if she is to be believed. Parnell accepted, but the situation was mollified by Katharine's sister, Anna Steele, who no doubt pointed out to O'Shea the political expediency of not burning his bridges with Parnell. Thereafter, the trio settled into their irregular but mutually beneficial arrangement. Katharine paid O'Shea £600 a year to leave her unmolested and acted as a political go-between, passing messages from him to Parnell on behalf of the Liberal government. In 1882, when Parnell was held on suspicion of 'treasonable practices' in Kilmainham prison, O'Shea was selected to secretly negotiate his release. In return, Parnell publicly supported O'Shea's bid to take Galway as an Independent Liberal in the February 1886 by-election – O'Shea having lost his Clare seat the previous year.

From time to time reports appeared in the press that threatened to upset the arrangement. One particularly ill-timed one – involving Stead, once again – appeared in the PMG on 24 May 1886 under the headline 'Mr Parnell's Suburban Retreat'. It announced that Parnell ventured nightly to a residence in Eltham, Kent, where he was to be seen in the mornings taking riding exercise. The O'Shea family home was in Eltham and the implication clear. The government could not afford another scandal: on 5 May, the Queen's Proctor had filed his petition in the Crawford suit. Dilke's fight for political survival filled the papers. O'Shea had become a political liability and was told he must go. On 8 June, he turned on Parnell, refusing to vote on the second reading of the Home Rule Bill and dramatically resigning his seat.

With no political position to uphold, O'Shea might have been expected to straightaway petition for divorce. Personal circumstances stopped him. Katharine had an elderly aunt from whom she anticipated a large inheritance. As her husband, O'Shea would benefit. The aunt died on 19 May 1889, but her will was still under dispute when O'Shea eventually filed his petition on Christmas Eve. Political expediency may, once again, have forced his hand. In mid-December 1889, Gladstone had invited Parnell to his home to discuss Home Rule. Parnell left feeling confident. Five days later, O'Shea's petition was filed. Parnell suspected Joseph Chamberlain's hand in it. Chamberlain had, by then, split with Gladstone to lead the Liberal Unionists and O'Shea, though no longer an MP, was still corresponding with him. It is also possible that an article that appeared in the *Evening News*, whether by accident or design, on 11 September 1889 played a part. The article stated unequivocally that the 'impenetrable mystery' of Parnell's Kent home had been solved: that prior assumptions that he lived there with *both* O'Sheas was wrong: it could now be revealed that since relations between the two men became hostile, Parnell had 'continued to board with Mrs O'Shea and her daughters' while the Captain 'has been so little at home for the past year that he can hardly be said to belong to the *ménage*'. The long-kept 'secret' was out. O'Shea now had no choice but to act.

Katharine answered his petition with allegations of connivance and collusion, and with counter-allegations of physical assault, neglect and habitual adultery with prostitutes and other women. Behind the scenes, she offered her husband large sums to let the case lapse: £20,000 was rumoured to have risen to £60,000 the night before the trial. In the course of proceedings, her answer was altered twice: first by order of the court to strike out the allegation concerning prostitutes and then by Katharine, who added an allegation of adultery with her sister Anna enacted at the very time Anna was acting as intermediary over the impending duel. If this was an attempt to intimidate O'Shea, it failed. On 15 November 1890, the nation braced itself for another long and scandalous trial. Said the *Morning Post*, 'Not since the days of the Parnell Commission, which for want of a better meeting place held its sittings in the Divorce Court, have the doors of that incommodious and inconveniently arranged justice chamber been so fiercely besieged or its half-dozen or so rows of oaken benches so early filled.' But when the court convened, all expectation was upset by the shocking announcement by Katharine's advocate, Frank Lockwood, that she would not defend the suit.

Sir Edward Clarke, representing O'Shea, was as surprised as anyone but proceeded on the assumption of her guilt. O'Shea went into the witness box and swore that since 1881 Katharine had repeatedly denied the affair; that the rupture in 1886 was purely political; and that he had acted swiftly following the *Evening News* report. He denied a liaison with Anna and she corroborated his evidence in toto. Witnesses testified to Parnell concealing his identity in Kent with the suggestion that it was to evade O'Shea rather than the press; and a housekeeper threw a thoroughly disreputable light on the affair by claiming that on one occasion when O'Shea arrived home unexpectedly while the lovers were locked in the drawing room together Parnell must have escaped by the window and down a non-existent fire escape at the rear of the property to enable him to run round the house and announce himself at the front door minutes later. With none of this challenged, how could the jury do otherwise than find for O'Shea? This they did without deliberation.

It is now generally accepted that what came out in court was not the whole truth. The judge, had he suspected any foul play, could have invited the Queen's Proctor to investigate when he granted the decree. He did not. In fact, Sir Charles Parker Butt – the judge who had given the ambiguous ruling in the Crawford case four years earlier – unequivocally stated in his summing-up that he could not see any evidence of connivance. A cynic might suggest that given Butt's close connection with the Liberals, the open secret of the O'Shea/Parnell arrangement must have been known to him and that he and the proctor alike must have been keen to avoid another Dilke debacle. There is no evidence to support such a theory. Parnell was undeniably guilty and without evidence of collusion or condonation the only question was whether there was undue delay in O'Shea petitioning the court. Undue delay was a discretionary bar to divorce and O'Shea answered (honestly or otherwise) every question concerning newspaper reports suggesting intimacy between Katharine and Parnell before 1889 to Butt's satisfaction. The decree was subsequently made absolute without hesitation. Custody of the children believed to be O'Shea's went to O'Shea and Parnell was condemned to costs.

Afterwards, Katharine stated that she had prevented Lockwood defending her because the night before the hearing Parnell had convinced her to let it go. Perhaps he knew that their best hope had always been that the dispute over the will would be resolved before the divorce suit was heard – that O'Shea would accept Katharine's bribe and not put in an appearance on the day.[6] The fact that it had not sealed his fate. By taking a married woman as his common-law wife Parnell had gone against the Catholic Church and British orthodoxy, both of which now turned against him; as did many of his followers. He fought hard to hang on to power as his party fractured beneath him, suffering in health as a consequence. On 6 October 1891, independent Ireland's great hope died in Katharine's arms.

While Parnell's domestic situation, lacking in salacious detail, might have provoked little interest had he not been a public figure, there were plenty of private individuals for whom the opposite was true. Among them, hitherto unknown men staked their professional reputations on a favourable outcome in the divorce court, drawing in the process unwanted negative press attention usually reserved for celebrities. Certain types of professionals seemed to draw greater attention than others. From the diverse body of middle-class professionals whose university education raised their social standing, doctors and clergymen were particular favourites for divorce court stardom. Perhaps it was because both held unusual positions in society. In ministering to the physical and spiritual needs of their community they were worldly and otherworldly figures who associated with all classes and in whom great confidence and trust was placed: the cleric as the conduit to God; the doctor as preserver of life.

A doctor's 'large experience of humanity', wrote Dickens about Mr Merdle's physician in *Little Dorrit*, made him 'an attractive man'. There were women who 'perfectly doted on him'. Here lay an occupational hazard. The realities of large families, multiple pregnancies and the fact that children's healthcare was the wife's province necessarily meant the general practitioner often had more to do with her than her husband. Moreover, most medical treatments, little understood and increasingly involving the latest scientific techniques, then took place in the home. Multiple rooms in the house – including bedrooms – became consulting rooms.

Occupational Hazards

The potential for suspicion, jealousy and the desire for revenge is immediately obvious and has been demonstrated to a certain extent by Dr Bird's involvement with the Campbells. But for all the publicity surrounding that high-profile case, perhaps the greatest public battle for professional survival fought in the divorce court in this era was between Birmingham accountant William Lomax Harrison and Solihull doctor Edward Sutton Page.

Harrison had been a chief clerk of the bankruptcy court in Birmingham, an auditor for the Birmingham and Midland Banking Company and a director of the Birmingham and Midland Insurance Association. He had acted as City of London Public Accountant and, by the time he filed his petition on 20 August 1883, had been a partner in the private practice of Messrs Lomas Harrison and Starkey for twenty years. The sixty-five-year-old was also thirty years a Freemason, president of the Arden Club – a social society for prominent local businessmen and gentlemen – and father to six children. The family lived in a large house, Uplands, in the countryside 5 miles outside what was then the village of Solihull.

Page was the son of a Gloucestershire landowner who had trained as a chemist before becoming a physician, graduating from the Faculty of Physicians and Surgeons in Glasgow in 1866. He had practised medicine around Solihull ever since, taking over a large parochial practice from a retiring physician in 1875. His practice was based at his home, Sutton Grange, in the centre of Solihull. It afforded him an income of about £1,800 a year on which he supported his wife and ten children. In addition to which, the forty-seven-year-old was medical officer at the Solihull Workhouse.

Both men were members of the Conservative Club. Both men's livelihoods depended on their good standing within their community. Both must have been painfully aware of negative publicity.

Most provincial towns and cities then enjoyed 'a vibrant and comparatively diverse parochial press'.[7] Birmingham was no exception, boasting three dailies and four weekly papers. Since 1870, when the telegraph was nationalised, news from London had flooded into the provinces to be reported by an increasingly cohesive regional press represented by the cooperatively owned Press Association. Larger papers also sent their own journalists to

London to gather news of local interest. For the 1895 high-profile divorce case of the Hon. Wilfrid Brougham, second son of the local Baron, for example, *The Mid-Cumberland and North Westmorland Herald* proudly announced under its headline that their coverage was 'Specially reported for the *Herald* by Mr W. Brewis Hodgson', their local correspondent – imagining, no doubt, that this would give them the edge over their rival, the *Penrith Observer*, which also extensively covered the case. In London, the provincials had the reputation of printing more prurient material than their London counterparts to entice readers to 'buy local'. Certainly, some of them printed in full letters read out in court that were only précised in London papers and gave additional information about the parties and the locations of liaisons that would not interest or mean much to a London reader. Moreover, reliable sources suggested that a lack of colourful local news encouraged editors to string out divorce reporting; while competition with London evening papers for working-class readers was so fierce that provincial titles that covered divorce extensively in their late editions profited thereby. Though equally scandalous material could be had from other courts – bastardy and indecency reports from police courts, for example, which they reported 'at nauseous length'[8] – Harrison and Page must have had grave concerns over what might be printed about them, particularly in the *Birmingham Daily Post*, which targeted the business and professional classes, and the *Mail*, the local evening halfpenny paper. Both these titles covered the whole nine-day trial extensively – and its effect on all concerned thereafter.

The trial began on 28 November 1884, by which time the two men were already deep in dispute. In August 1881, at Mrs Harrison's request, Harrison had, in the proper manner, interviewed Page in order to approve him becoming her physician. Harriet Harrison had long been under the treatment of various Birmingham doctors but wanted a physician closer to home. Since marrying Harrison in 1867, when he was forty-nine and she only eighteen, she had given birth to six children in nine years and, as a consequence, had developed ulceration of the uterus which required regular examination and intermittent topical applications of lunar caustic, a silver nitrate compound used to destroy diseased or damaged tissue. To control the pain, Harriet had been prescribed

Chlorodyne – a tincture of laudanum, cannabis and chloroform – which she took in ever-increasing doses. Its effect was soporific, rather like opium or morphia. By 1878 she was described as being 'almost permanently' under its influence and on 2 July 1880, Harrison had her committed to Tower House in Leicester, a home for higher-class female inebriates. On the way there, Harrison claimed in court, Harriet had admitted to having committed adultery with a young officer named Ernest George Martin. Harrison had previously found a letter addressed to 'My darling George' in a dress pocket and confronted Harriet with it. Now, drugged and angry, she told Harrison he would 'curse her name' if he knew all she *had* done and *would* do. Harrison searched her rooms at Uplands in her absence and found 230 empty Chlorodyne bottles.

Harriet's future looked bleak; but Tower House was unusual for its time. Its proprietor – a temperance advocate named Mrs Theobald – understood that intemperance was an addiction, 'a *physical impulse*, asserting its need, like a hunger'. Patients were treated kindly and with good results.[9] Harriet improved quickly and wrote her husband loving letters, thanking him for his kindness and saying he would never regret his forbearance if he let her come home. She made three or four short visits and returned home 'clean' at Christmas.

At his interview, Page was made aware of Harriet's history. He took over her care and treated the Harrison children for usual childhood illnesses without event until January 1882, when the eldest son, William junior, then nearly fourteen, told his father there was something 'suspicious' about Page's visits. Harriet and Page, he said, had been locked in her room together for over two hours that day. His eleven-year-old sister Mabel confirmed the story, only to change her mind after being taken to task by Harriet, reducing the visit to fifteen minutes and claiming its purpose was to examine the child's inflamed throat. Harrison, as a consequence, demanded that Page's home visits cease. In April, however, Harriet became desperately ill with gastritis and Page was summoned. Harriet feared she was again pregnant, but Page told her it was most unlikely. When she recovered, the family went on a Mediterranean tour and in June Harriet was examined by another physician who confirmed she *was* pregnant and had been for six months. They returned to England and on 20 July, a daughter was born. The moment Harrison saw the infant he doubted its paternity. Nevertheless, the child was baptised Hilda Lomas Harrison. Page looked after Harriet following her confinement and continued to treat her and the children until 5 November 1882, when he received a letter from Harrison asking him to desist and send his final bill. Page was so shocked he requested an interview. The meeting took place two days later.

On oath, the men gave very different accounts of this meeting. Harrison said that Page had asked for an explanation and Harrison had told him that his lengthy visits had made his house the talk of the neighbourhood. He complained that Page had prescribed morphia for Harriet despite his request that she should not be given narcotics. Page had explained that the bottle Harrison produced labelled 'morphia' actually contained a placebo and that his visits were not overly long and he never saw Harriet alone. Harrison then summoned a maid, Anne Chennery, who confirmed that Page's visits often lasted two to three hours. When Anne left the room, Page apologised, claimed there was nothing immoral in his conducts but admitted he had been indiscreet and said under those circumstances Harrison was justified in firing him. He said he would not communicate with Harriet again, directly or indirectly, and left the house.

According to Page, he'd told Harrison he made no apologies for giving Harriet morphia when she needed it: Harrison had never told him not to and he could not treat her if his hands were tied. He'd also made no apology for seeing her alone, which he did out of necessity because Harrison refused to pay an additional charge for evening appointments that he could attend. Page told him he'd only seen her with the door locked when an examination was necessary to prevent children and servants interrupting and that his visits were long because he was often kept waiting. In the course of the interview Harrison accused Page of fathering his youngest child, Hilda. Incensed, Page made to leave, saying he was sorry he had ever entered the house. He had been warned it was dangerous for any medical man to be there: Harrison had already let two go unfairly. Harrison admitted it and named them, but said it was no use Page getting upset: 'You doctors are like parsons and priests: You get such an influence over women that you can do what you like with them.' Page said Harrison then told him he did not believe *any* of his children were his own – especially Margery, the second youngest, and Herman, his second son, who he thought belonged to a tradesman who came to Uplands to put up a lightning conductor (laughter). His wife was 'a dear little creature' but most extravagant. Becoming even more heated, he produced an account book that showed expenses of £2,800 in nine months. Harrison claimed Harriet was unstable: that she had set fire to the house and that the children were terrified they would be massacred in their beds. Page suggested Harrison must be delusional to think such things. Harrison then calmed down, apologised for his comments, told Page to take no notice and he would send for him again when things blew over. They shook hands.

A fortnight after the conversation Page had received a letter from Harrison's solicitor accusing him of 'walking out' with Harriet and demanding he stay away. Page had denied the accusation. Then in January 1883, he'd heard that Harrison had been slandering him. Harrison had told one of Page's patients that Page had seduced Harriet while she was drugged and had attempted an abortion – claims he repeated in March in a speech at the Arden Club. Page was told of this at a trade dinner and immediately sued. In the meantime, Harriet had started using Chlorodyne again and by December was so under its influence that Harrison had sent her and her child away to her half-brother in London.

In gathering evidence for the slander suit, Page was given permission to put interrogatories to various potential witnesses. They contained questions that went well beyond the alleged slander, raising and making insinuations about Harrison's unusual personal history. They involved a woman named Sarah Ann Reach – Harriet's mother. When and for how long had she lived with Harrison and was she his mistress? Had Harrison paid for Harriet's education and had Sarah continued to live with them after their marriage until her death in 1874? It might not have occurred to Page when he put these questions to Harrison's acquaintances in the summer of 1883, but Harrison's barristers in both actions – in the slander suit heard in the Queen's Bench in March 1884 and the divorce trial the following November – were under no illusion that because it was well known that Harriet's brother was a half-sibling, the questions tended to imply not only that Harriet's mother had been Harrison's mistress when Harriet was a child, but that Harrison was in fact Harriet's father as well as her husband (sensation!). Page strenuously denied this was his intention and Harrison denied the allegation: both Harriet and her brother were born long before he met Sarah.[10]

Still, at the seven-day slander trial heard in the Queen's Bench in March 1884, Harrison was forced to explain that in 1859, when he was forty-one, he had been dangerously ill with rheumatic fever and Sarah had been his live-in nurse. Being then separated from her husband and in dire straits, Harrison had kept her on as a servant following his recovery in gratitude for her 'great care' and then paid for the ten-year-old Harriet's education. When Harriet turned eighteen, he'd married her. In a post-'Maiden Tribute' world such benevolence might imply that Harriet had been groomed by Harrison or some 'arrangement' reached with her mother in a 'respectable' version of the child-trafficking Stead denounced. Disparity in age, however, in 1867 was not uncommon (though, admittedly, few husbands were thirty years older than their wives) and perceptions regarding sexual propriety within marriage were different. Though the legal marriageable age without parental consent was twenty-one, the age of sexual consent was not raised to sixteen until 1885.[11] Harrison and his young bride relocated from Acton, north of Birmingham, to Knowle in the south-east and lived at Uplands perfectly respectably until the events here described.

Still, the interrogatories had consequences. At the slander hearing the judge condemned them as 'about as scandalous an abuse of privilege as anything he had come across'. Though the jury found for Page, the damages awarded him were only £150 – a sum described by Justice Butt at the divorce hearing as 'very inadequate' in his mind for a wholly innocent physician charged with adultery and betrayal of confidence. In addition, they'd undoubtedly provoked Harrison to file his divorce petition in the first place. In the petition, Harrison accused Harriet of adultery with Page and 'unknown men' since he sent her to London in January 1883 – where she had been continually watched by detectives – but not with Ernest Martin, the young officer Harriet had actually committed adultery with. Why not? One explanation might be that having continued to sleep with Harriet after her confession, Harrison thought the court would interpret this as him forgiving her and thereby condoning the adultery. His solicitor should have known better: a further offence was legally said to revive a former, thereby making it perfectly justifiable for Harrison to have named Martin as a co-respondent alongside Page. That he did not suggests either a certain incompetence on his solicitor's part (the low number of divorces meant many provincial lawyers were new to the practice) or that Harrison was certain of his case against Page (any 'unknown men' identified by detectives was something never to be relied upon; and, in this instance, was never mentioned again); or that he was consumed either by jealousy or revenge for the gossip and suspicion that had befallen him courtesy of the doctor. Harrison added to his plea a claim for £5,000 damages: nearly three times Page's annual income.

The whole issue of damages was rather thorny for the court. No matter how its judges tried to dress it up as being compensation for the personal and material loss of a man's wife and the necessity for him to provide a replacement maternal figure for their children, it was difficult to escape the uncomfortable notion that by definition damages treated a wife as chattel – particularly because she had no equal recourse. Claims were mostly made by middle-class husbands – understandable when it is considered that a middle-class wife was more likely to assist in her husband's business than wives at either end of the spectrum – and they influenced the manner in which a case was received. Juries tended to disapprove of excessive or ruinous claims and in successful cases award only a fraction of the sum claimed, if any at all. Suits with damages were also nearly seven times more likely to fail than those without.[12] Harrison therefore, whatever his motivation, was taking quite a chance.

In court, he brought forward the usual obeisance of servants to testify to the length of Page's visits and the locked doors, to hearing Harriet say she loved Page and hated Harrison and even, in one instance, to hearing her tell the infant, Hilda, 'Here comes your father (meaning Page); it is well to be you as you have two fathers.' Their female servants claimed that Harriet dressed herself in her best clothes to receive Page, that he often took tea with her after concluding his business, that they addressed each other with endearments and that Harriet sat unnecessarily close to him, looking at him adoringly. An audacious gardener even admitted putting a ladder to Harriet's window during one of Page's visits, but found he could see nothing because the blind was down. Harriet and Page both denied any suggestion of intimacy and Page produced both his coachman and his appointment book to prove that he simply did not have time to spend the hours suggested with Harriet.

A cabman claimed to have driven Page and Harriet to a certain house in Birmingham on two occasions; the proprietress of the house, a Mrs Porter, was called and claimed it was not a brothel, but admitted she let rooms by the hour and that Harriet and Page had been there. The house turned out to be opposite Queen's Hospital, giving Page a perfectly legitimate reason to be in the region, though he denied in his evidence he had visited it for twenty years. A second cabman who claimed also to have driven the lovers said he could tell 'some impropriety was going on inside' his cab because of its vibration! He was forced to concede he had seen nothing, and both Harriet and Page denied they had ever ridden in a cab together and claimed her visits to his house (where his wife was always present) were perfectly legitimate as his practice was based there. Her children needed to be seen and Harrison had banned Page from his house. That Harrison claimed he did not know Harriet went there caused some consternation.

For both men, the medical evidence was crucial. The last of Harriet's former physicians, a Dr Sproston, confirmed Page's diagnosis of uterine ulceration but said his own examinations had only taken fifteen minutes. Page said his examinations took longer because he found Harriet a difficult patient requiring a great deal of coaxing to submit to treatment. Examinations were carried out using a most alarming-looking instrument called a speculum, which was used to widen the vagina so that the lunar caustic could be applied to the ulcer using a caustic-holder or probe through the cervix. Both doctors used this technique but within the medical profession its propriety was debated. Opposers claimed that use of the speculum offended 'the natural modesty of women' and should therefore be avoided – especially with virgins.[13] Others argued that women who were never asked to submit to the indignity of the speculum were being exploited, paying huge sums to be 'drugged *ad nauseum* without receiving the slightest advantage'.[14] Sproston's predecessors seem to have been guilty of this. Though the efficacy of caustic applications is uncertain, their failure to do anything other than offer pain relief must have prolonged Harriet's suffering and triggered her Chlorodyne habit and much of the misery in the household that resulted from it. Medical ignorance and scepticism also heightened public prejudice against modern practices, not least, in this instance, because of the physical similarities between the caustic-holder and an instrument known as a sounder which was used by backstreet abortionists. Harrison's notion that Page had performed a bodged abortion on his drugged wife – alongside Page's insistence in April 1882 that Harriet was not pregnant and his failure to insist on a chaperone at his treatments – possibly stemmed from this. Page's expert witness stated in his evidence that, in his experience, women did not want anyone else present during such treatments due to embarrassment and shame. He put forward the opinion that, given what he'd heard of Harriet's symptoms, adultery would have been the last thing on her mind!

The 'unnaturally grave' nature of the evidence excited 'very great interest' among the legal profession and general public alike, commented *The Times*. At the centre of it all was the pitiful Harriet, whose stature against two forceful men, duelling for their reputations, produced the effect of her sinking so far into the background as to be almost invisible. In sharp contrast to their commanding performances in the witness box she appeared vague, uncertain and contradictory. She claimed, for instance, that when she saw Harrison after the slander allegation he'd asked her to write and sign both a denial of any adultery with Page and an admittance. Her barrister had to explain to the jury that Harrison had asked her to write the truth, whatever it was – so really, this was no contradiction at all. She had written a denial. Then, because the 'Dearest George' letter had been entered into evidence and in the witness box Harrison had said it was 'a certainty' that Margery was not his child and that Harriet had told him she was Martin's, Harriet had to answer for this too. She claimed not to have met Martin until after Margery's birth and that it was a passing acquaintance.

Martin entered the box and concurred. The one occasion when Harrison had seen them together, he said, he had met Harriet by chance and she had invited him to return with her to Uplands to have luncheon with her and the children. Harrison had returned unexpectedly from work and found them together. It was perfectly innocent, said Harriet: Harrison's suspicions were unfounded. How then had she come to write the 'Dearest George' letter? And why had she torn it up and thrown it on the grate when Harrison confronted her with it? She was vague on the first question but answered the second saying it was because she was ashamed. Her barrister said her countenance suggested as much, but Justice Butt said he had strong opinions of his own about it. He did not share them with the court, but to an outside observer the letter appears to be the result of a fantasy of a deeply unhappy woman falling under the influence of narcotics (especially when taken in conjunction with other comments later made about Dr Page: that she thought him a 'very nice man' who was good to talk to). Harriet otherwise appeared to have little adult company and, in answer to Harrison's petition, had alleged her husband was a man of 'foul and violent temper'.[15]

The number of servants who came forward to testify to seeing bruises on Harriet's body equalled those supporting Harrison concerning her adultery. Harrison, however, brought two doctors who said they had never seen or heard anything to substantiate this allegation. That's because Harriet had never spoken to them about it, she claimed – because she was ashamed. Such an answer today would garner sympathy and understanding. Then, it was interpreted as her being ashamed that *her conduct* had provoked the violence. And even though Harrison admitted one instance of violence – that he had horsewhipped her in the presence of their eldest son, having sent the fourteen-year-old to fetch the 'small riding stick' he used, and that the incident was the precursor to his banishing her to her brother in London – it was deemed by the jury that Harrison had been provoked sufficiently for it not to be cruelty – by Harriet sinking into an addiction that made her a poor housekeeper, culminating in an apparently irrational act in which she ordered 80 lbs of meat (which, she claimed, was because it was Christmas, and they always made gifts of provisions to the local community at Christmas) and the awful presence of the infant Hilda. In support of this verdict they cited the letter Harriet had written Harrison during her incarceration at Tower House thanking him for his kindness. Would she have written such a letter after years of cruelty? Harriet seemed unable to explain and failed to convey to the jury how desperate she had been to return to her children.

As regards the adultery the jury were less certain. Harriet, it seems, had only stayed with her brother in London for three weeks before using the 30 shillings a week Harrison allowed her from his annual income of £1,300 to take digs in London for several months before being drawn back to Birmingham by the thought of her children. There, the unfortunate lady had found herself at Mrs Porter's – the very house where she was accused of having gone with Page! Mrs Porter claimed other men visited her there, but there was no corroborative evidence. And as regards Page, though Butt told the jury they should have 'the courage of their convictions' if they felt there was 'conclusive' evidence against him, the judge had preceded his guidance with a warning that they should take 'especial care' not to ruin a man who belonged, in his view, to 'the greatest and noblest profession of all' on hasty conclusions drawn by servants. After two hours' deliberation the jury returned 'hopelessly at variance'. With no hope of agreement the judge dismissed them and the petition alike.

Back in Birmingham, the outcome and the strong rhetoric of the *Birmingham Mail* proved too much for Harrison. 'The Asmodeus of judicial investigation has unroofed this house' to reveal, where one would expect to find 'all the evidences of refinement and culture', a household stricken by 'some malignant spell', the *Mail* opined: whatever Harriet's faults, a father sending his son for a stick with which to beat his mother in his presence was 'too terrible for comment'. At a meeting of Harrison's prized Arden Club held during the trial there were 'unpleasant proceedings' and some threatened resignations.[16] Moreover, two months after Harrison had filed his petition, his business partner, Starkey, perhaps sensing a sinking ship, had reportedly drowned while canoeing in a freak accident only to rematerialise in Australia having absconded with a sizeable proportion of the firm's capital. Harrison's various court applications – to Chancery to recover his money, to the divorce court for a retrial and to the Queen's Bench for a retrial of the slander suit – were all granted but came to nothing. In November the reinstated divorce suit was dismissed for Harrison's non-payment of Harriet's costs of £699. Five months earlier he had set sail for Canada, taking his children with him. Margery was among them: Hilda was not.

Meanwhile, Page – refusing to 'repute himself a loser' – returned to Solihull and his practice, where he remained until his retirement sometime between 1901 and 1911. Whether his practice suffered is unknown. In response to the case the *Lancet* offered strong advice to physicians concerning their interactions with female patients but placed the bulk of the blame on ladies like Harriet who '*will*, unless they are kept at a great distance and treated with punctilious politeness only, confide in their medical advisers'. The very fact that women consulted physicians about their physical health precluded personal or social intimacy: 'We have no patience with, and little respect for, women who fail to realise this.'[17] The men had fought for professional survival, but Harriet and her children suffered nonetheless. Separated from their mother, the children 'whispered together about her' and, hearing nothing of her, told each other stories concerning her fate: she had run off with their violin teacher; she had returned to Uplands destitute and been turned away; she had died in a railroad accident in Spain; she had been murdered in her carriage on her way home from the doctor. The culprit might have been suspected but was not named.[18] The truth was never discovered. Harriet was believed to have died soon after the trial. Her daughter, Hilda, appeared on the 1891 census in the care of a couple in Acton with no apparent connection to the family. She was listed as the 'daughter of William Lomas Harrison: his deserted child'.

As the popularity of human-interest stories grew, middle-class cases like this were increasingly reported. The consequences for some were even steeper than loss of reputation and livelihood. Harrison's allegations if proved would have ruined Page professionally, but had another doctor – Bruce Edward Goff – been found guilty of cruelty following his wife's 1897 allegation that he had used a sounder on her to procure several abortions, he could have faced a criminal prosecution – something that was always pointed out to a jury during proceedings. In court, Mrs Goff's advocate drew direct comparisons between Goff's actions and those of a recently convicted backstreet abortionist found guilty of manslaughter and sentenced to seven years' penal servitude the previous month after the woman on whom he operated subsequently died of septic peritonitis.[19] The extent to which considerations like these influenced a jury is indeterminable. For Goff, it was fortunate he had retained a letter from his wife saying if he tried to divorce her (which he did) she would 'ruin him' and that the co-respondent in the case turned out to be such a heartless cad that the sympathy of the jury was all Goff's. Fortunate, too, for Dr William Anthony Nutt, accused in another suit brought by Mrs Marian Martha Money in 1883 of having provided her husband with ergot of rye which he forced to her take to induce an abortion and for having used various instruments on her at her husband's request for the same purpose, that her husband did not defend the suit and Nutt was not therefore called to account for his actions. Any loss of professional reputation for these men must have been a decidedly secondary consideration when they learnt of the charges levelled against them.

For clergymen – the other class of professional on which the press focused attention – the consequences were more clearly defined, but only after 1892. The rise of puritanism provided the foundation for the passing of the 1892 Clergy Discipline Act. Where previous disciplinary Acts had dealt with the breaking of ecclesiastical laws or ritual offences, this one dealt with misdemeanours and addressed offences 'against morality': drunkenness, lasciviousness and more general 'conduct unbecoming'. It was intended in part to bridge the widening gap between secular courts and Christian doctrine and to remedy situations like that of former curate Arthur Robert Morrison Finlayson. Finlayson had held an administrative position in the Church in 1885 which he promptly resigned when he was charged with adultery with Hannah Cookson, the wife of a Chester manufacturer. He was found guilty, condemned to pay £1,000 in damages and consequently found himself in the bankruptcy court. Afterwards, however, he was reinstated as a curate in Somerset, at a living in the gift of the Bishop of Bath and Wells – a position he held until his death in 1910. Though Finlayson was doubtless a valuable asset to his community, his presence and the presence of other offenders against morality raised difficult questions for the Church and, under increasing pressure, Parliament stepped in. After 1892, any clergyman having a bastardy order made against him or found guilty of adultery was rendered incapable of holding a preferment and could be deposed from holy orders. The ruling was non-negotiable, enacted within twenty-one days and no further evidence was required.

The broader consequences seemed to give juries pause. In the case of *Worrall v. Worrall and Jones* (1894) it took two attempts to find a young Manchester curate guilty of adultery despite several very compromising admissions. Hugh William Jones, the twenty-four-year-old son of a schoolteacher, admitted that he and thirty-six-year-old Mrs Louisa Worrall had had a secret rendezvous in the churchyard of St Mary's, Hulme, at her request after her husband found an affectionate letter she had written Jones stating that 'there never has been and never will be another like you in my eyes' and signed 'Your poorly darling Fuzzy Buzzy'. This letter had been preceded by a day out together in Chester; and Jones admitted he afterwards met her at a hotel in Saltburn-by-the-Sea where they both spent the night (separately) before an excursion to Redcar the following day. These might have been, as Jones claimed and half the gentlemen of the first jury believed, only the foolish and innocent actions of a young clergyman in his first post keen to offer solace to the unhappy wife of Henry Worrall, co-owner of J & J. M. Worrall, the 'largest velvet dyers and printers in the world', and, thereafter, his clumsy attempts to repair the damage done, but the visiting judge at the retrial – John Compton Lawrance, brought in from the Queen's Bench to assist in clearing a backlog of cases – was having none of it. Though the battle between Worrall and Jones was a little like David taking on Goliath, in his summing-up the judge said the consequences to Jones (loss of occupation and financial ruin) should have no bearing on the case: verdicts in the court had a serious bearing on everybody and they would be doing Worrall an injustice if they gave it much weight. After twenty minutes' deliberation, Jones's career was over. His family sent him to the Cape, from where he returned ten years later, married to a merchant's daughter, to live out his days on relatively slender means.

This case is broadly illustrative of the potential hazard for clergymen in their interactions with married women. Becoming an active member of the local church was a respectable occupation for a middle-class woman while her husband engaged in business. Research suggests that by the end of the century the majority of lay people involved in church work were women.[20] There was nothing remarkable, therefore, in Louisa Worrall's close involvement with Jones in organising a *tableaux vivant* for their parish or in farmer's wife Rosa Agnes Hern organising church entertainments for the parishioners of Dalwood in East Devon. She and her husband, William Henry Hern, who married in 1889, had moved from his father's farm in nearby Stockland back to her childhood home, Dalwood Mill, in February 1893 so that Hern could help his ageing father-in-law, Hermon Bromfield, in the mill and Rosa could care for her invalid mother. The men were pillars of their community: Bromfield was churchwarden and chairman of the school board; Hern was its secretary. Rosa played piano at choir practice and school events. The curate in the village, Alfred Baker Winnifrith, was also on the school board and was the eldest son of the vicar of St Mary, Mariansleigh in North Devon, who was considered 'one of the most respectable and conscientious clergymen in the Exeter diocese'.[21] Winnifrith was Oxford educated, had come to Dalwood from his first curacy at Shaugh near Tavistock in 1892, and was friendly with the Herns. They were all in their mid- to late twenties, were on first-name terms and the curate considered he and Hern were 'like brothers'; that was, until Hern filed a petition with the court on 2 October 1895 accusing him of adultery with Rosa.

Rosa had been unhappy with Hern and had confided as much to Winnifrith. She said they had made a mistake in marrying and were ill matched, and that she thought Hern shared this view. She had often told him she would leave but for their son, Stanley. On 29 October 1894, she saw her opportunity and took it. Rosa and Stanley had both been unwell and Hern suggested they go to his parents in nearby Colyford to convalesce. They left that morning, but never arrived. Two days later, Rosa's sister Jessie brought Hern a letter from Rosa saying she and Stanley were going to disappear and she hoped Hern would not look for them; that it would be a blow to him but it was for the best; and that so far as Rosa was concerned, he was free 'as if you had never seen me'.[22] To Winnifrith she wrote that he would be shocked but not surprised; that she was doing Hern the greatest kindness by leaving and she hoped it would not bring trouble on Winnifrith: it ought not to, but 'unfounded and annoying tales' around the village made her fearful. 'If people only knew how often you have tried to smooth things between

Will and me they would not have so much to say.'[23] This, claimed Winnifrith, was the first he knew of any gossip concerning him.

When the case came before Gorell Barnes and a common jury on 28 April 1896, Rosa was still missing. With the court's permission, Hern's petition had been served on her sister after Hern had sworn an affidavit detailing the numerous attempts he had made to find her. He had enquired of her brothers in London; of Winnifrith's brother Bertram, who ran a boarding school owned by their father in Hythe, Kent; of Winnifrith's mother in Mariansleigh; and of Winnifrith himself. Winnifrith claimed to have heard nothing more from her. He urged Hern to be patient – Rosa had promised to contact them if any harm befell her or Stanley – and to keep it from public knowledge; more specifically, he asked Hern not to discuss the matter with the Bromfields. There had been scenes with Hermon Bromfield, who had openly accused Winnifrith of causing and conspiring in Rosa's disappearance. Moreover, when in January 1895 Winnifrith wrote an angry letter to Hern from Mariansleigh complaining that Bromfield had been 'disseminating scandalous reports about me with diabolic persistency' and refusing to assist them further in finding Rosa, Bromfield had taken the letter to the bishop. Perhaps unwisely, Winnifrith had written in it, 'Pardon me saying, but my personal observation leads me to the conclusion that you were utterly unsuited to each other.' The cruel truth was that the 'sensitive' Rosa had made 'every effort to do her duty' until she was 'no longer equal to the struggle'. Winnifrith's further suggestion – that he would act as arbitrator or mediator in the Herns' separation should Rosa ever make contact again – did not go down well with the bishop. An internal investigation ensued. By the time the bishop responded in March 1895, Winnifrith had left Dalwood for Hythe where he assisted at his father's school. The bishop concluded that, although Winnifrith could not be 'wholly exonerated' from indiscretion, there was insufficient evidence to justify blocking him taking another position, assuming his experience rendered him 'more watchful in the future'.[24]

Lack of evidence was less of a problem for Hern. He had only one servant to call on but there was a gaggle of village gossips willing to make the excursion to London at Hern's expense to share what they had seen or heard. Though plainer in appearance than many who went into the witness box, their 'country ways' provided Londoners with a unique entertainment. Winnifrith's 'voluble and shrewd' charwoman, Mrs Mary Meers, for example, reportedly took a 'keen delight' in announcing she had seen Rosa and Winnifrith kissing 'thirty times' but had 'a canny reluctance to being led into stating her deductions' from seeing him unlace Rosa's boots one afternoon when she came to tea before helping her into the slippers she had brought with her. This 'funny old lady' asked the court to believe Winnifrith told her he loved Rosa and asked her to deliver notes for him – one of which she (untruthfully) told Winnifrith she had given to Rosa in her brother's presence, eliciting the response, 'My God, my God, you fool! I am a ruined man.' Another from Rosa to Winnifrith Mary said she read after it came open in her pocket: 'My own darling Alfred,' it said, 'I will be up this afternoon from two to three, as Will is not well, and we will embrace each other, won't we?' (laughter).

The witnesses' broad Devonshire accents made it difficult for counsel to understand them, the *People* told its readers, reporting their evidence in dialect to illustrate the point. A young miller named Burgess claimed to have met them out walking in a lane at 11 p.m., Winnifrith with his arm about Rosa's waist, but continued to go to church thereafter because 'it had naught to doo with mee'; and the wife of a cattle dealer claimed to have seen another note from Rosa addressing Winnifrith as 'Deeyur Ahlfred' and saying, 'Coom and haave some tea, thur's a deeyur.' But nothing delighted the *People* more than the 'rustic instinct' expressed by Bromfield when, after looking through his own window and seeing his daughter and Winnifrith 'clasped in each other's arms, kissing', he did not act promptly to put a stop to it, but went to tell his wife because he did not like to interfere without hearing what she had to say about it first! It was all very amusing, but when added to the evidence of a Sergeant Hastings – that he had seen Rosa and Winnifrith coming down a staircase he knew led only to bedrooms when they were otherwise alone in the Mill – and that of Hern – that five days before Rosa left he had seen her with her arm about Winnifrith's neck – it threw a different light on Winnifrith's appeal to Hern to separate quietly from Rosa: one that would take some defending.

The difficulty was that Winnifrith, as a mere curate, did not have the means to defend it. Hern's advocate was not a silk – he was represented by 'senior junior' Joseph Priestley – but Winnifrith could not afford even that. At the start of the trial he announced he would be defending himself. It must have thrilled spectators to see him cross-examine his accuser as to why he did not turn Rosa out if he'd seen them together as stated (A: because she said it wouldn't happen again) and why he stayed friendly with him thereafter (A: to find out where she had gone), but the thrill was short-lived. When the court adjourned at the end of day one, an unidentified gentleman in attendance took pity on Winnifrith and provided him with a silk and a junior.

James Alexander Rentoul QC had been a Presbyterian minister before being called to the bar in 1884 and was more at home in the City of London and Central Criminal Courts but gave Winnifrith a sterling defence. He attempted to discredit Mary Meers, first by calling her daughter's parentage into question and then by suggesting there had been local demonstrations against her after she gave what turned out to be false evidence in a slander hearing in 1893. He then called the only witnesses available to Winnifrith – his parents and brothers – to testify as to his friendship with the Herns and discredit Mary still further by stating she was 'a busy-body who did not mind her own business and interfered in everybody else's' (laughter); and, worse, that she had been implicated in a case of infanticide (sensation!) and was only retained by Winnifrith because he could not afford better. Finally, Rentoul gave an impassioned speech in Winnifrith's favour, saying the allegation was as serious for him as one for murder would be for another man: for just as a convicted murderer would forfeit his life, a negative verdict for Winnifrith would mean social and professional death to him. He asked that Rosa's absence should not prejudice the jury against the curate and that they should not destroy his career because he injudiciously befriended one parishioner over others.

Unfortunately for Winnifrith, it was not only Rosa's absence that spoke against him. Hern's advocate was quick to point out that Bromfield, in giving evidence for Hern, was attacking his own flesh and blood and that Winnifrith had been driven out of the village by his actions and was unfit for 'the cure of souls at Dalwood or elsewhere'. Nevertheless, Gorell Barnes summed up largely in Winnifrith's favour, saying it was not in Winnifrith's interest to conceal Rosa's whereabouts and there was no reason to suspect she even knew of the proceedings. No allegations had been made before she left, so she had not left because of them; it was unlikely that Winnifrith had confided in Mary Meers when he had not taken his own family into his confidence; and, moreover, Bromfield had continued to perform his duties as churchwarden despite everything. Still, after ninety minutes of deliberation, the jury found Winnifrith guilty and gave Hern custody of Stanley.

Winnifrith immediately appealed. Within weeks, Rosa reappeared. His solicitor had advertised for her in provincial papers across the country and she'd responded, claiming ignorance of the proceedings. She was granted an appeal alongside Winnifrith. But her reappearance presented the appeal judges with two quandaries: How could they allow a retrial for Rosa without allowing one for Winnifrith against whom there had been 'ample evidence'; and would it not be a 'gross injustice' to put Hern to the expense of a second trial? On 8 July 1896, they concluded that Rosa had deliberately stayed away for fear of losing her son; that the affidavit explaining her actions did not express enough indignation at the charges against her to make them think otherwise; that Winnifrith had come to court knowing she would be absent; that Barnes had summed up in his favour yet the jury had still found him guilty; and that his intimacy with Rosa gave sufficient grounds for assuming he *was* guilty, and if he wasn't, he only had himself to blame.

Had this been all, the case would have concluded with Winnifrith ending his days teaching at his father's school and Rosa giving up her son and being outcast. Both were bad enough. But Rosa's reappearance and evidence given for the appeal had revealed, despite their best endeavours, that Rosa and Winnifrith had been in contact all along. Such blatant manipulation of the court could not go unchallenged. Further investigations were undertaken and on 5 December 1896, Rosa and Winnifrith appeared at Bow Street charged with committing wilful and corrupt perjury and conspiracy to commit perjury: Rosa in an affidavit swearing she'd known nothing of the divorce proceedings, and Winnifrith in his evidence to the divorce court in which he said he knew nothing of Rosa's whereabouts.

Rosa's movements since leaving Dalwood provided treasury solicitor Mr Sims with an array of geographically dispersed witnesses whom Rosa, alone and living on her wits, had told similar incriminating stories. A pub landlord from Ashford in Kent – 14 miles from Hythe – knew Rosa as Mrs Vernon. She'd lodged with him for ten months until August 1895 and Winnifrith had visited her there half a dozen times and stayed three nights. Mrs North, a local nurse, had taken charge of young Stanley for 6 shillings a week while 'Mrs Vernon' travelled north to Liverpool to take up a position as temporary housekeeper to a Dr Hughes. Mrs Harper, who owned a newsagents in Liverpool, knew Mrs Vernon as a widow from Devonshire with a curate friend who looked after her financial affairs and sent her postal orders on a regular basis. She'd taken over Stanley's care in November when Rosa secured a more stable position as companion to a Mrs Cassell for 10 shillings a month. Coming across Rosa in a state of distress one day, Rosa had confided in Mrs Cassell that her husband was alive and had started divorce proceedings against her that she and her curate friend thought could not have gone ahead in her absence. Anxious to change her address again, 'Mrs Vernon' then took up a position as pianist and barmaid at the Lord Nelson Hotel in Barnsley in December 1895. There, she received letters from her curate friend, one of which she dropped and her resourceful landlady picked up and put in a drawer, eventually selling it to a Barnsley solicitor for a sovereign. The landlady said Rosa had had a photograph of Winnifrith in her room and had once told her he had sent some moss from her mother's Devonshire grave, she having died in Rosa's absence. Hern, too, gave evidence as to Rosa having left home with only £5, suggesting Winnifrith had subsequently supported her. Without hesitation, the magistrate committed the conspirators to trial at the Old Bailey, setting bail at £500 each – way beyond their means. Attempts by Winnifrith's father and a London publican to tender themselves for his bail were rejected on the ground that neither of them were considered sufficiently solvent.

On Wednesday 13 January 1897 at the Old Bailey, Rosa and Winnifrith pleaded guilty. Mr Justice Hawkins, known as 'the hanging judge' for his vindictive sentencing, told the pair that he considered Winnifrith at greater fault: he had brought disgrace and discredit on his parents, had encouraged Rosa to perjure herself to save his reputation and then not even done the decent thing and married her when she became a divorced woman!

Being a clergyman only worsened his crime. Rosa was sentenced to six months in Holloway and Winnifrith to eighteen in nearby Pentonville, both with hard labour.

While moralists raved in the press about the 'incalculable harm' Winnifrith's presence in the divorce court had done to the Church as a whole and others bemoaned the effect on his poor innocent parents of him having 'debauched' a parishioner, Winnifrith's family and friends rallied. The *Devon and Exeter Gazette* printed in full a letter written by Winnifrith to a Hythe friend from Newgate Prison the night before his sentencing maintaining his innocence of adultery. His brother Bertram made a statement saying Winnifrith was 'the truest and best-natured fellow' and had been misjudged. In February and March, London and provincial papers reported that signatures were being added to a petition for Winnifrith's early release at a rate of a hundred a day. The MP for Hythe had signed it, as had ninety-three members of the Devonshire Volunteers (in which Hern was a sergeant) and residents from both of Winnifrith's former parishes. Unusually, the press continued to show an interest in the prisoners' welfare during their incarceration, *Reynolds's* sharing a joke with their readers that Rosa was 'being taught macramé and to make bead blinds' and Winnifrith was working for the Post Office!

On Rosa's release, a parishioner from Winnifrith's first curacy who had moved to Croydon took her in and treated her as 'a dear adopted sister'.[25] Winnifrith returned to his family a year later. His convalescence was long. It took another year before he married Rosa at Croydon Registry Office on 22 November 1899. The family photograph in the plates section of this book, which shows Rosa and Alfred Winnifrith embraced by his family on the occasion of Winnifrith senior's 1913 retirement from the Church, speaks of a real Christian spirit extended to them both – something that cannot have been easy for Winnifrith senior as a High Church conservative with a stern moral code. In the front row sits their daughter, Alfreda – the key sadness in their otherwise happy life together being her death the following year, aged twelve. Alfreda's funeral service was performed by her grandfather.

The Alfred Winnifriths were remembered as 'a dear and loving couple' by his niece, the actress Anna Lee, who spent 'many happy times' at their Clapham home where 'Uncle Albert' ran a boarding school for boys and 'Aunt Rose' was 'exceptionally beautiful and a wonderful cook'.[26] Winnifrith died in January 1950 aged eighty-five; Rosa followed three months later.

The Winnifriths' story is touching and such humanity as was shown by their family and friends against convention rarely reported. The conventional view was that prosecutions such as theirs were necessary to counter the growing perception that in the 'Supreme Court of Lies ... witnesses know they can lie with impunity and that no proceedings will be taken against them'.[27] The fact that this observation was expressed a dozen years after Rosa and Winnifrith's imprisonment substantiates the argument that prosecutions were too few to be an effective deterrent and that other offenders, like Crocombe and Crook in the Howard de Walden suit, very publicly got away with it. The difficulty was in proving such offences to the satisfaction of the criminal court. For lying to constitute perjury it had to be a *wilful* statement spoken under oath or written in a sworn affidavit (or similar sworn document) and *material* to the outcome. How did one accurately determine whether a witness was lying or mistaken, whether their testimony was misleading or blatantly untrue without two witnesses to prove it or 'one witness whose evidence is corroborated by independent and material circumstances'?[28]

The public prosecutor, mindful of wasting public funds, only ever took on cases he expected to win. Available data shows that across all courts he only prosecuted a quarter of the fifty-eight applications for perjury prosecutions he received each year with a success rate of 54 per cent.[29] Augustus Stephenson, who became DPP in 1884, largely agreed with his critics who said that of all courts the divorce court required 'especial vigilance, as being the point of origin of the offence which poisons the stream of justice at its source', but also thought ill-considered prosecutions in cases of suspected but unprovable perjury would bring the law into contempt and justified his record with the opinion that the divorce court presented parties with unusual 'inducements' to commit perjury that must be looked upon 'with indulgence'.[30] In one attempt to resolve the issue, Charles Darling QP MP introduced a bill into the Commons in 1888 which, if enacted, would have made special provision for a divorce court judge and jury to pass immediate sentence on perjurers as if they had been indicted of the charge. The fundamentally flawed bill was short-lived but its existence has been described as testament to the degree in which the court was considered the 'playground of perjurers'.[31] Cases in the next chapter will show, furthermore, that the reputation of the court was threatened not only by parties willing to lie to achieve their desired ends or mischievous servants with their own agendas but by a host of shady and unscrupulous characters with no desire for 'respectable' reputations who were willing to exploit the system for their own gain.

6

Working the System (Pt 1): Dodgy Detectives

Then he turned his thoughts upon Bozzle, and there came over him a crushing feeling of ignominy, shame, moral dirt, and utter degradation, as he reconsidered his dealings with that ingenious gentleman. He was paying a rogue to watch the steps of a man whom he hated, to pry into home secrets, to read the letters, to bribe the servants, to record the movements of his rival, his successful rival, in his wife's affections! It was filthy...
Anthony Trollope, *He Knew He Was Right* (1869)

By the time the court moved from its old home at Westminster Hall into the Royal Courts, detectives were already a well-established 'necessary evil'.[1] There had been developments in the world of private inquiry in that time. There were still individuals like Trollope's fictional creation Bozzle – a retired policeman who 'had not lived without a certain reputation in the police courts'; who worked alone or with the assistance of shady associates at need and maintained an 'outer respectability' by always attending clients in 'a decent coat, and a well-brushed hat, and clean shoes' but lived a rather down-at-heel existence[2] – but there was also a growing number of agencies who advertised for business in respectable London papers and modelled themselves on the relatively recently established plainclothes detective department at Scotland Yard.

The detective department of the Metropolitan Police Service had been established in 1842 with little enthusiasm among commissioners, some of whom 'disliked detection on principle'.[3]

Working the System (Pt 1): Dodgy Detectives

It consisted originally of only eight detectives to cover the whole of what we now know as Central London supplemented by men put temporarily into plainclothes at need. The department grew slowly. It was not until 1869 that a newly appointed commissioner increased the core group of Scotland Yard detectives from fifteen to thirty-three and put a detective into each division of 'The Met', creating an additional body of some 189 men. By this time, there was great public interest in higher-ranking detectives who were immortalised by Charles Dickens, Wilkie Collins and others and whose skill and success with limited resources has become legend. At the other end of the scale things were different. Recruitment was difficult and there were complaints that many in the lower ranks were too illiterate to accurately report their proceedings. In the rougher districts, their skillset seemed to include little more than 'a certain amount of low cunning, a smattering of thieves' slang, and the knack of making believe they knew every evil-doer in London'.[4] Then in 1876, the Great Turf Swindle – a confidence trick involving scam bets taken on behalf of a rich client – tainted the reputation of the department through the associated corruption of three senior Scotland Yard officers and their conviction at the infamous Trial of the Detectives the following year.[5] A fourth officer was tried and found not guilty. He was Inspector George Clarke.

Despite the verdict Clarke was pensioned off and, following a short interlude as a publican, set up in private practice as the George Clarke Detective Agency in 1878 – the same year Scotland Yard reorganised its detectives into a Criminal Investigation Department. Clarke's was not the first private detective agency. In 1871, the PMG commented that 'the large increase in spy or detective agencies' that had sprung up alongside the official detective bureau was 'a not very pleasant feature of the period'. Not all private detectives could legitimately claim the credentials of Clarke and fewer still were above suspicion of dubious practices. Those who fulfilled both criteria were considered the best: deserving and respectable retired inspectors and superintendents whose reports were 'perfectly reliable and their charges fair'.[6] They formed professional relationships with solicitors and received private endorsements. Public endorsements were rare. Few were so fortunate as the Westminster Detective Agency, a partnership run by an ex-inspector and a lawyer, which was openly supported by

Truth proprietor Henry Labouchere (and returned the compliment by advertising in his journal). On the whole, commendable firms were in the minority; or, as the PMG put it, the profession had been over-glamourised in novels and much money was 'sunk in a perfectly useless manner by employing these persons' who, if not actually immoral themselves, surely created a general 'demoralization' of society.[7]

There is nothing glamourous about Trollope's fictional detective, but the demoralising effect of Bozzle can certainly be felt in the manner in which he influences events in the novel. His client, Louis Trevelyan, believed 'Bozzle, either by fair means or foul, *did* get at the truth', but soon after his introduction it becomes clear that he'd spent too long inhabiting the morass where 'affairs always secret, dark, foul, and fraudulent' were the norm to value strict veracity over the desire to feather his own nest at Trevelyan's expense. Thereafter the reader learns that for the right price Bozzle can be convinced to do more-or-less anything. That such attributes might also be applied to his real-life counterparts is implicit in comments found in Geary's *Marriage and Family Relations* (1892), a manual aimed at legal practitioners explaining the practical application of the divorce law. Geary notes that the evidence of detectives was rarely taken at face value by the court, especially if uncorroborated, gathered while the couple lived apart (a situation in which it might be supposed the husband was 'on the look-out' for evidence) or the detective was highly paid to collect it. While the employment of a detective to ascertain the truth of painful revelations for an unwitting husband living in happy ignorance with his wife was perfectly acceptable, hunting her down to pin offences on her was not.[8] This was amply demonstrated by Clarke's son and grandson in the Dunlo case described in chapter one, where the transcribing of their notebooks generated scorn at their ineptitude and the suspicion of fabrication. Society solicitor George Lewis – who, incidentally, defended Clarke in the Trial of the Detectives – may have known Clarke senior for many years by the time his agency was established and have considered him 'far from brilliant but almost certainly honest', but his descendants were another matter.[9]

Despite the difficulties of telling the good detectives from the bad, it was generally considered that having none at all was worse. Court reporter Fenn commented that suspicious spouses who

Working the System (Pt 1): Dodgy Detectives

chose to go it alone often made 'a deplorable hash of the whole business'.[10] George Thirkettle's experiences during his wife's 1888 suit is a case in point.

When Mary Jane Thirkettle, thirty-three, sued for divorce claiming that her husband of nine years was dangerously unhinged, the forty-six-year-old ex-solicitor's clerk chose to employ neither solicitor nor detective. His alleged cruelty included various attempts on Mary's life – an attempt to strangle her, to throw her out of a third-floor window and to set her bed on fire while she slept – and the reckless and wilful communication of a venereal disease from his adultery with an unknown woman eight years previously. Thirkettle filed a denial but only employed a solicitor when the suit was about to come to trial. He then filed a counter-petition of his own accusing Mary of adultery with a seventy-year-old retired Indian Army officer, Major General John Francis, based on evidence supplied by a cabman named Winser whom he'd paid to watch them. From Francis, Thirkettle claimed £1,500 damages. Four months and two lawyers later, Thirkettle amended his petition to include a second allegation against Thomas William Waller, the husband of Mary's sister and managing director of the successful Bradford brewery Waller and Sons. From him, Thirkettle claimed a staggering £20,000. By the time the suit came before Mr Justice Butt and a special jury on 4 December 1889, Thirkettle was on his fourth solicitor, having chosen to represent himself twice along the way.

Initially, each of the parties was represented by a silk. Mary's advocate was William Willis QC – later a county court judge – while Thirkettle had Mr Bayford; Inderwick appeared for Francis and Sir Henry James for Waller. After Willis's persuasive opening address and Mary's evidence, in which she explained that Thirkettle had increasingly restricted her freedom following a religious conversion and tried to have her declared insane and detained against her wishes, Thirkettle argued with his counsel and the second day opened with their retirement, citing 'very great divergences of opinion' with their client on how his case should be conducted. In all probability Bayford had suggested Thirkettle should settle out of court as Mary's case was strong, but he was having none of it. Thirkettle decided to defend himself and over the course of the next three days tested the patience of the court to its extreme.

Mary's sister and brother-in-law gave convincing evidence of Thirkettle's violence (including being alerted by Mary's screams in time to witness him attempting to push her out the window), corroborated by the hotel proprietor whose window it was. Two doctors attested to his venereal disease and mental state. Thereafter, Thirkettle brought forward his brother, Robert, and several members of his church to attest to what a marvellous man he was and how little Mary respected his views. He called several servants whose evidence the judge dismissed as inconsequential compared to Thirkettle's allegations against Waller and Francis which he did not even attempt to prove until the third day. When Thirkettle's witnesses to the adultery were called, much of what they said was vague or circumstantial and tended to prove nothing more than that Waller would greet Mary in a 'brother-in-lawly way' with a kiss on her cheek and that the elderly general, though somewhat 'spoony' over her, never overstepped the mark. A supposedly incriminating letter from Francis produced from a voluminous pile of papers on Thirkettle's table said nothing more than that the pair had decided after a short acquaintance not to meet again due to Thirkettle's unreasonable and unfounded jealousy. The only witness with anything like concrete evidence was the cabman Thirkettle paid to spy on them. He attested to driving Mary and Francis to his apartment on Duke Street on two occasions, where they let themselves in with a latch-key. When asked by Willis if he would swear on his oath that the people he followed were those in court, the eager would-be detective replied, 'Ain't I a-swearin'?' But unfortunately for him, General Francis lived in Bury Street and was a large man: the General Francis who actually lived on Duke Street was so unlike him as to be known at the club where they were both members as 'Little General'.

The final straw for Thirkettle came with his cross-examination of Mary. He pleaded with her, 'Will you in this public court, and before your God, will you now, Polly, listen ... it may be the last time you speak to your husband, have I treated you cruelly or not? Tell them the truth ... save your soul.' Mary curtly replied, 'I have spoken nothing but the truth.' When later in the day it became Thirkettle's turn to address the jury the magnitude of the task overcame him: his memory failed him, he claimed, and he could not continue. Yet during the summing-up he interrupted the

Working the System (Pt 1): Dodgy Detectives

judge so often he was banished from the courtroom and when the jury delivered their verdict in Mary's favour he became decidedly agitated and appealed to all those present to help him get justice until the judge ordered the usher to 'remove that man'.

Two days later, Thirkettle and his brother presented themselves at the Queen's Proctor's office complaining his solicitors and counsel had refused to act on his instructions and the court had declined certain evidence. It was true that Justice Butt had stopped him asking many questions but had explained it was due to the law of evidence and that if Thirkettle thought it wrong he ought to go to the House of Commons and have it altered! All this was recorded in the proctor's register, along with the proctor's instruction that Thirkettle should submit his complaint in writing. No further entry was made. Over the course of the next three months Thirkettle filed multiple written statements with the court from witnesses claiming Mary associated with the proprietors of a house of ill repute and affidavits declaring the veracity of his position and that the 'cruel and heartless' proceedings had 'almost ruined' him in costs of some several thousand pounds. He was fortunate, though, to escape the fate of the hapless cabman Winser, who was tried for perjury on the evidence of the Generals Francis and sentenced to twelve months' hard labour. If the PMG had had its way, Thirkettle would have been in the dock beside him.

Thirkettle had clearly clung to an obstinate determination to be right and an obsessive belief in his distorted view of the evidence before him – just like Trollope's protagonist, Trevelyan. It is not clear how he came to employ Winser beyond the fact that Winser acted briefly as a process server for one of Thirkettle's many solicitors. Doubtless, he got the cabman on the cheap. But had he instead employed a detective from the classified ads – even, or perhaps especially, one who advertised in the respectable papers – would he have been better off? Fenn would have told him that such a man was the last person he should have trusted, for not all those who advertised were as they seemed.

Taking at random a single day from a London newspaper – in this instance, *The Telegraph* of 12 November 1890 – and studying the five agencies offering their services reveals some interesting anomalies that immediately prove Fenn's point. All five listed 'divorce' as a speciality. The National Detective Agency, branding itself after the famous Pinkertons, claimed its founder, George John Binet, was an ex-Chief of Police and all its staff were 'skilled and experienced detectives'. Three years later *Truth* would reveal that the agency's only employment criteria was a guinea laid down to obtain a certificate stating that the holder was their only agent within a specified area. In the provinces, the specified area would have been a whole town, but in one provincial town alone *Truth* found four holders of identical certificates none of whom had been referred work. In addition, Binet himself was no policeman. He had formerly worked as a draper's clerk and when he joined the Freemasons in 1888 had described himself as a merchant. *Truth*'s exposé resulted in his prosecution for fraud and a term of twelve months' hard labour.

Slater's Detective Agency was established by 'Captain' Henry Slater in around 1886. Slater's real name was actually Henry Smith, but he had taken the name Slater to deliberately confuse himself with Henry *Salter*, a detective for whom he had previously worked; prior to which Smith had been a pawnbroker's assistant and then a solicitor's clerk. By 1890, Slater's had become the largest London detective agency and ran multiple adverts in numerous dailies claiming that through their network they could discover anything about 'any subjects and about any visitor' to the city and that they had been 'successful in every case wherein engaged in the Divorce Court for the past four years'. For each successive year this astonishing claim was extended until 1903 when after seventeen years their antics in the Pollard divorce case (on which more later) would result in their downfall.

With Adolphe de Gallo of Great Marlborough Street advertising his detective agency in the *Telegraph* while appearing at the same time in the London city directory as an interpreter and translator, that left only two that were actually run by former inspectors as advertised: Moser's and the 'old-established' Detective Agency. No wonder Herbert Trace of the 'old-established' (for 'old-established' read three years) felt it necessary to specify, 'No unscrupulous self-styled detectives here.' Meanwhile Moser's, who advertised themselves as being open day and night with agents in every city in the world, were Slater's main competitor and one of the first to introduce female private detectives. Maurice Moser's first female employee was Charlotte Antonia Williamson, housewife to a commercial traveller until her husband divorced her for her adultery with Moser.

The turnover of agencies also seems to have been high. The classified ads in the *Telegraph* for January 1883 when the Royal Courts first opened its doors lists six completely different agencies to that of the later edition. Of these, only Abbott's, boasting twenty-seven years' experience, was still advertising in 1890 and still going strong in 1905. Fenn points out that many private detectives did not advertise, obscuring the picture, though those that did advertised frequently in a range of papers – the *Telegraph*, *Morning Post* and *Evening Standard* most often. By 1890, the array of agencies that had come and gone and their exaggerated claims spawned the *Punch* cartoon 'The Divorce Shop', in which a fawning and unscrupulous-looking agent, standing in front of storage boxes containing 'circumstantial evidence' and 'keyhole notes', asks a gentlemen customer, 'Want a divorce, Sir? Certainly, Sir, – certainly! Any evidence you may require ready at the shortest possible notice!!'[11] The implication is as much fabrication of evidence as ease of acquisition, and in 1892 the Barrett divorce case demonstrated just how far beyond their brief some detectives were willing to go and just how necessary were others in uncovering their decidedly dodgy dealings.

In October 1890, thirty-seven-year-old John Barrett, an assistant conservator in the Woods and Forests department of the Indian Civil Service, met Gertrude Alexandra Bird, then eighteen, orphaned and working as a lady's companion in Lahore. They returned to England with his widowed sister Rebecca and her three children, were married in St Pancras on 14 June 1891 and thereafter they all lived together in Bedford. On 20 July, Gertrude appeared at a local solicitor's office in a dazed state claiming Barrett had been violent. In September she left her husband and went to Paris, to a house recommended by the solicitor. Two weeks later Barrett travelled to Paris to beg forgiveness and bring her back. Gertrude agreed to return on the understanding that he would be kind and they would no longer live with Rebecca, there being a certain animosity between the two women. In October they holidayed in Hastings, where Gertrude appeared at another solicitor's office armed with a broken parasol and bloody handkerchief. The parasol, she claimed, Barrett had broken over her back, but her injuries from the assault were no longer visible because he had then locked her in her bedroom until her bruises subsided. In November, she claimed, he threatened to poison her with arsenic and say she had committed suicide. In December they took rooms in Belgravia and on 15 February 1892, after further violent episodes in each of the intervening months, she left him in fear of her life. She then consulted a third solicitor, Ernest Greenwood of Sergeant's Inn, who filed a petition for judicial separation on 18 February and a claim for alimony pending the suit. On 11 March the court ordered Barrett to pay Gertrude £44 a year on a weekly basis and on 30 March Barrett filed an answer denying cruelty.

Two weeks later, Barrett filed his own petition alleging one single instance of adultery committed at a boarding house on Wellington Road, St John's Wood, on 28 March with 'a man named Wilson'. On 28 April, Barrett filed a motion for his suit to go ahead without a co-respondent as 'Wilson' could not be found nor further identified. The motion was supported by four affidavits sworn by Herbert Muskett of Wontner and Sons, solicitors; Sarah Muchmore, keeper of the boarding house; Henry John Clarke, of George Clarke's Detective Agency; and George Such, presumably Clarke's subordinate. The go-ahead was given by President Jeune on 3 May and on 8 August the case came before Justice Barnes. Barrett was represented by Frank Lockwood and Gertrude by senior-junior Henry Kisch.

Despite the fact that the various solicitors Gertrude contacted gave evidence as to her visits and the housekeeper from Hastings recalled hearing Gertrude scream on one occasion and said that Gertrude had shown her bruises on her arm and was locked in her bedroom so often the lock broke (laughter), in the face of Rebecca's and Barrett's denials and Barrett's assertion that Gertrude was foul-tempered and jealous, Barnes ruled that it was 'difficult to know the truth' as regards Barrett's cruelty but that Gertrude's case had not been sufficiently proved and Barrett was consequently found not guilty. Conversely, the evidence against Gertrude and 'Wilson' was strong. Sarah Muchmore described how Gertrude had come to her boarding house with a gentleman she called her husband to inspect her rooms. The gentleman put 10*s* down to reserve three rooms on the same floor and left his card on which was the name 'Wilson'. The 'Wilsons' then took up residence on

Working the System (Pt 1): Dodgy Detectives

28 March. They had dinner in the evening and then went out, returning about midnight. The following morning Sarah took them hot water at Gertrude's request. Gertrude came to the bedroom door in her nightgown and Sarah could see Wilson in bed behind her. They then went out for the day. Gertrude returned about 6 p.m. and Wilson later. They had an almighty row. Gertrude called Sarah upstairs and said she wished to leave but she could not find her hat or nightgown, which was afterwards discovered in the coalscuttle (laughter). Gertrude left, and roughly an hour later Sarah heard Wilson creep out of the house. She had seen neither of them since and their bill remained unpaid. Shortly after, Clarke came to see her inquiring after the couple. Sarah gave him Wilson's card and a pipe inscribed with the same name which had been left on the bedroom mantlepiece.

Sarah's evidence was corroborated by her daughter Minnie and compounded by Barrett claiming Gertrude had lived immorally in India before they married. It was also confirmed to some degree by Gertrude, who only denied the actual act of adultery but fully admitted being at the boarding house with Wilson and explained how she came to be there.

After leaving Barrett she had taken lodgings on Earl's Court Road where she met a lady who went by the name Countess Carina Faringo. Carina befriended her and introduced her to an Ellen Watson. Ellen told Gertrude she was married to an electrical engineer who was currently working abroad and that she was looking for a female companion. Gertrude, who was short of money and had already pawned some of her jewellery, accepted the position. The two ladies moved together to a house in Pimlico and on their first night there Ellen suggested they go to the Empire Theatre, borrowing money from Gertrude to buy the tickets. After the performance, Ellen introduced her to a stockbroker named Stephens. They all drank champagne together and Stephens asked Gertrude to go to a private hotel with him. She declined. Instead they all went for dinner at the Café Monico. Afterwards, Stephens kissed Ellen goodnight: Gertrude refused to be kissed.

The following day Ellen went out leaving Gertrude alone. On her return, she invited Gertrude to go to the theatre again. There, Ellen said that if they were lucky they might find another gentleman to buy them champagne. After the performance, she spotted Wilson. She told Gertrude he was the son of Charles Henry Wilson, head of the major shipping company Thomas Wilson & Co. and Liberal MP for Hull. They again went for dinner and Wilson boasted about his carriage and horses, his yacht and his friends Lords Wolseley and Kimberley. He pressed Gertrude to meet him again the following day at Hyde Park Corner. He told her he wished to spend time with her, promised her jewels and enticed her to go to the boarding house with him. She went to view the rooms as Sarah Muchmore described. When she returned that evening to Earl's Court Road, Ellen seemed pleased at what she told her and suggested Gertrude 'make the most of her chance'. But the following day Gertrude changed her mind. Ellen became angry and called her a fool. Gertrude said she was married and the risk was too great, but Ellen assured her no one would know. Eventually, Gertrude relented and went with Wilson, claiming she only did as Wilson and Ellen directed because she was broke and otherwise friendless: a perfect stranger in London who had not known the city before her marriage.

On the first night she claimed Wilson got drunk and slept on the sofa in the adjoining sitting room. When Sarah brought the water, Wilson dived into bed when she went to answer the door. On the second night she said he returned to the boarding house intoxicated. She told him she was disgusted with him and wanted to leave but he hid her clothes. The rest of the scene was as Sarah described. When Gertrude returned to Earl's Court Road she upbraided Ellen for introducing her to such a man. Ellen laughed and said it was 'experience gained'. Then she said her husband was returning to England and she would have to find Gertrude new lodgings. She put her up in a room on Buckingham Palace Road and left. After she had gone Gertrude discovered that the rest of her jewellery and her pawn ticket were missing. She went to the pawnbroker's and found her other jewels had been redeemed. She reported the theft and a month before the divorce hearing, with the assistance of Detective Sergeant Edwards of Scotland Yard, Ellen was indicted for stealing £50 worth of jewels. Ellen, whose real surname was not Watson but Lyon or Lyons, denied the theft and was granted bail. Her bail was paid by Henry John Clarke.

Working the System (Pt 1): Dodgy Detectives

At the divorce hearing it transpired that after the Wilson episode Gertrude's solicitor, Greenwood, had recommended she employ Slater's to locate Ellen Lyons. Their agent, William Hamilton, not only discovered Ellen's whereabouts and true identity but also recognised Countess Carina – or Madame Carina, as she was better known – as an 'acquaintance' of Moser's. He identified the stockbroker Stephens as none other than Henry Clarke himself. On the strength of Hamilton's evidence and Lockwood's refusal to put either Ellen or Clarke in the box because he 'did not trust theirs', Justice Barnes concluded that though Gertrude *was* guilty of adultery (because it was difficult to think that a woman of 'purity and respectability' would have willingly done as she did) she had been entrapped. There was no suggestion that Barrett was complicit and Barnes readily acquitted him of knowing or authorising his agents to act as they did, but he did rule that those actions were despicable and should bar Barrett's success. Barnes dismissed both petitions and condemned Barrett to costs.

Soon after the hearing, Barrett returned to India alone. Gertrude stayed in London, taking lodgings on Vauxhall Bridge Road and pursuing her manipulators with the help of CID. Ellen disappeared but Henry Clarke, whose father George had died in 1891, continued to trade on his father's professional reputation and work under his name. CID kept him in their sights but took more than two years to find Ellen, despite her moving no further than Tooting. Eventually, on a tip-off, she was discovered living with Clarke at 12 Artillery Buildings in Westminster under the name *Wilson*. She and Clarke were arrested on 12 January 1895 and tried at the Old Bailey on 30 March and 1 April. By this time, Gertrude's circumstances had considerably worsened. Her alimony from Barrett had ceased when the divorce hearing ended and since his return to India he had not supported her. She had pawned all her possessions and in 1893, with nothing left to sell, entered the workhouse where she trained in the hospital to become a nurse. At the trial, DS Edwards testified that when Clarke was approached he'd admitted posing as Stephens and that after the indictment for theft Ellen had admitted assisting Clarke 'only where a stylishly-dressed person is required'. The question of a conspiracy rested on Gertrude's evidence. Her former landlady gave her a good character and the judge expressed the opinion that the fact she had not resorted to prostitution added weight to her testimony. Though the prisoners' barristers argued that whatever Clarke and Ellen had done to bring about the meeting between Gertrude and Wilson, the responsibility for her going with him was solely Gertrude's, the jury disagreed. The prisoners were convicted of attempted procurement and conspiracy to procure Gertrude to have carnal connection with Wilson. Clarke was sentenced to two years' hard labour in Pentonville for masterminding the plan, Ellen to twelve months in Holloway.

The Barrett case and its outcome clearly reveals the moral ambiguity of the divorce law. Barnes was absolutely right to deny Barrett his divorce and considered himself morally justified in describing Gertrude's behaviour as unrespectable, but by his judgment had left her unprotected. Thereafter, how could the law have helped her? Her only option would have been to petition the court for restitution of her conjugal rights, but how could she do that with Barrett in India? And even if he had remained in England, the fact that she had accused him of cruelty and been found technically guilty of adultery would have given him a strong defence. And what of her financial position? There were provisions for paupers to approach the court but they were protracted and considered largely inadequate. And even if she made use of them, what could she hope to achieve? Assuming she was awarded a restitution order and Barrett did not comply with it, she could sue again (if she could again secure paupers' assistance) for a judicial separation on the ground of his desertion. A change in the law in 1884 allowed that this could be done within a fortnight. But even if Barrett did not defend such a suit, what would Gertrude gain? The court could award her permanent alimony. But how could she enforce such an order? Ultimately, she was on her own. Quite literally, in Gertrude's case: orphaned and then separated, still only twenty-three and, as she described herself, 'a perfect stranger'. This condition, in the court's opinion, she had brought about herself by her actions during the six-week period between meeting Madame Faringo and accompanying Wilson to the boarding house. Despite her recognised entrapment, these actions were interpreted as representing the start of a descent into immorality, no matter what Barrett had done or not done to bring about their separation and even if her most grievous offence was actually naïveté or foolishness.

Working the System (Pt 1): Dodgy Detectives

By 1901, Gertrude found protection in an 'irregular marriage' with a fifty-year-old retired Indian civil servant, Frederick Kinsman, who gave her a home and a son and, one would hope, some happiness. Henry Clarke, meanwhile, did not return to Ellen on his release from prison – she'd disappeared again – but to the wife he had married in 1883 and their two children, becoming first a publican and then keeper of a lodging house. His detective agency had been brought down by the Barrett case. But if Slater's role in it gave them cause for celebration, it was short-lived. In 1903 their involvement in the Pollard suit put them in a similarly dubious position.

It was discovered that Slater's had made several attempts to induce Thomas Pollard to commit adultery for his wife's benefit. When these attempts proved unsuccessful they had paid a prostitute, Maud Goodman, to swear Pollard had been a regular client. Mrs Pollard denied all knowledge of their antics, repeatedly pleading in the witness box that she 'just wanted to be free', but the actions of her solicitor, Henry Albert Osborn, were dubious. One of Slater's employees swore to hearing Osborn tell the agency's manager, George Philip Henry (known as 'Slater junior', though no relation), that he would go to Plymouth where Pollard was living to 'see what he could do' when the detective told him he was not getting on very well at securing evidence against him. It then took Osborn only twenty-four hours to secure the necessary statement from Maud; and Maud herself testified that when she later began to doubt her role in the affair Osborn bullied her into submission and told her what to say. He was charged with soliciting and inciting her to give false evidence. The manager and three employees were charged with conspiring to pervert the course of justice. The employees received sentences of up to six months' hard labour and Slater junior got twelve months, but after an hour and twenty minutes the jury remained divided as to Osborn's role in the affair and he was eventually acquitted – a fact which tends to support the view that little credence was given to the testimony of prostitutes.[12] Neither was 'Captain' Slater found to be directly involved in the entrapment, though it was proved that both he and Osborn were aware that Slater junior had instructed the three employees to arrange everything. In his closing address, prosecution barrister Edward Carson condemned the agency for having perpetrated seventeen years of falsehood and of having been manufacturers of illegal evidence from 'beginning to end'.[13]

The sentences were not the longest sentences for divorce court antics in this era – that honour went to Manchester detective Henry Fennemore George, who got five years' penal servitude for presenting false evidence in the 1902 Worsley suit – but Slater's Detective Agency was finished and the dark age of the private investigator as *agent provocateur* finally brought to an end.

7

Working the System (Pt 2): Scheming Solicitors

The prosecutions of the Clarke and Slater detectives to some extent helped the 'Court of Lies' repudiate its reputation for being soft on perjurers, but only to a small degree. The detectives, the Winnifriths, parties to two other suits in 1891 and 1897 and those that follow in this chapter, account for all major prosecutions related to divorce court activity in the late Victorian and Edwardian eras.[1] They were newsworthy because readers thirsted to hear how criminals got their comeuppance, not how their victims were affected.

The prosecution of Osborn in relation to the Pollard suit demonstrates the close relationship between detectives and solicitors and the manner in which the unscrupulous of each profession naturally gravitated towards one another. The failure to convict Osborn also represents a pattern in which solicitors came off better than their more dubious associates. At the criminal trial of Henry George – the detective in the 1902 Worsley suit – Manchester solicitor Edgar Crossfield Pearson was given a tough time in the witness box for 'not recognising' that the evidence of detectives was not to be relied upon unless corroborated. He was probably fortunate that a prospective witness named Cochrane had not been so easily manipulated as the prostitute in the Pollard suit. When Cochrane had first been taken to Pearson's office by the detective to give a statement and been asked if he had seen the co-respondent lift Mrs Worsley's skirt he'd replied, 'No.' At the Old Bailey, he stated that the detective then took him outside and told him, 'Mr Pearson really wants you to say that you did.' They'd gone back into the office and when Pearson repeated his question, Cochrane still said, 'No.' With no stronger evidence against him, Pearson's actions in the case were interpreted as incompetence.[2]

Incompetence was then a perpetual problem, largely due to inexperience. When one considers that in 1875 there were 11,728 practising solicitors in England and Wales and in 1900 there were 15,500, and that in those years there were only 580 and 747 petitions filed respectively, the number of solicitors handling matrimonial suits for the first time must have remained high.[3] A provincial solicitor had to engage a London-based counterpart to act as his agent with the court but was still the main point of contact for his client and their witnesses. His theoretical knowledge came from 'how-to' guides such as *Divorce Practice* (1885) by chief clerk of the Divorce Registry T. W. H. Oakley. Practical assistance came from the London agent, but mistakes were still made and on the whole solicitors were shown a degree of latitude by the court as an organised professional body finding its feet in a new field. Yet there were occasions when even the most experienced had their methods called into question.

Solicitor and man of letters E.S.P. Haynes said of the relationship between solicitors and barristers that it was not unlike that of husband and wife: the solicitor being the silent support while the victorious barrister took the credit and glory. Barristers jealously guarded their territory and in general regarded themselves as morally and intellectually superior. As a body they enjoyed a long tradition of honesty and integrity which solicitors did not. Haynes asserts that this was due to the more obscure nature of solicitors' work and 'to the fact that barristers have never been exposed to the temptation of handling large sums of money entrusted to them by confiding clients'.[4] A certain tension, therefore, existed between the professions that sometimes overspilled into the courtroom.

In 1899, society solicitor George Lewis acted for Mrs Kathleen Chandos-Pole in her divorce petition against husband Samuel. Kathleen brought allegations of her husband's adultery with a maid, but during his investigation Lewis unearthed a more scandalous possibility: adultery with a lady named Inez Broom who, by the time the petition was filed, had become the honourable Mrs Rupert Craven. When the suit came to trial, Lewis was cross-examined as to his actions by Bargrave Deane. First, Deane insinuated there was something underhand in Lewis choosing to visit the maid in person after she'd denied the charge. Had he done so to apply pressure to secure her confession? Then, Deane accused Lewis of having dropped the charge with the maid in favour of the one with Inez. At best, this implied Lewis had attempted to intimidate Chandos-Pole into not defending a suit that would become very public with Inez involved; at worst, that Lewis had bribed witnesses for their evidence against her. There was 'somewhat of a scene' when Lewis took offence and then refused to allow Deane to withdraw his comments, challenging him instead to prove what he had insinuated.

The situation was compounded by the fact that at the start of the suit Kathleen Chandos-Pole had taken the unusual step of distancing herself from the allegation against Inez, unequivocally stating that she had no personal knowledge or suspicion of any misconduct between her husband and Inez and that the allegation was all down to Lewis. It was compounded further by the reading of letters from Chandos-Pole to Kathleen in which he'd begged her, 'Don't listen to Lewis and Lewis, they are the biggest scoundrels out'; by Rupert Craven unequivocally stating in the witness box that witnesses against his wife *had* been bribed (though he had no personal knowledge of the fact); and finally by the evidence of the thoroughly modern and unconventional twenty-six-year-old Inez herself who, on taking the stand, demanded her right to a controversial lifestyle: to go hunting with men and smoke and drink with them in hotels afterwards without being offended by their coarse language; and to allow Chandos-Pole to sleep it off afterwards in her hotel bedroom without it being assumed she had slept with him.

Deane came out of the contretemps on the wrong side and, the next day, retired from the trial through 'ill-health', leaving his junior to defend Inez's corner alone. After five rather fraught days, Justice Barnes asked the jury in his summing-up not to be swayed by personal prejudice against Inez's lifestyle or side issues, calling Deane's suggestion 'ridiculous' for one in Lewis's position, but the jury proved unequal to the task. After an hour's deliberation they were completely divided as to their verdict and dismissed. At the retrial, though the second jury were equally bemused by Inez's protestation that she did not have to question whether her lifestyle was respectable because *she* was respectable, they found her not guilty all the same; and on his return to court Deane made a public apology to Lewis for an allegation he admitted was based on his 'mistaken' reading of the evidence.

Lewis's biographer would no doubt be the first to say the famous solicitor sometimes trod dangerously close to the line, but when a solicitor had a vested interest in a suit, the temptation to overstep it must have been especially hard to resist. In 1891, Francis Edward Fox of Hickin and Fox, 29 Lincoln's Inn Field, found himself in just such a situation when he was reunited with his former fiancée who had deserted him in 1882 to marry budding artist John Nelson Drummond. Fox had first met Marie Alicia Wright, as she was then, in Devon when she was fourteen and he eighteen. While she had married, relocated to London and had four children, he had remained single and true to her memory. They had been reacquainted only a week when he declared he still loved her. Thereafter he became a regular visitor at the Drummonds' Dulwich family home while the artist passed most midweek days and nights at his studio in Great Russell Street, Bloomsbury. In May 1891, after Drummond's suspicions had been roused by their manner towards each other on a group outing to the Naval Exhibition, he spied on the couple and found them in a compromising position: Marie sitting on Fox's lap, kissing and caressing his face. The two men fought and Drummond banished Fox from his house. Thereafter, Fox and Marie plotted her divorce.

The first part was straightforward. The fact that the Drummonds had a tempestuous marriage meant there were plenty of episodes in their history that could be distorted to appear as if Marie were the innocent victim of Drummond's cruelty. The second required some planning. Fox first employed two detectives to watch Drummond in Bloomsbury. When they discovered nothing, Fox arranged for the detectives to entrap him. As Drummond described events when the case came before President Jeune and a special jury in February 1893, on 10 September 1891 a woman identifying herself as Miss Lamb of Charlotte Street called on him at his studio late at night and told him she had information about Marie that might be of interest to him. He invited her inside. She asked for money, and then more money, upon which Drummond asked her to leave. She was with him for about half an hour. Five days later he was approached by

Above: 1. The controversial new Royal Courts of Justice sketched on Lord Mayor's Day, 9 November 1882 (*The Graphic*, 2 Dec 1882).

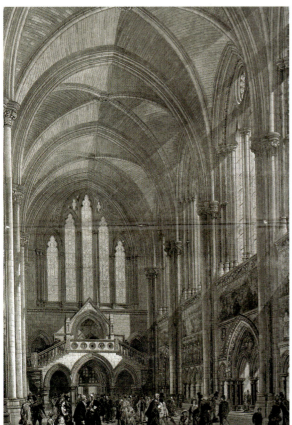

Left: 2. The magnificent cathedral-like Central Hall showing one of the passages to the courts, judge's rooms and chambers (*Illustrated London News*, 9 December 1882).

Opposite: 3. Several divorce court regulars appear in this *Vanity Fair* cartoon of 5 December 1891. Grouped around Lord Justice Coleridge in the bottom left corner (clockwise from left): Charles Gill, Sir Richard Webster, Sir Edward Clarke and Sir Charles Russell. In the centre, to the right of Lord Halsbury, the Lord Chancellor, is the 'gargantuan' Patrick Murphy; and in the bottom right corner with Mr Justice Collins are (clockwise from left): Mr Justice Jeune, Frederick Inderwick and Frank Lockwood.

Clockwise from top left: 4, 5, 6. Legal personalities left behind impressions as vivid as their *Vanity Fair* caricatures (clockwise from left): The President, Sir James Hannen; his successor, Sir Charles Parker Butt; and society lawyer Sir George Lewis.

7, 8. Completing the late-Victorian divorce bench: Sir Francis Henry Jeune (above), photographed for *The Sketch*, 1902; Sir John Gorell Barnes (below), whose portrait became a 1913 postcard.

Above left: 9. Campaigning editor of the *Pall Mall Gazette* and father of investigative journalism, W. T. Stead (undated photo, Library of Congress).

10, 11, 12. These stars of the stage became divorce court celebrities (clockwise from top right): Marie Tempest (Mrs Izard) as 'Dorothy', the eponymous heroine of the show that made her lover's fortune; Miss Edith Chester (Mrs Carew); and Belle Bilton (aka Lady Dunlo).

13. A dubious cast of characters: the 'brutal and disreputable blackguard' Howard de Walden and the wicked conspirators, the Count's valet Crocombe and the lady's maid Crook, as they appeared in *The Sketch*, 15 March 1893.

14. In the witness box, Joseph Tasker likened himself to Mr McGoosely (shown here on the left), the drinking companion of popular comic drunkard Ally Sloper. (From the collection of Jason Lineham)

15–18. The 'year of filth' 1886 saw the perfect storm of salaciousness, celebrity and scandal involving (clockwise from left) Virginia Crawford, as she appeared in the 'Verbatim Report', Sir Charles Dilke, pictured here with second wife Emilia, Lady Dilke (Rijksmuseum); the chronically infirm Lord Colin Campbell and his beautiful and accomplished wife, Gertrude (Rijksmuseum).

Left: 19. *Punch* satirises the role of the private enquiry agent in divorce suits, 11 January 1890.

Below: 20. Winnifrith family photograph, 22 December 1913, showing Albert and Rosa Winnifrith (seated left) alongside Alfred's parents, his brothers and their wives. Their daughter, Alfreda, sits on the floor between her cousins. (Courtesy of Tom Winnifrith)

another woman on Shaftesbury Avenue who said she was desperate and asked if she could model for him. It being the second time she'd asked him and he needing figures for a street scene of London, he took her back to the studio and did some sketches. She identified herself as Miss Spinks of Southampton Row. She was with him two hours and was paid half a crown before leaving. Unbeknown to Drummond, he was watched on both occasions.

William Crittenden worked for an inquiry agency run by Adolphus Hermann Louis whose prosaic business traded under the poetic name Flowerdew and Co. Crittenden described the company as 'a miscellaneous business' acting in matters 'entrusted to them by solicitors'. Whether his boss had any connection with a qualified practising solicitor named Frank Flowerdew or simply traded off his name is uncertain, but clearly he was not a man above shady dealings. In April 1891 he was prosecuted by the Law Society for acting as a solicitor though unqualified. He was not convicted but the judges of the Divisional Court observed that he 'certainly sailed dangerously near the wind'; so too did his employees. Crittenden claimed in court to have investigated the two visitors to Drummond's studio and discovered they were well-known prostitutes whom he'd subsequently followed to their residences. 'Miss Spinks' was identified as a Mrs Purella and 'Miss Lamb' as Clara Davis. Clara had been questioned by his colleague and confirmed she'd been with Drummond and said he afterwards gave her one of his paintings. She sold the painting to the detective for 22s. This version of events was corroborated by a second detective, who produced a receipt for the picture, and by Clara, who'd signed it. The presence of Mrs Purella in Drummond's studio was corroborated by a cabman who said he remembered driving them from Shaftesbury Avenue to Great Russell Street because, as he'd set off, Crittenden had jumped up on the cab and then paid him to follow the woman home.

So far so good. But if Fox had thought this was all the evidence they would need, he had not counted on Marie. Her relationship with Drummond was as passionate as it was tempestuous. Soon after the set-up, she'd argued with her husband over money (Drummond's income was always precarious) and they'd made up in the time-honoured fashion. In this one lapse all Fox's endeavours were undone by Marie condoning her husband's 'adultery'. A subsequent visit from the bailiffs to seize goods in lieu of Drummond's many debts, however, provided the potential solution. Fox felt they could argue it proved Drummond's cruel neglect and therefore revived all former marital offences. He convinced Marie to file her petition. The solicitor she used was a man named Byrne.

The petition immediately brought a torrent of letters from Drummond denying the offences and desperate to save his marriage. On the night of 5 January 1892 Drummond returned to the family home with Marie's eldest brother, Henry. She and Drummond spent two nights together. They had sex on both occasions. Later, Marie would swear that when the two men left she heard Drummond say to Henry, 'I have done it, old chap.' Marie's other brother, Ned, was also a solicitor and Marie interpreted Drummond's comment to mean that by sleeping with him she had once again condoned all his 'offences'. She immediately contacted Byrne, who arranged for a doctor to come and examine her and specifically told her not to have any more contact with Drummond until arrangements could be made for her. Unfortunately, Drummond returned that evening. Marie let him in and somehow, when he left the following morning, he took with him a document signed by Marie and witnessed by the children's nurse unequivocally stating that they had returned to cohabitation and that she withdrew all charges against him.

The following day Byrne collected Marie and installed her in the Inns of Court Hotel under a pseudonym. Though Fox stayed away, he wrote to her there. The children remained at home with their nurse. By the end of the month Marie had filed a supplementary petition alleging that when Drummond had returned to the house with Henry he had plied her with a sleeping draught and taken her by force while she was under its influence, rendering the document he had made her sign worthless. Only after this did Drummond file his answer to her petition alleging her adultery with Fox and asking for a divorce to be granted him, along with custody, costs and a claim for damages of £5,000.

At the trial, Drummond's barrister, William Willis QC, more than lived up to his reputation of being as aggressive, zealous and indignant in his client's interests as he might have been if 'his own honour and property were at stake'.[5] Under his vigorous cross-examination he revealed inconsistencies in the testimonies of those involved in setting up Drummond and pushed Marie hard on all aspects of her evidence but particularly the question of forcible cohabitation. The two days she spent in the witness box must have been a horrible ordeal for her. Much of what she said about her and Drummond's sex life appeared in the papers, justified as necessary for readers to understand the question of condonation. Willis read aloud letters from Fox to Marie which revealed not only Fox's excessive antipathy for Drummond, who appeared in the letters as 'the hound', but also that, though Byrne was nominally Marie's solicitor, it was Fox who pulled his strings and who schooled Marie in her evidence. Willis also read a very touching letter from Drummond to Marie in which he begged her to 'throw away those wretched fancies' of a life with Fox 'and begin a good motherly, honest, sweet life worthy of you without those penny tragedy novelette imitations'. The net effect was that the sympathy of the court gradually swung away from Marie and her claims that life with her husband was dismal and precarious. Drummond faced some difficult questions from Marie's advocates – Inderwick and Deane – and Fox's – Lockwood – about the extent to which he left Marie short of funds and unprotected while he was at his studio, but these he at least answered honestly while Marie's case was increasingly weakened by the revelations of Fox's manipulations. On the eleventh day Marie crumbled. When directly questioned on the nature of her relationship with Fox she admitted having kissed him on four separate occasions. The jury decided they had heard enough. The foreman brought proceedings to a sudden dramatic conclusion, intervening with a unanimous verdict in favour of Drummond.

This left only the question of damages to consider. Any expectation that the claim of such a large sum might be hotly contested quickly evaporated on the morning of day twelve with announcements by Lockwood and Inderwick that they were retiring from the case, reserving their right to appeal on the ground that the jury's intervention had prejudiced the case before Fox and his eighteen witnesses could be heard. All prospects of the spectacle of Willis cross-examining Fox vanished with them, but Willis took full advantage of his opponents' capitulation by expressing such sympathy for Marie for her courtroom ordeal and such censure of Fox's behind-the-scenes involvement that the blame for the whole palaver was laid firmly at his feet. In summing up, the president expressed himself particularly regretful that the charge of forcible cohabitation had ever been brought and guided the jury that in assessing damages they must remember that the evidence against Drummond had clearly been fabricated. After forty minutes' deliberation they awarded Drummond £4,000.

The matter of damages is interesting. The claim in this instance was high, but so too was the award. The 1881–1900 sample shows that three-quarters of claims in this period were under £2,000 and those above that sum were predominantly filed by aristocrats or wealthy businessmen. Often claims were either withdrawn during the proceedings or juries awarded a fraction of the claim: a third, on average. In any and all suits involving damages the judge always reminded the jury that awards were not intended to punish the co-respondent but to compensate the husband for the pecuniary loss of his wife, the injury to his feelings and hurt to his family life. Though the concepts of punishment and compensation are, by definition, difficult to entirely separate, the reminder was intended to prevent excessive and vindictive awards. The judge could also order how the award was to be spent – i.e. for the care and education of the children of the marriage, or even to maintain a wife divorced from her husband if she was deserted by her lover. With all this in mind, what can be said about this award? Marie had not been abandoned by Fox, so the damages were not needed for her future maintenance and £4,000 was an incredible sum to claim from a man of Fox's standing to maintain Drummond's children in their accustomed manner, even if an additional governess or nurse were required to look after them to enable Drummond to continue at his studio.

It can only be assumed therefore that a large proportion of the figure was intended to recompense Drummond's personal injury. Moreover, though there was plenty of evidence that Fox's actions were comparable with those of the detectives in the Barrett case, the public prosecutor declined to act. Though Fox's actions no doubt stretched the prosecutor's tolerance of the 'inducements' to parties to commit perjury that he looked upon 'with indulgence', Fox's public exposure and the £778 costs he was condemned to pay were considered punishment enough for his crime. Indeed, they ruined him. The partnership of Hickin

Working the System (Pt 2): Scheming Solicitors

and Fox was immediately declared bankrupt and dissolved. Fox appealed both the verdict and the decree absolute. He lost. He then married Marie within days of the decree being granted but continued to fight the order for damages. That was only settled in 1895, when a benevolent cousin when a benevolent cousin agreed to pay his outstanding costs and the court accepted a guaranteed payment of £40 a year payable to the children's guardian until the youngest turned twenty-one. By this arrangement, the maximum Fox could have expected to pay was £720 – a fraction of the original £4,000 award. He and Marie thereafter emigrated to New Zealand where Fox became a journalist. Drummond died in 1897, aged only thirty-seven. The children were separated and left to the care of his siblings.

Behaviour such as Fox's angered the court but, human nature being what it is, it was an inevitable consequence of a system that pitted separating couples against each other, failed to adequately punish perjurers and allowed divorce only for a marital offence. Manipulation of the system – to a certain acceptable degree, anyway – must therefore have been expected. What the court did not expect and what incensed it intensely was when litigants flaunted that manipulation under its nose in the manner Louis Clavering Clovis Bonaparte did in December 1891. In this instance, to make matters worse, Bonaparte's manipulation involved a sister court from our own United Kingdom: the Scottish Court of Sessions.

The inequities of the English law compared with the Scottish, which for three hundred years had allowed divorce for simple adultery by either spouse or four years' desertion, had long been a bone of contention and became seriously so towards the end of this era. The first significant attempt at reform of the English law came from a Scottish MP, William Hunter, in a bill presented to the Commons in April 1892. Hunter argued that with so many Scots and English intermarrying it would be sensible for the divorce laws of both countries to be the same, and he judged the English law to be immoral. Neither point was well received. A scathing attack from the attorney general and widespread resentment among politicians that a Scottish lawyer should attempt to rewrite English law saw the bill easily defeated. But the continued existence of different grounds for divorce between the two countries unwittingly provided

Decadent Divorce

opportunities for the unscrupulous. When Bonaparte wished to rid himself of his wife Rosalie – the divorced wife of music director Norfolk Bernard Megone – he did so by admitting to the English court not only that the Scottish court had been manipulated into giving Megone a divorce it had no grounds or jurisdiction to give but that he, Bonaparte, had conspired in the whole affair with the help of a young Glasgow solicitor named Lang.

Louis was the illegitimate son of Lucien Bonaparte, a prince of the late French empire long domiciled in England, who had married his mistress late in life and acknowledged their son in 1891, thereby legitimising him by French law and bestowing on him his illustrious name. Louis Bonaparte's involvement with Rosalie was suspect from the start. On 20 December 1884 Rosalie Barlow, as she was then, had married Megone in Hampstead. Nine months later he had filed a petition for divorce, alleging her adultery with an old friend of her family named O'Hagan, committed while she was staying with her father's relations on the Isle of Man. This was an allegation neither could deny. O'Hagan was a wealthy director of various public companies and wished to avoid publicity, so he proposed that he pay Megone £1,000 and settled a further £5,000 on Rosalie for the petition to be dropped and another co-respondent found. Enter Bonaparte who, when approached by O'Hagan's solicitor, agreed to be that man. On 16 October 1885, he and Rosalie travelled to Sutton Coldfield where they spent a fortnight together. On 9 November Megone dropped his petition against O'Hagan and four days later filed another against Bonaparte.

If it is true that there is no honour among thieves, it appears there is also sometimes none among divorce conspirators. On 8 February 1886, Bonaparte decided to defend the action and filed a motion with the court to amend his answer to include an allegation of collusion, along with an affidavit exposing the whole arrangement. The matter came before President Hannen on 22 February, during which Megone practically admitted the charge. The angry president warned him that when the suit was tried his petition would almost certainly fail.

Then came another twist in the tale. For reasons known only to himself, Bonaparte reversed his position once again. Having first offered himself as the means by which Megone could get his divorce and then tried to stop it, he now decided he wished it to go ahead. His counsel would later suggest it was because he had grown 'fond' of Rosalie and wanted to marry her. Whether this was true or not, it was suddenly Bonaparte driving the divorce ahead, not Megone. In 1887 an engineering contract took Bonaparte to Kilmarnock and, ahead of this move to Scotland, he made enquiries of twenty-four-year-old Glasgow solicitor John Stuart Lang as to the possibility of Megone divorcing Rosalie there. Lang had been in practice less than a year. He corresponded with a writer in the Scottish Supreme Court named William Officer for guidance. Officer informed Lang that if Megone domiciled in Scotland for forty days he would be entitled to approach the Edinburgh Court of Sessions for a divorce. In May 1887, Lang – who now acted for both Bonaparte *and* Rosalie – wrote directly to Megone proposing he withdraw his London petition and take up residence in Glasgow. It would not be necessary for him to actually be in Scotland for each of the forty days, Lang advised him, so long as he could prove it was his main residence. For appearances it was suggested he could argue that the move from London to Edinburgh was to save himself expense as Rosalie had also relocated to Scotland by this time and was living with her mother in Ayr. In reality, the whole thing would be financed by Bonaparte.

By this time, Megone had his own reasons for wishing to expedite his divorce. He had been living with a musician named Lucy Maria Tilt and in December 1886 she had fallen pregnant. He agreed to the terms and Lang secured business premises for him in Glasgow where he might establish himself as a tea merchant. (In 1881 Megone had been clerk to a tea merchant but, so far as it is known, had no further experience in this field.) A long correspondence then ensued between Lang and Bonaparte, Lang and Officer and Lang and Megone. Lang, driven by Bonaparte, held the whole thing together as Officer started to get cold feet and Megone resisted the move to Glasgow, saying work commitments kept him in London. In the end Megone spent only three of the forty days in Scotland and no business was ever carried out at the Glasgow premises. At one point it was suggested that the conspirators might have to revert to London which, the sly solicitor stressed, might be facilitated by Hannen's imminent retirement, but the Scottish petition eventually went ahead. It was filed in December 1887 and summons served on Bonaparte and Rosalie at a Glasgow hotel by arrangement.

Bonaparte was named on the petition as 'Joseph Richards' – Joseph being the name he had taken at confirmation and Richards being his mother's maiden name. Keen to avoid publicity, he had insisted on this; being illegitimate, Richards was a name to which he could legally swear.

As required by Scottish law, on Christmas Eve Megone went to Edinburgh to swear before the judge that the facts of the petition were true and that there was no collusion. Then on 10 March 1888 the case was heard. Rosalie's mother gave evidence as to Rosalie's 'disappearance' from her house the previous December; a resident of 365 Sauchiehall Street, Glasgow, attested that Bonaparte and Rosalie subsequently lived there as Mr and Mrs Joseph Richards; and the decree was granted. With no necessity under Scottish law to wait six months for the decree to be made absolute, Megone immediately married Lucy in Edinburgh and on 30 May 1888, Bonaparte and Rosalie married on the Isle of Man. A clause in the Scots law stated that a divorced wife could not marry on Scottish soil a co-respondent with whom she had been found guilty of committing adultery. This only applied when the co-respondent was expressly named in the decree (something that was not a legal necessity in Scotland) and in practice simply not naming them in the summons was 'a policy frequently resorted to'.[6] It required a level of cooperation between parties that in England would have been considered collusion. They were, however, allowed to marry elsewhere if they could establish a proper domicile. Bonaparte's pseudonym and the Isle of Man marriage were attempts to cover both bases.

Unfortunately, Bonaparte soon discovered that he was not so 'fond' of Rosalie as he thought. Neither, it seems, was she very fond of him. In January 1891 she admitted adultery with a man named Coghill and by September Bonaparte wished to marry a fellow engineer's daughter, Laura Scott. Rosalie was induced to sign a confession and Bonaparte and Laura eloped. Bonaparte then used the confession to extort money out of Coghill with the threat of divorce proceedings against him; and persuaded Rosalie to give back valuable Bonaparte family jewels which presumably had been part of the inducement. On 29 October, he married Laura in Reigate.

Working the System (Pt 2): Scheming Solicitors

Rosalie immediately filed a divorce petition on the ground that Bonaparte's marriage was bigamous. The document was poorly written and her application immediately dismissed. Had it not been, it would have been easily defeated anyway. All Bonaparte needed to do was admit the conspiracy with Megone, if he had the gall to do it. The filing of his own petition in London on 16 December 1891 asking to have his marriage to Rosalie annulled on the ground that her Scottish divorce was obtained illegally proved that he did.

Their suit, which was heard on 30 July and 1 August 1892 by Justice Barnes, presented the judge with a problem. It is a generally accepted principle of English law that no man may take advantage of his wrongdoing, yet here was Bonaparte flaunting the fact that he was entitled, by law, to do just that. How could Barnes refuse the petition if Rosalie had not been legally divorced from Megone? The short answer is he could not. Rosalie's advocate tried to argue that she was ignorant of the manner in which the Megone divorce came about, but Barnes ruled that it was immaterial and a contention that would not hold water. He annulled the Bonaparte marriage but ruled that in the circumstances Bonaparte should be condemned to all costs.

The only other penalty Bonaparte incurred for his daring was the publicity he had once been keen to avoid. *The Times* reported the entire proceedings with the lengthy correspondence between the conspirators in full across four columns. No further comment was really necessary, but the Scottish press took the manipulation of their court system by a French aristocrat domiciled in England personally. 'Seldom has a writer of the lowest class of fiction produced from his practiced imagination a story of social vice, rascality, and intrigue more disgraceful,' wrote *The Scotsman*. 'An infamous imposture' had been perpetrated on the court in which adultery, for once, played a minor part 'in the procession of contemptable vices'. Lang's lack of scruples, Megone's readiness to participate so long as it cost him nothing and Officer's willingness to assist were all roundly criticised.[7] Bonaparte – prince of the late French Empire – was shamed in papers across the United Kingdom. He married Laura and lived with her until his premature death from meningitis in 1894. His co-conspirators all suffered for their involvement with him. Rosalie returned to her mother. For the rest of her life she went by the name Rosalie Clovis though by English law she remained married to Megone. By 1939 she had entered East Sussex County Mental Hospital. She died there in 1945. Megone and Lucy lived together until the early 1900s before separating. In 1910 Lucy (legally) married again; in 1922 Megone quietly (and illegally) married his long-term mistress, Ethel Phillips, on his deathbed. Both Officer and Lang were prosecuted by their respective governing bodies and tried in the Scottish Supreme Court. Both were suspended from practice for a year. Lang subsequently became a partner in a Glasgow firm. In 1908, the partners were indicted for embezzling a client's trust fund and Lang was sentenced to four years' hard labour.[8]

Bonaparte's open manipulation of the system was an embarrassment, but even coming so soon after Hunter's reform bill did nothing to reopen the question or tighten the law as to domicile. The Scots law remained unchanged until 1938 when cruelty was added as a ground for divorce. In the meantime, parties attempting to cheat the English system found themselves confronted with another obstacle which their Scottish counterparts did not: they had to outwit the Queen's Proctor.

8

Working the System (Pt 3): 'Clean Hands', Collusion and the Queen's Proctor

> Divorces aren't given away in this country. They are dragged out of an unwilling Court by main force. And when you've got your bone, there's no knowing if the King's Proctor won't stroll up and take it off you.
>
> Arnold Bennett, *Whom God Hath Joined* (1906)

The office of King or Queen's Proctor was known to have existed in the Middle Ages. It was held by a barrister trained in canon law who acted for the Crown 'in all causes and matters, maritime, foreign, civil, and ecclesiastical, whatsoever' which concerned the Crown or its interests, rights or prerogatives.[1] In 1860, following concerns about the high number of divorce cases that went uncontested, the role was expanded to include the investigation of possible collusion by couples whose behaviour barred them from obtaining a divorce decree under the terms of the 1857 Matrimonial Causes Act. The necessity for a petitioner to approach the court with 'clean hands' and outright horror at the thought of divorce by mutual consent had resulted in the enacting of several bars to divorce: connivance and condonation, which were absolute bars, and certain discretionary bars including adultery of the petitioner, undue delay in presenting a petition and behaviour sufficient to conduce a respondent's adultery (usually desertion or negligence).

When it became clear in the years following the Act that the bars did not prevent petitioners trying to hoodwink the court, Lord Brougham – the great Whig reformer and one-time advocate of Queen Caroline in her defence against attempts by George IV to strip her of her title on the ground of her alleged adultery – proposed that any unlawful practice should be investigated by the attorney general or someone representing him on the part of the Crown – a system similar to that in Scotland where the Lord Advocate policed collusion. Concerns about the increased workload for the attorney general if it was left to his office ultimately saw the task go to the proctor acting under the attorney general's discretion in one of two ways: he could either intervene at the court's invitation at any point during proceedings if collusion was suspected; or, following the granting of a decree *nisi*, he could 'show cause' why a decree should not be made absolute by reason of it having been obtained by collusion or by the withholding of material facts. In such a situation, with the attorney general's permission, he could retain counsel and subpoena witnesses for what amounted to a second trial.[2]

The first Queen's Proctor to perform this function was Francis Hart Dyke, who held office until 1876. In also being Registrar of the Province of Canterbury he offered continuity between the new system and the old and interpreted collusion in the manner of the ecclesiastical courts as either a straightforward agreement between parties that one of them would commit adultery for the purpose of getting a divorce or an agreement that they would prosecute a false petition. He was essentially a passive recipient of information that came to him either from a suspicious judge or from interested persons, such as friends and relatives of one of the parties involved or their solicitor. There had aways been people willing to 'shop' colluders – Lord Brougham openly acknowledged the difference that whispers to individual members of the Lords had made in preventing divorces under the old system – but information from a judge was considered of the 'highest authority'. Unfortunately, with further changes in the law in 1878 that condemned the proctor to costs whenever his intervention was unsuccessful, such communication from judges 'practically ceased' and, in conjunction with the appointment of Augustus Keppel Stephenson as Dyke's successor in 1876, the proctor's function perceptibly changed.[3]

Stephenson was a forceful character who had also been appointed Treasury Solicitor in 1876 and zealously pursued both roles, adding a third to his portfolio in 1884 when he was additionally made Director of Public Prosecutions, bringing divorce court deception entirely within his jurisdiction. He changed the manner in which the proctor's office functioned in two fundamental ways: firstly, by actively seeking out wrongdoers instead of passively waiting for information to come to him; and secondly, by shifting emphasis away from collusion to focus on the more straightforward question of the petitioner's 'clean hands'. Legal historian Wendie Schneider has argued that by thus focusing on one single discretionary bar to divorce – adultery – Stephenson 'rewrote the substantive law of intervention' to create 'a harsher regime than even England's conservative lawmakers had intended'.[4] At the time, the legality of this shift was questioned, as shall be seen; and certainly, a petitioner's adultery was rarely overlooked as a bar to divorce unless it was determined that the petitioner was driven to it by the respondent. (An abandoned wife driven into prostitution to survive might fall into this category.) But whether a petitioner's adultery was condemned any more than before the proctor became active is uncertain. The point is that it was more readily exposed and certainly successive proctors continued to practice in this way until the function was made obsolete by the introduction of divorce by mutual consent in 1971: returns for 1961–70 show that 88 per cent of interventions were on the ground of undisclosed adultery versus only 3.4 per cent for collusion.[5]

The fact that collusion, by definition, was difficult to prove makes the shift understandable. The fact that the definition of collusion was not easily agreed upon made matters worse. Bargrave Deane – by then a judge in the division – told the Barnes Commission in 1910 that the only real collusion was when parties agreed that one would commit adultery to enable the other to sue for divorce. Another possible interpretation was when one offered the other an incentive not to defend a suit. Faking adultery was not collusion because you can't collude in something that doesn't happen. This, he said, was more like connivance. George Lewis, on the other hand, said there was nothing wrong with couples discussing and agreeing not to defend, and if they faked adultery that was neither collusion nor connivance but conspiracy to defeat the ends of justice – a criminal offence. The Earl of Desart, who replaced Stephenson in all his offices on Stephenson's retirement in 1894 and was the sitting proctor at the time of the commission, said he had no doubt collusion occurred in cases of desertion following an order for restitution of conjugal rights.

The 1884 change in the law that dispensed with prison sentences for spouses who refused to comply with such an order, ruling instead that noncompliance within a fortnight without good cause amounted to desertion, allowed the aggrieved party to file a petition for judicial separation or, if adultery could also be proved, for divorce. Deane agreed with Desart that 'the whole thing is a collusive arrangement from beginning to end' but, Lewis argued, you cannot condemn couples for collusion created by law! Asked how he detected collusion, Deane said, 'You can only smell it', before telling the story of how Lord Ludlow, when he was seconded from the Court of Appeal to temporarily sit on the divorce bench, said he knew the court to be 'brimful of collusion' and meant to put a stop to it, but then went a whole term without discovering any, though Deane was 'perfectly certain there was plenty of it'![6] Many got away with it; some even flaunted the fact under the proctor's nose.

One such was the second Earl Russell, who in his 1923 memoirs readily admitted collusion committed in sheer frustration at his prior experiences with the draconian law. Having failed to secure a divorce from first wife, Mabel, after a ten-year struggle involving three very high-profile court cases, he had taken the law into his own hands in 1900, emigrating with his affianced second wife to America where he divorced Mabel under the laxer Nevada laws (securing, most probably, the first celebrity Reno divorce) before remarrying. Back in England, Mabel received the news with 'exclamations of horror and surprise' in an episode Russell admitted was completely staged. He had leaked the story of his American marriage to the press having agreed with Mabel beforehand that she would receive the news in public and feign surprise before suing for divorce on the grounds of his 'technical' bigamy and adultery, knowing there was £5,000 waiting in a bank account for her on the day the decree became absolute.[7] That authorities saw nothing 'technical' in the bigamy and indicted Russell for the offence, resulting in his spectacular trial in the House of Lords and subsequent imprisonment, is another story. Mabel's theatrics worked and the collusive divorce was successfully secured.

Though Russell's arrangement was hardly unique, most other perpetrators were too mindful of their reputations to admit they had broken the law. Russell had his own reasons for doing otherwise, as shall be seen. But given that rooting out collusion was intended to be the proctor's primary function, when a seemingly reliable source approached him categorically stating that a certain Mr and Mrs Carew had obtained their 1892 divorce by collusion, Stephenson must have thought that here for once was a straightforward case in which he could demonstrate his effectiveness against such conspirators. It turned out to be anything but.

Frank Murray Maxwell Hallowell Carew was a racehorse owner and man of fortune – his wealth principally gained by land rents and moneylending. After his wife secured her decree *nisi* in an undefended suit heard on 8 February 1892, the PMG had no scruples about referring to him as 'a man of loose propensities' – both before and after marriage – who associated with prize fighters and attended race meetings with women of 'loose morals'.[8] Perhaps, in part, this candour was encouraged by the relative position of his wife. Mrs Carew was better known nationwide as Miss Edith Chester, the doe-eyed darling of the stage who, the year before her 1887 marriage to Carew, had been described by *The Era* as possessing 'a profusion of personal charms ... sweet, pure, and tender, almost beyond the reach of printed praise'; a talent whose star had continued to thus shine right up to the hearing.[9] The proven facts of her case were that Carew had thrown her down on several occasions, punched her on another and committed adultery with one Alice Seymour, a woman with whom he cohabited. But following Edith's easy win, the requisite six months before her decree could be made absolute came and went without any application to the court to make it so. Not until 17 December 1892 was the application finally filed. A week later, the proctor intervened.

His informant was Carew's business partner, Reginald St Feré Vaile – a man so close to the Carews that both their sons were given middle names in his honour: one 'Reginald', the other 'St Feré'. Vaile told the proctor that since the decree *nisi* Edith and Carew were often seen together. The proctor's further investigations revealed that this had been the case throughout the whole of the proceedings; that the Carews had remained on apparently friendly terms despite the fact that Carew resided with Alice. Such amicable relations being both inconceivable and monstrous between divorcing spouses, the proctor readily believed they must have colluded. The fact that Edith had allowed Carew to sleep at her house after the decree was granted and, the proctor alleged, had conjugal intercourse with him, meant that in legal terms she had also condoned all his marital offences.

The intervention came before Justice Barnes and a special jury on 23 November 1893. Proceedings were bizarre from beginning to end. Sir Edward Clarke had been retained by the proctor with Bargrave Deane and the proctor's son, Guy Stephenson, as his junior, but when the time came Clarke was unavailable and the job went to Montague Hughes Crackanthorpe QC, who was not often seen in the divorce court. His opponent was the infinitely more at-home Frank Lockwood. Crackanthorpe's two key witnesses were Carew's valet and his housekeeper. The valet testified to the Carews' friendliness, to Edith's visit to Carew's home after the divorce and to hearing her tell Carew in a friendly manner that now he had his divorce he could marry whom he liked. The housekeeper claimed Edith always called Carew 'Franky, dear' and he always called her 'darling'; that following their divorce, on the occasion of their wedding anniversary, Edith came to his house and dressed it with flowers to remind him of their vows; and that Edith had told her she was pregnant, still loved Carew and would, if not for Alice, forgive him everything.

Lockwood had no difficulty in dispatching both these witnesses. The valet, it transpired, had been sent to Vaile by Carew under the impression it was Edith he was helping. When she came to Carew's house, he admitted, it was always with the children and a companion. Edith's solicitor later testified this was to fulfil the terms of an access agreement ordered by the court. The housekeeper also admitted under cross-examination that her main consideration was the children and that as a good Catholic she considered it her duty to try to reconcile the Carews. She could not say for certain that her conversation with Edith wasn't before the divorce or that any affection witnessed between them was after it. Thereafter, so thoroughly did Lockwood expose the exaggerated claims of each of the proctor's subsequent witnesses that he seemed to toy with Crackanthorpe. For every one who claimed to have seen Carew and Edith together, Lockwood cross-examined as to whether they hadn't also seen him with Alice. Invariably – much to Crackanthorpe's growing frustration – the answer was yes. In some instances, they even confused them. For much to the amusement and curiosity of the popular press it was revealed that Alice fashioned herself on the actress: dressed like her, wore her hair like her, and adopted her deportment. Were she not a couple of inches taller, she would have been Edith's spitting image, though temperamentally they were very different. While Edith was placid, Alice was fiery and appeared to have a curious hold over Carew who seemed infatuated with her.

So destructive were these revelations to the proctor's case that, eventually, a thoroughly exasperated Crackanthorpe complained that Lockwood was spending too much time focusing on an irrelevant aspect of the case. In so doing, Crackanthorpe seemed to suggest that Lockwood was merely diverting attention or playing up to the crowds in court. The thoroughly unsensational *Times*, however, pointed out that he was not: Lockwood was simply trying to prove that if Edith had condoned Carew's adultery by sleeping with him after the divorce hearing, the fact that Carew had continued to misconduct himself with Alice revived Edith's former grievance, thereby entitling her to her divorce!

With proceedings increasingly reminiscent of the latest Gilbert and Sullivan farce, Crackanthorpe, in sheer desperation, stated that if Lockwood continued in such a manner he would, if pushed, bring similar charges on behalf of the proctor against Edith (sensation!). Barnes asked if he meant adultery. Crackanthorpe said he did, and immediately the judge challenged him to bring forth his evidence. By the time the court reconvened the following week, Edith had been formally charged with having committed adultery with Mr Loftus William Earle, the twenty-eight-year-old owner-manager of the Lyric Club where (and to whom), it may be remembered, Marmaduke 'Marmy' Wood had so unwisely cast aspersions on the character of another actress, Belle Bilton, so sensationally in the Dunlo case.

Edith's adultery was alleged to have occurred at a weekend party aboard Earle's houseboat moored on the Thames near Hampton

Court Palace the previous summer. The allegations rested on the testimony of two servants who claimed that Edith and Earle were known to each other as 'Edie' and 'Lofty' and had spent all day Saturday alone together in the onboard saloon while other guests ventured out on the river and that at one point 'Lofty' may or may not have had his arm about Edith's waist. It was hardly the most damning evidence and, it transpired, had been secured after Carew's solicitor suggested to the proctor three months previously that detectives be put on Edith's trail as a back-up. A week ago, those detectives' reports were handed to the proctor who, presumably, authorised Crackanthorpe to use them as a last resort. Crackanthorpe called the servants only after having made a huge show of calling Carew, who did not answer and was not in court, but whose solicitor stated he *had* been told he would be wanted that day, but had declared instead his intention of making for the railway station (laughter).

Crackanthorpe thus closed so feebly that the rest of Lockwood's task was easy. In his opening address for Edith he employed every bit of his famed wit and good-humour to ridicule the theatricality of Crackanthorpe calling Carew as if he was trying to raise 'spirits from the vasty deep' (laughter), commenting that he thought nothing would have shocked his learned friend more than if Carew had responded (loud laughter). He insisted that Carew's open and flagrant conduct with Alice outweighed any indiscretion on Edith's part in remaining in contact with her husband, firmly laying the blame for the destruction of their 'sweet and happy marriage' on Alice's domination of Carew and concluding that as the possibility of Alice and Carew marrying had been talked of, he hoped the jury would give them every opportunity of doing so!

With that Edith entered the box and denied all the charges against her. If the jury were nearly ready to conclude that Carew had instigated the proctor's intervention to avoid having to marry Alice – the bubble of his infatuation having finally burst – Edith's evidence gave them an even stronger motive. On the night Carew spent at Edith's house after the divorce hearing, he had arrived on her doorstep late at night, his face scratched, pleading for sanctuary, claiming Alice had threatened him with a knife and that he was afraid of her. A bed was prepared for him in the spare room and Edith's housekeeper took him tea in the morning before he left.

Working the System (Pt 3)

For two years, Edith claimed, she had tried to release him from Alice's clutches and had failed. Now she had her divorce he was attempting to strip her of it to save his own skin, not to reconcile. As for Earle, she said, he was an old friend of Carew's who had visited her that summer and extended her the hand of friendship, nothing more.

Crackanthorpe was forced to accept Edith's denial and concede that the proctor had been misled. Magnanimously he announced that, not wishing to act in a half-hearted manner, he would withdraw the whole intervention. The foreman spoke up, saying if he did not they would intervene to stop the case. Lockwood insisted, for the sake of Edith's reputation, that all charges – collusion, condonation and adultery – be put to the jury who immediately found her not guilty, the foreman receiving a round of applause when he added that the last charge should never have been made.

It was a 'most unfortunate and deservedly unsuccessful intervention', said the *Daily News*, and 'monstrous' for Earle who, despite having secured the services of the gargantuan Mr Murphy QC to speak on his behalf, had been denied the right to intervene in his own defence. The general consensus in the press was that the whole intervention had been a 'serious blunder'. The evidence was 'very amusing', said *St James's Gazette*, but they agreed with a smart young city clerk on the Underground who was overheard saying, 'There was not a bet in it.' The *Yorkshire Herald* called for Carew's partner, Vaile, to be punished for involving the proctor in the first place and the *Weekly Dispatch* and other radical titles called for reform of the law that encouraged couples 'to resort to trickery, and often open immorality' to escape the unhappy bonds that bound them. It was thought incredible that as DPP Stephenson should have prosecuted the case at all on such flimsy evidence.

But though his actions in this instance were wrong, his instincts were not. When Edith returned to the stage in August 1894 playing opposite Charles Hawtrey in *Hot Water* – a farce about a scheming servant who plots to separate his master from his new wife in a bid to return their household to the bachelor status the valet infinitely preferred – it was as Mrs Loftus Earle. The couple had married quietly a month after Edith's divorce was made absolute. Three months later, Lockwood's hope became a reality when Carew married a gentleman's daughter by the name of Florence Harriet Rhind, who turned out to be none other than Alice Seymour in yet another guise. But to what end? The designing young lady who had been born Harriet Jane Rhind to a garden labourer and charwoman on the Isle of Wight twenty-four years earlier returned there seven years later married, as she wished to be, but in name only. Her temperament proved too much for Carew, who abandoned her.

In light of Carew's attempt to manipulate the proctor, Stephenson's decision to hunt down cases of petitioner adultery might seem thoroughly sensible, although in this and in his methods he increasingly came under attack. In 1880, when the suave Sir Henry James QC became attorney general under Gladstone, he had immediately come into conflict with Stephenson over the proctor's duties and responsibilities. Their correspondence extended into 1883 and gives a fascinating insight into how Stephenson operated.[10]

James's main gripe was that at 'considerable expense to the public' the proctor was initiating investigations off his own bat *before* seeking the attorney general's permission to proceed. In so doing he was exceeding his brief and the practice ought to stop. James denied a wider personal or political agenda but the timing of his complaint is interesting given that the discourse takes place just as the opposing voices of puritanism that favoured tighter controls on immorality on the one hand, and reformists who would in time call for the abolition of the proctor's office on the other, were starting to be heard. In response, Stephenson put together a memorandum outlining and justifying his methods.

The employment of investigators was necessary, he argued, to enquire into the 'various communications' he received to determine whether there was a case to answer. Most frequently, these communications came in the form of anonymous letters from 'the lover of justice' who professed the purest motive and disclaimed personal hostility to either party involved. Second to these were communications from respondents or co-respondents after verdicts had gone against them or other interested parties. Least frequent were communications from independent, disinterested parties or, after 1878, from judges. In addition to this, he received details of all successful undefended cases from the court. The practice of enquiring into *all* these had 'recently been adopted' and had confirmed his longstanding view that material was suppressed in 'a large portion' of them. In addition, his office made full use of newspaper reports of cases and enquired into those that seemed to him or his assistant suspicious. In all such cases, discrete enquiries were then made – usually by solicitors local to the petitioner on the proctor's behalf, of whom there seemed to be a ready supply. Thereafter, the proctor proceeded on the principle that if a petitioner appeared to be of 'good character' in his neighbourhood no further enquiries were made, but if he were 'a notorious evil-liver' Stephenson considered it would be a dereliction of his duty and bring the court into disrepute if he did not enquire further.

By this method Stephenson claimed to have been most successful at very little cost. Where his predecessor had intervened in sixty cases in his last five and a half years of service and been successful in only forty at a cost to the public of £33,692, Stephenson had intervened in fifty-seven but been successful in forty-eight (84 per cent) at a cost of only £11,239. His method of pursuing adultery over connivance, he concluded therefore, was cheaper, more efficient and more effective. Stephenson also reminded James that under section 7 of the 1860 Act, *any person* could 'show cause' or present reasons to the court as to why a decree *nisi* should not be made absolute without reference to the attorney general. Stephenson had interpreted this to mean that under this clause, where collusion was not suspected but other crimes were, he was at perfect liberty to show cause as a member of the public. In a final comment that reveals the tension between the two offices he argued that in such a situation, in strict accordance with the statute, he need not refer to the attorney general at all, but in practice he always did as was required by his office.

Stephenson was perfectly accurate in stating that any person could show cause. In practice, however, virtually nobody did. The only instance in this era appears to have been in *Edwards* v. *Edwards* (1897). Dr David Edwards of Cemmaes, Montgomeryshire, Wales, had accused his wife, Catherine, of having a child by another man. He also accused her of adultery with a man named Edward Wilson but did not name him as the father of the child and later withdrew the charge as unprovable. Neither did he include in his petition the fact that his wife had allegedly confessed to committing adultery with Caernarfon MP and future prime minister David Lloyd George on 4 February 1896, but this came out in court (sensation!). The child was born on 19 August 1896 and the adultery was alleged to have taken place between July and December 1895, but there were very few particulars. Catherine counter-sued for judicial separation alleging cruelty, which included the fact that on 9 August, before her confinement, Edwards had pulled her around the room by her hair and stamped on her stomach causing premature labour and the birth of a female child who then died on 17 September. Also that on 13 August he had threatened her with a knife and made her sign 'a document'. She had not known what the document was but had signed it in fear of her life and was then banished from their house. When the case came to trial Catherine withdrew her charges of cruelty and did not defend the allegation of adultery. Catherine's confession regarding Lloyd George did not tally with the delivery of a full-grown child in August, so a decree *nisi* was awarded on the ground of adultery with an unknown man, President Jeune commenting that he had never heard of a woman confessing adultery with one man to protect the identity of another. Though this is exactly what Dilke alleged happened in the Crawford case, it was not the official version.

Thereafter, Catherine was treated by a Dr Thomas Pugh Beddoes and eventually became his secretary. She told him her sorry story and at the eleventh hour Beddoes decided to show cause. There was no suggestion he ever contacted the proctor. At the second hearing, Beddoes argued that the mysterious 'document' signed was the confession; that it was false and had been taken by force; that Edwards had been cruel in banishing Catherine when she was heavily pregnant; that there was evidence to suggest that the baby was not full-term (and so could equally be her husband's or, indeed, Lloyd George's – sensation again!); and that he was concerned, therefore, that justice had not been done. Having heard evidence from all parties the president ruled that this one action of Edwards in itself did not constitute cruelty; that Catherine had withdrawn other charges of cruelty at the first trial; and that her now claiming her confession was false did not change the material fact that she had had a child by another man (Edwards denied paternity). He dismissed the intervention.

Beddoes' failure cost him dearly. In court, the judge had secured from Catherine an admission that her advocate had advised her not to give evidence at this hearing but she had chosen rather to listen to Beddoes. Reading between the lines it seems that before the first trial she had thought she had made a private arrangement with her husband whereby he would get his divorce, pay her costs and give her custody of their older daughter, Gwen. When that turned out not to be the case – the judge awarded Edwards custody – Catherine and Beddoes attempted to stop it. The judge obviously did not appreciate Beddoes' intervention and awarded costs against him amounting to £505 6s 4d.

With such a bruising experience, it is unsurprising few private individuals chose to intervene; and James's answer to Stephenson's argument that he was entitled to show cause as a private individual was that he was indeed, but that the public should not be expected to pay for it. The matter was referred to the Treasury financial secretary, who involved the Lords Commissioners, who, after due consideration, determined that the costs were 'trifling' and Stephenson sufficiently competent to use his discretion. He ought, they thought, to be able to continue as he was even though it was open to opinion whether he was working strictly in accordance with the statute. His 84 per cent success rate spoke for itself and no one wished to rock the boat.

Though the majority of cases the proctor pursued were undefended, the defended suit of Harding Edward de Fonblanque Cox – he who accused his wife of adultery on the 3.46 from Winchester to Basingstoke – might be considered typical of why Stephenson first and Desart after him preferred to pursue petitioner adultery over collusion and why the Lords Commissioners supported his right to do so.

Harding Cox was another wealthy racehorse owner and a successful newspaper proprietor. He owned *The Field*, *The Queen* and *The Law Times* outright, held large stakes in *Exchange and Mart* and was well known in sporting, theatrical and press circles. On 13 October 1881, he had married gentleman's daughter Hebe Gertrude Barlow and on 13 January 1893 filed a petition for divorce alleging her adultery with John Dyball, himself a married man, onetime land agent for Lord Chesham and Cox's 'bosom friend'. The adultery charged was not only on the aforementioned Basingstoke train, but at a string of hotels in Sussex and Devon as well as the Cox family home, Denham Court in Winchester, over a period of eighteen months. For this Cox claimed £10,000 damages and custody of their three sons. In answer, Hebe charged Cox with condoning the adultery (if any) by 'reconciling' with her at a Brighton hotel after he'd accused her; and also of conduct conducing the adultery: firstly, by undue attention paid to two ladies over a period of years despite Hebe's objections; and secondly, by his own subsequent adultery with five women, four of whom Hebe named (the other being resident in Paris, outside the court's jurisdiction).

From the outset theirs was a bitter feud. Greenwood & Greenwood of Sergeant's Inn (for Cox) and Wontner & Sons of Ludgate Hill (for Hebe) went to war on their clients' behalf, making alternate demands for further and better particulars and amending and re-amending their respective petitions and answers to include allegations that Hebe and Dyball had continued their affair even after the petition was filed; a further count of adultery on each side; and a second claim for £10,000 damages against a Wolverhampton gentleman of fortune named Edwin Butler whom the Coxes had first encountered at a hydropathic establishment in Hertfordshire some years previously. With all this wrangling it took nearly two years for the suit to come to trial on 16 November 1894, by which time Butler had died and his name been officially struck out. Still, with three of Cox's alleged mistresses given permission to intervene in their own defence and an estimated sixty witnesses subpoenaed, to say nothing of the evidence of others taken on commission, it promised to be a real spectacle.

The evidence against Hebe and Dyball was damning. Following Sir Edward Clarke's opening address for Cox an 'endless' procession of witnesses entered the box to testify to the hours Dyball spent alone with Hebe in her boudoir late at night and to their being seen alone together in each other's rooms in the various hotels. Letters were produced that strongly implied Hebe had established a false alibi for at least one encounter and, said *The Star*, the 'golden-haired and fresh-cheeked lady' becomingly dressed in black velvet and feathers looked 'quite entrancing enough to have inspired the impassioned outpourings of "Yours for all eternity, Jack"' – a reference to a deeply affectionate letter Dyball had written Hebe that was read out in court and recounted in full in newspapers across the country. Dyball was represented by counsel, but the man himself had absconded to the Cape before the trial. His absence and Cox's substantiating evidence on the fourth day left the impression that it would be impossible for

Hebe to successfully prove her innocence; sure enough, the fifth day opened with a declaration by her advocate that he would not put her in the box and the judge and jury must infer from that what they would in light of evidence already given. With her refusal to appear went her counter-charges. Cox and one of the interveners – a Mrs Jane Minton Goode – entered the box anyway to deny any wrongdoing. The two others, who had been in court all week, did not, having decided not to attend when they heard Hebe's case had collapsed. Clarke announced that Cox would not pursue damages as Dyball had absconded, but would instead provide Hebe with £1,000 a year from his own pocket 'to secure her from temptation'. In addition, she would retain custody of their youngest son provided she 'behaved herself'. These 'gentlemanly' terms President Jeune countenanced and the decree *nisi* was granted.

Unfortunately, this was exactly the sort of arrangement that excited the proctor's suspicions. He immediately sent enquiries to four London solicitors, one of whom had offices in Paris. On 24 April 1895 he put his evidence before the attorney general. On 11 May he entered an appearance and on 31 May filed his plea alleging Cox's collusion, condonation and multiple adulteries. When the intervention came to court on 19 November 1895, the jovial Frank Lockwood's opening address on the proctor's behalf revealed that when the solicitors had drawn up the agreement following the first trial, Cox's solicitor, Greenwood, had insisted on specifying that its terms were dependent on the decree *nisi* never being rescinded. When Wontner argued that this would look like collusion, Greenwood refused to capitulate and unsurprisingly, when the proctor intervened, Cox's monthly payments to Hebe stopped. A representative of Wontner's was subpoenaed to swear that there had been no such bargaining between the solicitors before Hebe had withdrawn but that Cox himself had insisted upon the proviso afterwards. In addition (and most unusually), Sir Edward Clarke, who was in court, was asked to make a statement as to the nature of the arrangement he had been authorised to make on Cox's behalf. It certainly did not include the proviso, said the indignant silk. Lockwood's only hope of proving collusion, therefore, rested on the inconceivable possibility of an admission under oath from either Cox or Hebe.

But Lockwood was not fazed. The very fact that Cox had added the proviso told him Cox anticipated the proctor's intervention, which meant he had something to hide – the exact nature of which Lockwood immediately revealed. He would prove, he said, that Cox *was* guilty of adultery with Mrs Minton Goode and also with May Sherbrooke (aka Mrs Smith or Mrs Gore); with Rosamond Annie Farmer (aka Mrs Rosie Waller) of Carlisle Mansions and Monte Carlo; with Adele O'Connor at a house in Paris which, he thought, he would have no problem convincing the jury was not an establishment visited by the aristocracy for the sole object of gratifying their artistic tastes, whatever its proprietrix might say; with Madge Middleton (aka Mrs Robertson); and with an unknown woman at a notorious house in Bessborough Gardens, Pimlico. In this single statement, Lockwood presented Cox not only as a serial womaniser but as a frequenter of brothels and a man who kept poor company: only one of these 'ladies' was respectably married – the other three were well-known courtesans.

Over the next three days a succession of witnesses – Hebe included – further besmirched Cox's good name and those of several others besides.

Rosie Waller described how Greenwood had sent a detective to her in Monte Carlo to offer her £500 to stay out of England until the trial was over. She'd bartered with him. 'If Mr Cox wishes to buy me, let him consider he is buying a horse, and pay me a couple of thousand,' she'd told Greenwood before writing to a solicitor friend that Cox would have to pay her 'very well' to prevent her going into court to 'speak the truth'. In the end, she'd received nothing but had stayed away anyway because she did not want her name in the papers (laughter). Now, she openly admitted two occasions on which she had 'misconducted' herself with Cox.

Ronald Barlow – Hebe's brother – described how he'd accompanied Cox to Monte Carlo and Paris and how Cox had asked him to give Rosie 500 francs to compensate her losses at the tables. Both Barlow and Rosie denied Cox's assertion that the money was to assist her claim against a former paramour, Lord Francis Hope, for breach of promise to marry. The following night, Barlow continued, Cox had stayed out all night. On his return, he told Barlow he'd slept at Rosie's rooms. They'd then travelled to Paris where they'd gone to the 'artistic' establishment and bought champagne for the women before being taken into a grotto at the back where 'a number of scantily-dressed girls came'. Cox went upstairs with one of them and returned more than two hours later. On their return to England, Cox told Barlow he was going to see May Gore and boasted that he had a latchkey to the home provided for her by his good friend Lord Sudley – though if Sudley ever found out he'd get a good thrashing (laughter). He'd told Barlow that Dyball was another of May's conquests (a fact repeated by her 'good friend' Rosie Waller), which annoyed him. Several servants corroborated Cox's evidence by recalling that Cox was frequently May's guest and that she called him her 'little pig' (laughter) – one maid adding that she had on one occasion run a bath for Cox and afterwards brought him and May tea and toast in May's bedroom.

Hebe and her sister both described how they visited May after hearing rumours of her relations with Cox and how May 'confessed all'. Cox had burst in while they were there and, after expressing surprise at their presence, had seized Hebe and cursed her, saying she had no evidence to support May's supposed confession.

Following this, a number of witnesses – a housekeeper, a builder, the owner of a coffee stall and the verger of a nearby church – all claimed to have seen Cox enter the Bessborough Gardens house in the company of a tall, dark, closely veiled lady. It was a 'bad house' said the verger, who claimed to have seen Cox enter it a dozen times. Collectively, their evidence proved incontrovertible but it also gave Cox the 'out' he needed. Knowing that he now faced the potential retribution of a number of disgruntled patrons at his dubious involvement with their mistresses, Cox accepted counsel's recommendation that he admit this last count of adultery and spare everyone's further blushes. It would mean his decree *nisi* would be rescinded but would spare him any additional expense than the victorious proctor's £901 9s 11s costs, for which Cox's guilt made him liable.

It was a triumph for the proctor that would most likely have eluded him had his jurisdiction extended only to collusion, and might have been a disaster for Cox had newspaper editors not remained unusually quiet. But what had the proctor achieved? 'The Harding Cox divorce case reminds us once again of some of the stranger anomalies of our divorce law,' wrote the *Westminster Gazette*, before explaining to its readers that because both Coxes had sinned they were denied a divorce because divorce was seen as a 'purely penal measure'. But the law could not force them back together; and 'what if the separation was not a punishment, but a relief to both?' And what if Dyball would have righted his wrong by marrying Hebe, which, by the proctor's intervention, he now could not do? 'We cannot see that these proceedings are required by either justice, common-sense or religion,' they concluded.[11]

In the years following Henry James's criticisms of Stephenson's modus operandi such comments were increasingly heard. Grafting the investigative component of the proctor's intervention onto the adversarial system of the court had produced something that historian Wendie Schneider concluded was 'neither fully investigatory' – because, as seen in this case, collusion was often dropped in favour of the more easily proved adultery – 'nor adequately responsive to the parties' interests'.[12] In the wake of the Cox case, Hebe emigrated to South Africa to live openly in Cape Town with Dyball as his wife. In 1897, Cox petitioned the court a second time, seeking a divorce on this ground, but was again denied relief due to his former sins. Ultimately, Hebe and Dyball separated. By the time they did so, Mrs Dyball had secured her divorce for the same offence (though she'd had to wait two years longer than Cox to apply due to her need to also satisfactorily prove Dyball's desertion); and following which Lord Francis Hope successfully divorced his wife despite his relations with Rosie Waller having been openly discussed in court in the Cox case! Mrs Minton Goode was also divorced by her husband in 1897 despite defending the suit with charges of cruelty and acts of familiarity with Juliette Nesville, a woman 'he well knew' to be leading 'an immoral and unchaste life'. These charges she dropped at the hearing when it became clear she could not defend those against her in a situation remarkably similar to that of Cox and Hebe. The affidavit filed in application for Goode's decree *nisi* to be made absolute was filed alongside another giving the proctor's assent.[13]

Such cases demonstrate the extent to which, win or lose, the proctor's was a thankless task. But to the supporters he did have, the proctor did more than simply prevent lawbreaking. If the permanent divorce court judges were considered arbiters of acceptable behaviour within marriage, so the proctor prevented a descent into immorality by acting as custodian to the institution itself by ensuring that those who were disentitled to relief by their own nefarious behaviour did not get it. The increasingly powerful puritan lobby upheld his right to defend society's stake in the marriage bond, arguing that second marriage, coming as it often must after a dissolution, 'is no longer permanent marriage, and does not stand on the same moral footing'.[14] Permanent marriage needed its defender, therefore: someone who encouraged every possibility of reconciliation, even though that meant interventions which unfortunately, being widely reported, subjected the populace to more filth in the process. On rare occasions, he even rescued marriages when the judge's hands were tied. In *Bastard* v. *Bastard and Brunton* (1894) – a case in which it must be said morality was thin on the ground – he was able to overturn a decree Justice Barnes had felt compelled to grant.

Stockbroker John Bastard and his wife Olivia had separated after fellow stockbroker Spencer Brunton's long-suffering wife Janet sued for divorce in 1891 on the grounds of wilful and reckless communication of both syphilis and gonorrhoea at various times throughout their marriage and Brunton's adultery with the outrageously flirtatious Olivia. Some years previously Janet had found the offset of an affectionate letter from her husband to Olivia on his blotting pad and had asked Bastard to intervene. Bastard had declined, saying Janet was being paranoid. But after the Bruntons separated and Janet got her divorce in January 1893, largely on the evidence of Brunton's housekeeper as to the goings-on at numerous parties held at Brunton's Suffolk home, Rougham Hall, over a six-year period, Bastard petitioned to divorce Olivia, citing in his particulars the exact same dates and occasions given in Janet Brunton's housekeeper's evidence. His case went undefended and Barnes had no choice but to award the decree.

The evidence was incontrovertible but in accepting it Barnes expressed misgivings as to Bastard's role in the affair and proclaimed that he would be sending the case to the proctor for further examination. Remarkably, the proctor discovered that neatly fitting between the housekeepers dates were numerous holidays abroad – to Paris, Carlsbad and Monte Carlo – enjoyed by Bastard, Olivia and Brunton, during which the Bastards slept separately and Olivia and Brunton had adjoining bedrooms. Over the six-day trial witnesses aplenty attested to the presence of all three of them in a state of semi-undress in Olivia's bedroom, where they came each morning to discuss the day's entertainments, and numerous occasions on which Bastard left Brunton alone with his wife while he went off on his own. Though initially Bastard claimed this was because he tired of Brunton's company and went in search of more 'serious society' – alone, because he was unable to convince Olivia to do likewise – on the sixth day, on counsel's advice, he admitted to conduct conducing their adultery and his decree was rescinded with costs.

The unravelling of such entanglements justified the proctor's function both for those who upheld the law and for those whose quintessential goal was the protection of the sanctity of marriage. In being widely reported they gave the impression that his intervention was inescapable where, in truth, he was a figurehead, albeit an intimidating one. The number of unhappy couples deterred from petitioning the court at all for fear of his intervention is indeterminate, but of the 300-or-so each year who did and were successful – a figure that rose to nearly 500 by the end of the century – he intervened in only 3 to 5 per cent, though he enquired into all undefended decrees (approximately three-quarters of those granted). He was restrained by resources, but also at times by the attorney general. Lord Alverstone (better known in legal circles as Sir Richard Webster) told the Barnes Commission that during his tenure as attorney general he had been 'unduly strict' in deciding which cases the proctor could investigate and suspected that the proctor, by the methods he employed, was only able to halt about a tenth of those divorces that were illegally obtained.[15] As such, unhappy spouses who had the means, guile or gall to run the gauntlet of his scrutiny stood a fair chance of success. Still, the stakes were high, both for the parties involved and their families, as the personal papers of the Brougham family reveal.

Wilfrid Brougham was the second son of William, 2nd Baron Brougham and Vaux of Brougham Hall, Penrith, whose brother had been former Lord Chancellor Henry Brougham, the man who had been so instrumental in establishing the role of the proctor in divorce proceedings. Wilfrid Brougham had filed his divorce petition on 21 November 1891, alleging his wife Francesca's adultery with Captain Coleraine Robert Vansittart, late of the 11th Hussars, survivor of the charge at Balaclava and owner of

Shottesbrooke House, Berkshire, the Vansittart family seat since the early eighteenth century. His case had all the hallmarks of lawbreaking. The Broughams had separated more than twenty years earlier and in 1871 Francesca had absconded to Paris. In 1876 Wilfrid instigated a suit for restitution of his conjugal rights which Francesca defended with allegations of cruelty. The nature of the allegations were such that the case was heard in camera. In addition to acts of physical violence spanning the whole of their seven-year marriage, Francesca alleged that Wilfrid was guilty of 'filthy and indecent and disgusting acts' and of compelling her to commit the same (which most likely meant masturbation or oral sex); that he had wilfully and recklessly infected her with parasitical vermin and on two occasions had taken her by force while threatening to kill her if she cried out.[16]

When it came to trial in 1877, Francesca appeared but did not defend the suit. The restitution order was granted, but Francesca immediately returned to Paris and Wilfrid to Brougham Hall. The order was never enforced. Despite the fact that three months later Francesca was found by the court to be in contempt for not returning, no further action was taken through the court until Wilfrid's divorce petition was filed fifteen years later. At the undefended hearing on 8 August 1893 the delay was explained as being due to Wilfrid's difficulty in finding Francesca, who lived under a pseudonym. His allegation of adultery was substantiated by evidence suggesting she had been delivered of two children by Vansittart before his death in 1886. With as little publicity as might be expected for a gentleman in his position, the decree *nisi* was granted. But the long separation, the charges against Wilfrid that went unprosecuted and the unenforced restitution order raised the proctor's suspicions. He immediately sent enquiries to three provincial solicitors, including a firm on Guernsey where Wilfrid had lived since his father's death in 1886, and the Brougham family solicitor in Penrith. In the proctor's plea filed on 16 February 1894 Wilfrid was charged with withholding material evidence, collusion, unreasonable delay in filing suit and adultery.

The family papers reveal how little of what went on behind the scenes ever came out in court or was reported in the press and how often a system that was intended to uphold morality trapped people in hopeless marriages by its procedures. Wilfrid Brougham had met Francesca in 1861 having purchased a commission in the 10th Hussars, then quartered near her family home in Ipswich. Underpinning the story of their marriage was debt – a situation not at all uncommon with young officers whose prospects were dependent upon their ability to purchase their way up the promotions ladder, to say nothing of mess bills and the difficulty of stretching a meagre income to keep up with the extravagant lifestyles of their wealthier colleagues. Moneylenders targeted them, knowing there was often an anxious father in the background willing to carry the debt to avoid the indignity of his son having to sell out to repay it.[17] Wilfrid's father had already repaid £11,000 of Wilfrid's debts before learning his son owed a further £2,000 in 1867 – a sum he could ill afford to pay. Brougham Hall had been extensively enlarged by the first baron and the second was struggling to maintain it. Unusually for this divorcing couple, their money was all Francesca's. Her father, Gaetano Francisco Vignati, a trader in Russian goods, had provided Francesca with £800 a year from a trust set up as part of their marriage settlement to support the Wilfrid Broughams and their eventual three children. Despite this, in 1868 Wilfrid sold out of the army and in late July 1870, after numerous begging and self-piteous letters to Brougham Hall, was declared bankrupt, his father named as a creditor. A week later, after an altercation in which Francesca claimed Wilfrid attacked her in front of friends, she left saying she would 'rather die' than live with him.[18]

For all Wilfrid's faults, it seems he genuinely loved Francesca, who was described by Vignati as having been 'fearfully spoiled' by her mother, then 'exceedingly so' by Wilfrid.[19] He refused to accept she had left for good and spent the next few years bombarding her with what the Penrith press would later describe as 'pathetic' letters through her solicitor begging her return while his father, increasingly burdened by financial pressures, pressed him to pursue her for assistance with their upkeep at Brougham Hall. It all became too much for Wilfrid and his health gave way. Prescribed morphia for recurrent abscesses, he spent the next two years fighting one kind of addiction or another and lamenting that 'this lonely life is hard to bear without some stimulant' as his doctor attempted to wean him off morphia by substituting a diet of strong coffee and brandy.[20]

On his recovery the Broughams were horrified to discover Wilfrid had gone outside the family, engaging a solicitor of his own who recommended petitioning the court for the 1876 restitution order to force a settlement from Francesca. Once the order was obtained Wilfrid's older brother Henry, a clerk in the House of Lords who was destined to become the third Lord Brougham and was already taking the lead in family affairs, impressed upon him the need to monopolise on it privately: '[The] most important thing I have to call your attention to is the great scandal to the family such a litigation would cause,' he wrote, believing that Wilfrid would be tempted further into the court system.[21] But Wilfrid was hesitant to irrevocably finalise a separation from Francesca and with four different lawyers now involved – Wilfrid's, Vignati's, the Brougham family's Penrith solicitor and their London agent – it took until July 1880 before a settlement was finally reached, by which time Wilfrid had again been declared bankrupt and his father had come to believe he should 'be forced to shut up Brougham & to live & die elsewhere ... and a very cruel ending it will be for me'.[22] Both were eventually rescued by Francesca agreeing to pay Wilfrid £300 a year, rising to £600 on Vignati's death, on the understanding that he did not enforce the restitution order or pursue her in any other way.

None of this was of any consequence to the Queen's Proctor, whose only concern was that details of this settlement were subsequently withheld from the court during Wilfrid's 1886 divorce hearing and that the 'pathetic' letters implied Wilfrid knew Francesca was cohabiting with a man in Paris as early as 1873. So strong was the proctor's evidence that he withdrew his additional allegations of collusion and adultery before his intervention came to court. Undue delay in presenting a suit was, by precedent, regarded as anything over two years. The proctor could account for eighteen. Wilfrid, of course, denied the charge, saying nothing about Francesca's behaviour had been 'authenticated' until 1890 when he'd sent investigators to Paris after his children, by then in their twenties, had opened his eyes to their mother's mode of living. But under cross-examination he was forced to admit that his son – also Wilfrid – had 'mentioned it' in 1880 and that his real reason for petitioning for divorce in 1891 was that with all three children by then married, and having spent many years living as a virtual recluse at Brougham Hall, he wished for a companion in his old age and had met a lady he wished to make his wife.

Wilfrid's advocate argued that this was entirely reasonable: Francesca had deserted him twenty years earlier and made wild accusations which she'd then withdrawn, while Wilfrid had done nothing morally wrong. But neither he nor Francesca got any sympathy from the court or press. Francesca had chosen an immoral life over her obligations as Wilfrid's wife and Wilfrid had acted in an 'unmanly' fashion by not confronting the situation sooner. The only sympathy meted out was to their son, Wilfrid junior, subpoenaed by the proctor and forced to give evidence against his father; during which he'd revealed that he had first become aware of his mother's shame through hearing rumours at school when he was just fifteen that were confirmed by his grandmother when his father refused to discuss it. The final sting in the tail for Wilfrid was his son's other revelation that the proctor had been alerted to his deception of the court by members of his own family. Fear that a divorce would negate Francesca's settlement at their daughters' expense – one of whom already lived in 'very poor circumstances' – finally overcame the Broughams' fear of publicity and triggered the four-day hearing that was reported nationwide in devastating detail and that put Wilfrid junior into the witness box to deny his father a divorce and thereby do what he described as 'my duty ... to my father's family, my mother and my sisters'.

The proctor received no immediate criticism following this case, but increasingly successes such as this contributed to the growing perception that he wasted time and money saving marriages that had already irrevocably broken down, forcing parties into 'irregular unions'. This is true of both these last two cases: Olivia Bastard and Spencer Brunton lived together unmarried until the destructive effects of tertiary syphilis affected first Brunton's mind and then his heart, resulting in his death in 1901; and Maria Sophia Faunce – the lady Wilfrid Brougham wished to make his wife – was forced to wait ten years before Francesca's death made way for her officially. Francesca's own children with Vansittart were never publicly acknowledged by their father. How often, even in the relatively few cases examined in this book, did unsuccessful suits end this way? The fault was not the proctor's, but neither was the remedy and his legacy suffered in any event. As the twentieth century progressed he became in Gail Savage's view 'a contemptible and pathetic figure, a lightning rod for pointed satire directed at the divorce law' as calls for its reform increased: an 'official Peeping Tom' whose activities were condemned as 'degrading, un-English, and anti-social'.[23]

Damning as these criticisms are, they are nothing compared to the conclusion of one who had actually held the office. While Stephenson vigorously defended his actions, the Earl of Desart told the Barnes Commission after sixteen years' service, 'I have felt over and over again, at any rate in a considerable number of cases, that my intervention has done more harm than good.'[24] His conscience was pricked by the number of couples he had punished by effectively denying them the chance of happy remarriages: a punishment court reporter Fenn described as 'the cruellest ... certainly'.[25] Following Stephenson's zealousness, it is difficult to know how it could have been otherwise; but Desart took upon his office the responsibility that adultery had become 'by practice' virtually an absolute bar. Reform would come – had to come, he acknowledged – but with 'very great difficulty and very great hesitation' the man responsible for rooting out petitioner misconduct told the commission that 'in the present state of public opinion the law should not be changed' – yet.

9

Nullity Suits:
The Letter of The Law

> ... Yet twenty white rabbits will not make a black rabbit.
> *The Law Journal*, 20 November 1886

On 12 June 1895, Armand Emile Augustin Dieval gave evidence in support of his petition to have his year-long marriage to Elizabeth Loton annulled on the ground that she was his late wife's sister. Dieval was a club steward and naturalised Frenchman who had lived and worked in England for twenty years. When he met the Loton sisters they were both ladies' maids at Hampton Court Palace where their father was senior warden. The prohibition of marriage with a deceased wife's sister dated back to the Reformation and had found its way into the statute books in 1835. By the 1870s it had become so contentious an issue and its repeal had occupied Parliament so frequently that in 1882 Gilbert and Sullivan satirised it as the 'annual blister' every reformer worthy of the name felt compelled to prick.[1] Their failed attempts were widely debated in the press.

Despite all this, Dieval claimed not to have known when he married Elizabeth that the ceremony was illegal. He claimed her family had pressured him into it. He claimed as soon as he realised he had broken the law he filed his petition for annulment. President Jeune did not believe him. He thought Dieval had married Elizabeth of his own free will and, finding her afterwards not to his liking, was now using the law to rid himself of her. The president called it 'disgusting'. Elizabeth's barrister argued Dieval would profit by his wrongdoing if the marriage was annulled and that he should, at very least, provide Elizabeth with an allowance. The president declared himself powerless to refuse the annulment or make Dieval pay anything other than costs. In passing sentence the indignant judge called Dieval's actions dishonourable, continuing that he would say nothing against the fact that Dieval was a Frenchman as he thought no honourable Frenchman would have acted as Dieval had done but, with that reservation, he was glad to know Dieval was not English! The spectators in court burst into applause.

This case demonstrates that it was not only the Queen's Proctor who was dissatisfied with the state of things: even the permanent judges of the court sometimes felt restricted by the terms of the law they practised, particularly when the verdict they were compelled to give conflicted with what they believed to be morally right. In this instance the press were sympathetic. Monsieur Dieval deserved his dressing-down, said the PMG: it was the least a British court could do in exchange for a public declaration of his freedom.

The marriage being illegal, the verdict was little more than that. The decree was not strictly necessary but it was quite usual for the court to hear suits for annulment of illegal marriages, usually from those who found themselves in bigamous unions either wittingly or otherwise, like Ellen Gilder in chapter one or the Eustons or Bonaparte. They accounted for almost a third of all nullity petitions, served to clarify the legal position of the parties and were largely successful. If the documentation was sound and the parties adequately identified there was no defence. A nullity suit of any description could not be defended by allegations of marital offences: the question of the marriage's standing always came first. Neither were all the bars for divorce extended to nullity suits. Collusion was subject to prosecution by the proctor but delay was no bar, though the longer the delay the stronger the evidence must be to prevent it looking like collusion. Otherwise, only a prior private agreement to remain married but live apart under specified terms, including not to sue or molest each other, was regarded as a distinct bar.

Beyond illegal marriage, the other grounds for nullity were nonconsummation due to impotency, mental incapacity sufficient to render a person incapable of contracting marriage and marriage induced by fear or force. Collectively, nullity pleas account for only

4 per cent of all petitions filed in this period, with nonconsummation accounting for two-thirds of nullity petitions.[2] They are generally less scrutinised by historians, perhaps because it is considered the social implications were less than with divorce, but they still represent a decision to end a marriage: in all except illegal marriage, their grounds rendered a marriage voidable but not by definition void. Nullity suits alleging impotency were equally the focus of little attention at the time, possibly due to the delicacy of the issue at stake or because, being heard in camera, they were not reported in the press and therefore produced little sensation or controversy. It makes them difficult to analyse now beyond acknowledging the recognised consequences at the time. Barrister Nevill Geary, writing in 1892, stated that the lack of 'advertising' through newspaper reporting meant that many a woman lived for years with an impotent spouse unaware that she was entitled to a decree on this ground.[3] This, he asserted, was 'the experience of every practitioner'. It is something that's difficult to verify, though it may be worth noting that in the 1881–1900 sample, the two petitioners in unconsummated marriages of the longest duration – eighteen and twenty-eight years respectively – were both women, and that few books then treated the subject in any great depth. In McQueen's 1858 *Treatise* the section is brief and in Latin![4] Geary sought to correct this by dedicating a whole chapter to it in his book.

Like many of the grounds for divorce, annulment on the ground of nonconsummation was another remnant of canon law and to qualify had to be directly due to 'malformation and impotence of [the husband's] parts of generation' or malformation or 'incapacity ... arising from nervous affection' in the case of a wife.[5] Geary spelled out the law's requirements in layman's terms. Consummation meant 'complete intercourse' (though in 1854 Dr Lushington ruled 'that any degree of imperfection' in the intercourse would not 'deprive it of its essential character') and the respondent's incapacity must date from the time of the marriage and be incurable (though if a man had successfully had sex with another woman either before or since the marriage that did not necessarily preclude the annulment as he may be deemed *impotens quoad hanc* – powerless as to this – with his wife). Simple wilful refusal was insufficient to annul a marriage until 1937, though if it were the wife's and continued long enough it might be deemed 'hysterical' and an annulment granted. The magic number was three years, which was considered time enough for a couple to overcome any 'temporary obstacle' to intercourse 'such as nervous feeling on the part of the man or resistance from fear on the part of the woman' and thereafter annulment became easier. For marriages of less than three years it rested with the petitioner to prove that the marriage was unconsummated due to the respondent's incapacity; more than three years and the onus of proof shifted to the respondent to disprove the facts or demonstrate that they were not due to his or her impotency. Moreover, a presumption of impotence accompanied the removal of the question of temporary obstacles.[6]

That three years might be considered necessary for some couples to overcome temporary obstacles says much about sexual awareness at the time and the difficulty of getting advice. The shyness of women in particular is demonstrated by the fact that two of the six husbands in the sample who brought petitions alleging the nonconsummation was due to their wife stated she would not explain her refusal, let alone seek medical help. But it is important to note that impotency had nothing to do with infertility: a woman did not have to be of childbearing age to petition for nullity on this ground. In this sense, despite the Church's position that marriage was decreed by God to provide companionship and for procreation, the canon law recognised and the statute law carried forward the notion of the importance of sex within marriage in its own right. Geary noted multiple cases in which it was suggested that a wife's health was apt to suffer without marital intercourse. To avoid suspicion of collusion both parties underwent a physical examination by two independent medics. Obviously, the clearest evidence of nonconsummation was for the wife to be found *virgo intacta*, but even so it must be demonstrably due to a physical defect in her or her husband to qualify. The husband, therefore, submitted himself to inspection to prove himself capable if he were the petitioner or reveal himself incapable if he were the respondent. Refusal to be inspected spoke strongly of impotence and an oral confession to the inspector might be accepted in lieu of examination.

Beyond this, the only real obstacle to securing an annulment was that which Lord Stowell called 'sincerity' – that is, that the impotency of the spouse must be determined to be the principle reason for the failure of the marriage. Any ulterior motive spoke of collusion or withholding material evidence on which the suit should fail. The question produced some interesting results. In the 1885 case of G. v. M., when the wife answered her husband's divorce petition to the Scottish court with an application for annulment on the ground of his impotency, he alleged she was insincere because she had committed adultery and given birth to an illegitimate child and her primary purpose was to marry the father. The court disagreed and annulled the marriage. The husband appealed, but the verdict was upheld by the House of Lords – the Lord Chancellor, Lord Selborne, asking what could be less fraudulent and dishonest and more sincere 'in a reasonable sense of the word' than the wife's desire to free herself from her impotent husband and legitimise her child according to Scottish law by marrying her lover.[7] Had she been seeking divorce there would have been no such understanding.

The least straightforward nullity suits were the rare applications for annulment on one of the two other allowable grounds: mental incapacity or marriage induced by fear or force. Each type produced one highly sensational case in the 1880s to challenge the practical application of the law. On 12 May 1884, John George Lambton, 3rd Earl of Durham, petitioned for annulment on the ground that at the time of the ceremony and prior to it his fiancée, Ethel Elizabeth Louisa Milner, was of unsound mind and incapable therefore of contracting marriage; and on 27 May 1886, Miss Lina Mary Scott, daughter of the deceased 3rd Baronet Scott of Lytchett Minster, sued on the ground that she had been induced to marry Arthur Edward Saunders Sebright by fear and terror of him and by false representations fraudulently made to her as to what would happen to her if she did not. President Hannen heard the Durham suit and Justice Butt heard Miss Scott's.

Mental incapacity from idiocy to insanity was, of course, something of a Victorian obsession and quite rightly. The horrifying spectacle of eighteenth-century restraint may have given way to a more rational approach but efficacious psychiatric and drug therapies were still some way off and the rhetoric of the London physician who in 1808 had written that 'Madness strides like a Colossus in the country' and who had spoken of 'atoms, or specks of insanity, which cannot be discerned by the naked or uneducated eyes' was still reflected in the medical profession's inability to stem the tide of ever-increasing numbers of committed lunatics as the nineteenth century progressed.[8] The spectre continued to play on the public's imagination. The predominant view was that insanity was 'a disgrace as well as a hereditary "taint" which might bring scandal and social ostracism to the victim's family'.[9] The desire to want to conceal it was considered 'both natural and commendable'.[10] The marriage prospects of relatives of the afflicted were significantly reduced and those who found themselves bound for life to a spouse who subsequently became insane were greatly to be pitied, but their misfortune was widely believed to be their own cross to bear.

It was generally frowned upon, therefore, that the divorce law gave Lord Durham the potential means to dispense with his insane wife; though again, it did not do so readily. Since the court gained jurisdiction in 1857 it had allowed only one annulment for insanity. In the Hunter suit of 1881 the marriage between Robert Hunter, a journeyman organ builder, and Emma Edney, a publican's daughter, was determined to be the cause of exciting a hereditary taint in the young wife. Emma's symptoms began immediately after her engagement and were new to her but reminiscent of those for which her father had previously been restrained. She'd entertained 'morbid delusions' about her forthcoming nuptials, considering herself 'unfit' to become a wife, though her mother said she was a 'virtuous' young woman. She'd become taciturn and agitated and following the marriage sat wringing her hands and could not be made to say or do anything beyond asking her husband to slit her throat. She was admitted to Bethlehem Hospital where the physician determined she was a suicidal lunatic who might improve but never recover. The marriage had never been consummated and as President Hannen believed the petition had been brought in good faith the decree was granted without hesitation.[11]

There were certain similarities between this suit and Lord Durham's which his advocate Sir Farrer Herschell highlighted when it came before the same judge on 25 February 1885. Ethel had also become cold and distant following her engagement to Durham in August 1882 and had barely spoken to him. She'd become dull and depressed following their lavish October wedding and less than two years later and a year after doctors declared her of 'unsound mind' had attempted suicide by endeavouring to throw herself from the first-floor window of her aunt's house. The result was that she was committed to Barnwood private asylum in Gloucestershire where it was noted she was subject to paranoid delusions: that she was guilty of murder and that she had succeeded in committing suicide.[12] A month following her committal, her widowed mother, Charlotte, who had been severely agitated by Ethel's decline and the likely impact of it on the marriage prospects of her younger daughter, Emily, was found hanging from a window catch in the water closet of Armagh Palace, the residence of her father, the Archbishop of Armagh. Following the coroner's verdict Durham's cousin, the political diarist Edward Walter Hamilton, noted that Charlotte's suicide 'ought to make matters easier' for Durham, who had filed his nullity petition in May 1884 – before both attempts.[13] But the timing was problematic: though everything that had happened since the marriage was deeply tragic for all concerned, the law was only interested in the existence and degree of insanity at the time of the ceremony and the extent to which it rendered its victim incapable of understanding the nature of the contract they were entering into. What followed thereafter was of little consequence. 'The contract' was deemed to have been initiated by the engagement and finalised by the marriage. If, as in the Hunter suit, it was determined that the engagement had upset the balance of Ethel's mind, this was sufficient to indicate impaired understanding of what she was committing herself to. In the former suit Emma Hunter had been present in court and stated that events were as her husband described them. With Ethel unable to participate but the Milners determined to defend the suit on her behalf, would Durham be able to convince the judge likewise?

The involvement of the Milners, the subject matter and the relative positions of the Durhams to the Hunters inevitably made this suit a considerably greater spectacle. The nine-day hearing involved a dazzling array of titled witnesses. Lord Durham himself had considerable wealth and was a gentleman of standing in the north where he was a major employer, with some 30,000 men working in his ships and coalmines to say nothing of those who farmed his 30,000 acres of agricultural land. He resided at the magnificent family seat of Lambton Castle which stood in 1,000 acres of park and woodland overlooking the River Wear Gorge to the north-east of the town of Chester-le-Street. He had been an officer in the Coldstream Guards, was a dynamic and influential member of the Jockey Club and, by 1884, Lord Lieutenant of County Durham. Ethel, meanwhile, as well as being the granddaughter of Marcus Gervais Beresford, Archbishop of Armagh, was granddaughter to the 4th Baronet Milner on her father's side. Her elder sister Mary was the wife of William, soon-to-be 2nd Baron Gerard, and was known to be a 'great friend' of Edward, Prince of Wales who, behind the scenes, intervened on her behalf to attempt to stop the hearing.[14]

In the summer of 1882 Mary had taken Ethel to Ascot, Newmarket and Goodwood and to a ball at Marlborough House where the twenty-one-year-old danced with the prince, was greatly admired and declared a 'bashful beauty'. Thereafter, Durham moved quickly to secure her. In mid-August they met again at the home of Lord Castlereagh where Durham proposed. Ethel accepted and was, thereafter, taken on a whistlestop tour of his family and introduced to his closest friends ahead of their October wedding. The ceremony at St Peter's, Eaton Square, was performed by Ethel's grandfather and, following a wedding breakfast at the Milner residence in Prince's Gate, the couple honeymooned at Lord Rosebery's seat at Epsom before returning to Lambton where a crowd of thousands turned out to greet them. There was a band and a procession through Chester-le-Street, for which their carriage's horses were removed and the carriage was pulled through the town by the people. At Lambton, Durham's servants and a deposition of local tradesmen presented them with a testimonial and some silver plate and a writing set for which there had been a local subscription. It was a grand and much-anticipated occasion equal to the status of a princely earl of the north country. But a fairy tale it was not. Behind the scenes the cracks were already beginning to show. Durham would later claim they had not been married two days when he realised he had married 'an idiot'.

His case hinged on his ability to prove that multiple examples of what was described as Ethel's 'odd' behaviour before and after the engagement and on their wedding day were seeds of her later affliction. In the witness box Durham described the extent to which she was unimpressionable and unresponsive: how when spoken to she would only ever reply yes, no or I don't know; how at dinner she would barely eat, mumble inaudible responses and otherwise sit mute; how when they walked out together she would walk as far away from him as possible or suddenly turn back without explanation; how they would later miss her indoors only to find she had immediately gone out again without telling anyone; how she never wore weather-appropriate clothing and seemed insensible of it; how she could sit for hours with an open book staring into space, never turning a page; and how in writing letters she would start over half a dozen times beginning each draft with exactly the same words as the one she had just discarded. After he'd proposed and she'd accepted she had remained completely passive when Durham kissed her; and on their wedding day she'd appeared dazed throughout the ceremony and at the breakfast stood motionless in the middle of the room, taking no notice of their guests or any interest in their wedding gifts. Then, and again on their arrival at Lambton, Durham virtually had to drag her from the carriage. She took no interest in the Chester-le-Street festivities or her new home and thereafter appeared totally unable to issue instructions to the staff. Three weeks before the wedding Durham had written to her, 'I wonder if you will talk to me when we are married', but virtually the only thing she had volunteered from that time to this was twice saying she had 'something dreadful' to tell him but then not what it was.

After her committal Durham began to associate this statement with her recognised delusions. He had also begun to reassess an incident that occurred the day before the engagement in which a match had dropped on Ethel's dress, setting it alight. Initially it was thought to be an accident but Durham came to believe it was intentional. Ethel had fled the room and was absent for some time before she summoned her maid. She had then reappeared in a new outfit as if nothing had happened. The following day they went out riding and Ethel had worn a tight habit despite the fact that her chest had been burned sufficient to leave a 2-inch-long scar, suggesting she was as insensible to pain as to temperature. Out of sheer desperation, on Ethel's twenty-second birthday, when they had travelled by train to London and been joined by Durham's very good friend, the beautiful socialite and patron of the arts Gladys, Lady Lonsdale, who presented Ethel with the gift of a puppy that Ethel would not touch or thank Gladys for, and whom subsequently she refused to look at or speak to, Durham had tried to break the atmosphere in the carriage by asking Ethel, 'Would you like to see me kiss Gladys? I have often done so.' The joke fell flat. But underpinning it was a growing sense that the Milners had known that Ethel was of unsound mind and had concealed it. Before Durham had proposed he had asked Mary why Ethel was so unresponsive towards him and Mary had told him Ethel was naturally reserved but increasingly so with him because she was very much in love with him: that she had been equally shy as a child but had got over it. Durham believed her wholeheartedly. Love is proverbially blind, his barrister told the court: and never more so than when a peculiarity is attributed to affection.

Under cross-examination, Durham came in for some tough questioning from Sir Henry James, not least about a mistress he had had prior to his engagement. He had told Ethel about her but she had seemed to not understand until he spelled it out. Durham was certain she was no different in her manner towards him before and after this revelation. James's questioning tended to imply Durham had been impatient of Ethel's reserve. It was to James that Durham said he had so swiftly come to the conclusion she was an idiot. 'But you consummated the marriage anyway?' the wily barrister asked.

Such an array of titled witnesses as the court had rarely seen came forward to corroborate Durham's evidence – his 'Honourable' brothers; his sister, the Marchioness of Carmarthen; his grandparents, the Duke and Duchess of Abercorn; his aunt and uncle, Lord and Lady George Hamilton; and from Ethel's own family, the Marchioness of Waterford – a relation by marriage. Then came the requisite obeisance of servants and some of the local tradesmen called in to discuss with Ethel any changes she might wish to make to the interior of Lambton after she became its mistress. Inevitably, there were none. Much of the medical evidence was heard in camera, but two witnesses who did give evidence in open court were the nurse and companion who'd had Ethel in their care between her diagnosis and committal. For nine months they had supervised her at a house called The Knoll on Kingston Hill near Kingston-upon-Thames, taken by Durham after he concluded in October 1883 he could no longer live with her. They spoke of how Ethel's condition worsened during that time and of the difficulty they had in handling her: of how latterly she would run away from them or bite or kick them; of how she once locked herself in the bathroom, laughing hysterically. From the companion, Mrs Vaughan, James secured the admission that she thought Ethel an imbecile and had treated her as such from the first.

The Milner family's correspondence shows that they considered the whole affair, from the taking of The Knoll onwards, a 'very deep laid plot' by Durham to rid himself of Ethel.[15] As early as January 1884 – five months before Durham filed his petition – they sought legal advice from family friend Edward Pollard QC as to whether Durham could have Ethel committed and what they might do to prevent it. At very least, Pollard wrote, they should get her away from Vaughan, whom the Milners considered a destructive influence. But the damage was already done: Ethel was taken to stay with a beloved aunt, Mrs Laura Vernon-Harcourt, in July 1884 yet would still attempt suicide a month later.

In Ethel's absence Mary became the Milners' chief witness, and an arduous experience it was. She spent the best part of two days in the witness box – though her stay there was undoubtedly lengthened by the fact that the extent to which she had got over her early shyness had given her the reputation for loquacity! Under cross-examination, she too came in for some tough questioning, particularly concerning the conversation with Durham that had prompted his proposal. Mary's belief in Ethel's love, she told Herschell, came from Ethel telling her that Durham was the first man she had met who put out of her mind a former attachment to Anthony Fane, Lord Burghersh – the 12th Earl of Westmorland as he would become – whose attentions she had received between her coming out in 1879 and his eventual rebuff in 1881. The Milners had objected to Burghersh because his family estate was known to have accumulated debts as a result of his father's gambling habits and Ethel's older brother had refused his permission for them to marry. Herschell asked Mary if it was not the case that, witnessing the effect of the separation on her sister's mind and fearing Ethel would be left on the shelf, she'd exaggerated Ethel's feelings for Durham to secure him before Ethel's madness could show itself. But Mary was adamant: Ethel had not been especially attached to Burghersh and had taken a 'sensible' view of the separation; and Mary had welcomed Durham's proposal the following year truly believing it was a means of securing happiness for her beloved sister. It was a protestation Durham's family would never believe and one that did not correspond with the notion that Ethel was still thinking of Burghersh a year after their separation.[16]

Other inconsistencies in Mary's evidence made Durham's supporters question her motives further. In the witness box Mary said she'd observed Ethel's coldness to Durham increase after the revelation about his mistress which, in turn, coloured Ethel's reaction to Gladys (whom Mary said Ethel disliked). This, said Mary, was because Ethel was not *in*sensitive but *over*sensitive, though she struggled to express it and consequently came across as obstinate. So concerned had Mary been about the change in Ethel's mood, she claimed, she'd asked her if she was really fond of Durham: an intervention Ethel apparently resented. Yet at the same time, under cross-examination Mary would say that Ethel took the news of Durham previous paramour 'sensibly' and that Durham had thought her rather stupid for not minding very much.

Collectively, the Milners sought to imply that any insensitivity was Durham's. Mary recounted a conversation she'd had with Ethel soon after the marriage in which Ethel had allegedly commented how 'curious' it was that 'things one has longed for most are often most disappointing when one gets them'; and family and friends attested to the fact that, despite her painful shyness of strangers, with patience and sensitivity Ethel could always be encouraged to speak one-to-one in company as well as any young lady. They countered the evidence of Durham's physician, who declared that his examination led him to conclude that Ethel must have exhibited signs of imbecility in childhood, with statements from an old governess as to Ethel having learnt French and German well enough to translate Schiller's plays, and called relatives who spoke of Ethel's teenage performances in family theatricals. The image portrayed of a kind, thoughtful, amiable but self-willed young lady was a world away from Durham's 'idiot' and reinforced the notion that Ethel's insanity had begun after the marriage as a result of Durham's insensitive treatment. One by one the Milners entered the box to attest to a marked deterioration in Ethel's mental state six months after the marriage following her return from a six-week sojourn in Cannes with Durham and his sister Katharine. The holiday had been prescribed by the Milners' renowned physician,

Sir William Gull, who had been called in to see Ethel in February 1883 and found 'not a trace of insanity, idiocy or imbecility' but rather that she was in 'an unsettled, passive state and depressed in health'; though he conceded he had not been called in to examine her state of mind.

To Durham's friends it appeared that the Milners only fixed on Cannes after Sir Henry James had tried and failed to get the doctors to say in camera that 'having a sensitive woman for the first time would drive her mad'.[17] Yet they could not deny the persuasiveness of James's argument that in confessing to Ethel about his mistress and in sleeping with her when she became his wife Durham had treated her as 'a person of full mental capacity', not an imbecile unfitted for the role of wife and mother. In response Sir Farrar Herschell argued that the marriage contract was unique in carrying with it certain binding rights and duties and it was evident that even if Ethel understood the words spoken, she had not really appreciated their meaning. Either that, or she had married where she had not loved which was 'calculated to affect the mind of a girl of somewhat unstable organisation'. Both interpretations pointed to an incapacity for which Durham was entitled to an annulment.

In passing judgment, President Hannen felt the difficulty of not being able to hear from Ethel or adequately express the 'standard of sanity' which he felt was necessary to fully appreciate what he described as the 'very simple' contract of marriage. That said, he pointed to five facts that emerged from the evidence to clarify Ethel's state of mind at various points in her history. The first was the evidence of family friend, the Hon. George Curzon, who stated that in 1879 he had spoken with Ethel about her shyness and Ethel had told him that the presence of strangers impeded her expression and flow of ideas, making her appear stupid. The statement, said the president, shows that she was then capable of forming a judgement on her own condition. The second was the fact of the engagement itself, not so much for Ethel's acceptance but for Durham's proposal. To understand this the president had looked to John Milton's observation, 'who knows not that the bashful muteness of a virgin may ofttimes hide all the unliveliness and natural sloth which is really unfit for conversation' and Milton's comment that 'the soberest and best governed men' are least practised in the affairs of the heart and might easily be 'mistaken in his choice'.[18] To the president, Durham was not 'unpractised' having already had a mistress and ample opportunity to form his own opinion of Ethel during their stay at Lord Castlereagh's home before his proposal. Thirdly, he looked to the fact that Ethel had herself raised the alarm after the match incident as evidence that she had her wits about her; and fourthly, to comments made to her younger sister, Emily – that when she became Lady Durham she would take Emily out into society as Mary had taken her – as evidence that Ethel understood the difference in social standing between a married and unmarried woman. To support this Hannen cited Ethel's letters written to 'My dear Lord Durham' before their engagement and 'My darling Jack' afterwards; and those signed 'Ethel Milner' before the wedding and 'Ethel Durham' afterwards. Lastly were some comments made to Durham's sister Katharine which, no doubt, Katharine had thought strengthened Durham's case but which the president took otherwise: that in February 1883 – before the trip to Cannes – Ethel had told Katharine that she suffered from melancholia and kept imagining things that made her unhappy, that were 'the kind of things that sent people mad'. This told the judge not that Ethel was then insane but that she was still capable of reasoning about her condition.

In all respects, the president conceded, the marriage was hopeless but in his verdict he was bound by the law and he acted accordingly to deny Durham his annulment. Yet in additional comments made in the course of his judgment the worldly-wise judge also proved he was only human. The temptation to speculate on the true course of events and evaluate the actions and feelings of those involved was too strong for him. It was his belief, he told the court, that Ethel was still attached to Burghersh when she accepted Durham and the 'something dreadful' she could not tell him was most likely that she could not and did not respond to his kiss having already felt the lips of another and spoken words of endearment to one whom she did love. In continuing with the marriage while feeling this she did Durham a great wrong. But likewise Mary must share the blame for telling Durham that Ethel's coldness was due to love when this was by no means certain. By her actions Mary 'assisted in wrecking the happiness of two lives'; while Durham, for his part, somehow persuaded himself that Ethel loved him when there was so much evidence to the contrary and afterwards demonstrated how little he knew how to win his young wife's affections through gentleness and patience.

The comments provoked indignation, particularly on Mary's part. Though *The Times* praised Hannen's 'elaborate judgment' for being 'a minute psychology study on the evidence', others echoed the opinion of John Hassard, Principle Registrar of the Province of Canterbury, who wrote to Mary, 'Every Barrister, – & indeed *every gentleman*, – I speak to is of the opinion that the judge was *utterly unjustified* in his closing lines ... He had *no business* to introduce such words into a judgment; – his own idea, on the point, was quite outside *the law* of the case, – & what was requisite.'[19] *Vanity Fair* agreed, pointing out that 'many successful marriages start with love on only one side ... Ninety-nine ladies out of a hundred would have acted in the same way.'[20] But would ninety-nine men have acted as Durham had? After 'two years of misery and worry' he at least felt he had done all he could in an impossible situation. He wrote to Ethel's cousin Edith, the daughter of aunt Laura: 'I very soon found out that my affection was as powerless to stir her mind as kindness is wasted on an obstinate mule. And I would rather have been married to a real statue of stone than to a living woman who had not one spark of love or duty or pleasure that my devotion could fan into life.' It had been 'very painful' to lay bare the details of his married life but he still believed it was 'the obviously clear duty of Ethel's family to tell me that she was not in a fit condition to marry'.[21]

The extent to which Ethel's attachment to Burghersh was the cause of her breakdown and the wider consequences of his name having been introduced into proceedings can be surmised from the joint facts of James asking immediately after Hannen's judgment to be allowed to read a statement clarifying Burghersh's relations with Ethel as newspaper reports of the proceedings had 'caused pain' (Hannen would not hear of it); and the contents of a letter written by Ethel's companion at the asylum to Durham two days later: Ethel, she wrote, 'is now aware of Lord B's engagement having been broken off, is highly delighted, & I feel convinced it will help in a great measure towards her gaining ground'.[22]

In the course of the proceedings it had been stated that Ethel had received another proposal of marriage two weeks before she accepted Durham. The eager press jumped to the conclusion this was Burghersh, though James refuted the suggestion the following day. Perhaps Hannen thought the same. Either way, criticisms that he had (unusually) gone beyond his remit by introducing points that were irrelevant to the verdict were tempered with praise for his at least having stayed within the letter of the law, however unsatisfactory some commentators thought that law was. In a case of a very different flavour Justice Butt would be criticised for acting in an almost exactly opposite manner.

The suit of *Scott orse Sebright* v. *Sebright* came before him on 12 November 1886. In her petition, Lina Mary Scott claimed that on 30 January at the registry office in South Audley Street, Middlesex, she had been induced to marry Arthur Sebright by fear and terror of him and false representations fraudulently made to her by Sebright and others that if she did not marry him she would be made bankrupt. When particulars were sought by Sebright's solicitor, Lina elaborated that Sebright had used 'undue influence' to bring about the marriage, not least by saying he would 'accuse her to her mother and in every drawing-room in London of having been seduced by him' if she refused to go through with it.[23] Sebright denied the charges and answered the petition with a demand for restitution of his conjugal rights.

From the outset curiosity was roused by the remarkable nature of the allegations brought by the 'strikingly handsome brunette well-known in London society' as the daughter of Lady Selina Scott and among her more intimate acquaintances as 'Giddy'. They cast immediate aspersions on the character of her husband – 'a distinguished member of the Bachelors' Club, and evidently well-known in more than one grade of London society'.[24] There was also the mouthwatering prospect of seeing the sitting attorney general, Sir Richard Webster, and the sitting solicitor general, Sir Edward Clark, going head to head for the prosecution and defence respectively. Curiosity was further roused by the attorney general's opening remarks: that he and the solicitor general had consulted and that 'certain details' – by which he meant the allegation that Sebright had said he would badmouth Giddy across London – would not need going into, which *The Times* interpreted to mean Sebright did not intend to put up much of a fight. The couple had never lived together, announced Webster, and Sebright would not bring any allegation of impropriety against Giddy.

Justice Butt replied that he did not see how their living together or not made any difference but the attorney general said the judge would in due course: it was the strongest evidence that Giddy never consented to the marriage but was frightened into thinking it was her only option. In which case, the judge continued, he doubted he had the power to annul it, but if Webster thought otherwise he might continue.

The story that then unfolded was truly remarkable. The pair had first met in 1878 when Sebright was nineteen and Giddy fourteen. Sebright was the son of the 8th Baronet Sebright, orphaned at seven and whose guardian had died when he was sixteen. He then found himself, as he later described it, with two misfortunes: being 'a gentleman at large about town looking about five years older than I was, and although still a minor, yet able to borrow money repayable on my coming of age' and having no older sister or similar female figure to guide him. Lady Scott for a while filled that void. The young Sebright considered her 'a very beautiful woman' and an 'intimate friend'.[25] She was then thirty-three, separated from her husband and living with daughters Giddy and Mabel in Cadogan Place. Mabel would later become the unfortunate wife of Earl Russell.

Sebright first proposed to Giddy when she turned sixteen and again the following year when he came of age and into an inheritance of £20,000. On both occasions he was rejected on account of Giddy's age. He then entered a firm of private bankers and financiers and, spurred on by his brother's wife who 'became smitten with a taste for speculation on the Stock Exchange', dabbled in the stock market where, it seems, he rubbed shoulders with a number of dubious characters and learnt a few tricks of the trade.[26] Giddy didn't see him again for several years, but in 1883 they finally became engaged. Giddy said she did this without her mother's consent and it was short-lived, but Sebright continued to see her and, apparently, to pursue her. When Giddy turned twenty-one and came into her own trust fund of £26,000 in February 1885 he proposed again (and was refused) and in June there was a family meeting with her trustees where it was put to Sebright that he could not possibly hope to secure Giddy without settling £10,000 on her to keep her in the manner to which she had become accustomed. Sebright hesitated and it was arranged that he would not see her for six months to give them both time to decide whether they wished to embark on married life together, but that he could write to her. Sebright insisted that his letters should not be seen by Lady Scott. In court, Lady Scott said she did not object to this because 'she did not wish to prevent the marriage if things could be settled in a straightforward manner', but this, alongside Giddy's repeated acquiescence in allowing Sebright to renew advances she perpetually repelled – and much more of the evidence heard – was never adequately explained, leaving the press to conclude, 'Heiresses are generally weaklings, but it is rare to find such a complete specimen of feminine incapacity in matters matrimonial.'[27]

In Giddy's evidence she said Lady Scott didn't know in June 1885 that Sebright was already 'heavily in debt' and had secretly persuaded Giddy to put her name to a bill of exchange in his favour to the tune of £500. Moreover, that by December 1885 she had signed bills totalling £3,350. It is not clear from the reported evidence whether these bills were drawn by Sebright in his own favour with a view to them being settled from Giddy's trust fund or by a third party or were bills he traded in as a 'financial agent', but by accepting them Giddy became liable when they matured. Sebright, of course, told her that he would settle them before then but somehow all the bills she signed ended up in the hands of moneylenders and bill discounters. A thriving backstreet trade then existed in bill discounting. A discounter, as his name suggests, effectively 'bought' the bill from the person who had drawn it at a discounted price thus becoming the acceptor's creditor. He could then hold onto it until it matured or sell it on again at a further reduced rate to recoup his money early. Thus bills could change hands multiple times and the person who had initially accepted them – in this case Giddy – could find him or herself being chased for payment by a person entirely unknown to them and often more unscrupulous in their methods of collection than the original drawer. It was in this manner that in September 1885 Giddy received a writ from a Mr Williams for the non-settlement of bills to the tune of £1,000 and, in due course, the threat of another from a Mr Lee.

Giddy appealed to Sebright but he said he could not honour the bills and would not help her unless she finally agreed to marry him. He went further: he booked the registry office and was furious when Giddy declined to go. Instead, she wrote for advice to a solicitor named Joseph Guedalla who had previously arranged for her to borrow money against her trust fund before she came of age. The letter reveals her desperation:

> I have been putting it off and off trying to think what I am to do ... The only thing for me to do is to ask Mr Rose [her trustee] to find the money for me, and if he will not, the only thing for me is to marry him, which means despair, as after the way he has treated me how can I like him? ... no wonder I am ill and wretched, and nearly mad from despair. Cannot you think of anyone who would lend it to me? ... I have nobody to confide my troubles in but you, as I never want anyone to know how disgracefully he has behaved towards me ... it is simply eating my heart out ... I am nearly wild with grief.[28]

At home it was noticed that Giddy looked sickly. She cried a lot, lost her appetite and was perpetually agitated but would tell no one the cause. She was seen by several doctors, one of whom mentioned Sebright to her, but she would say nothing about him. The doctor spoke to Sebright who said Giddy was 'dying of love for him ... and mark my words, she will die'.[29] She sent repeated daily appeals to Guedalla, who eventually sent her to an Arthur Burr of Burr & Co, 47 Pall Mall, who advertised himself as an insurance agent. It later transpired he was a man with whom Sebright had done 'considerable transactions'.[30] At the time Giddy was told Burr might be willing to lend her the money to get out of her present difficulty. They arranged to meet at Guedalla's office on 13 January where an agitated Giddy claimed Burr said he would only help her if she married Sebright as it was not seemly for him to deal with an unmarried lady. Guedalla – who had also overseen financial transactions for Sebright, had introduced him to Mr Lee and did enough business with Burr to warrant a private telephone line between their offices – refuted this, claiming Burr said it was *easier* to deal with a married woman but he did not want to influence her either way. He claimed that, seeing her agitation, he asked Burr to step out of the room and advised Giddy to come clean to her mother. She was frantic, calling on God to help her, but repeatedly stated she could not do so. She wrote to Williams begging him to hold off. He agreed to wait until 30 January so long as she could guarantee payment on that date.

On 29 January she received a letter from Sebright asking her to meet him the next day and to come alone. She went in a cab with her nurse. Sebright directed the cab to the registry office in South Audley Street. Giddy was so distressed, she said, she did not hear the direction and when they ascended to the office, claimed she did not know what it was or what she was there for. In the office was a friend of Sebright's named Count Valhermey. Sebright told her he had brought her there to marry her. She tried to leave and Valhermey blocked the door. Sebright told her if she did anything to show she was not acting of her own free will he would shoot her. She claimed he had threatened her with a gun before. She said she went through the ceremony barely aware of what she or others were saying. When the ring was put on her finger she flung it off before it could pass her knuckle. She tried to leave before signing the register but Sebright grabbed her arm and brought her back saying he would ruin her if she did not behave. She signed and went downstairs. At the door, Sebright told her to go home to her mother: he'd got what he wanted. She got back into the cab where her nurse had waited and returned home but did not confess anything to her mother until March, by which time Burr had declined to lend her the money but had said he would act as 'security' for her.

Giddy's testimony was substantiated as far as was possible by the doctors, her nurse and Lady Scott, but somewhat contradicted by the registrar, called by her own counsel, who said she seemed a bit excited and annoyed with Sebright (who explained it as being due to anonymous letter she had received that morning), that she kept her head averted from him the whole time but repeated the declaration without hesitation or demur and signed the register when called to do so. The ring, he said, she flung off just before she left. The trustees were called to give evidence as to their impressions and the terms of the meeting, but no evidence was offered to substantiate the claim that Sebright threatened to ruin Giddy and there had been no mention of a gun threat in Giddy's particulars. The former, certainly, Justice Butt said he would need to hear more about or else he would have to refer the case to the proctor for possible collusion. In the end it was settled that Sebright would go into the witness box to deny ever having had 'improper relations' with Giddy before the marriage or marital relations after and the judge accepted medical evidence that Giddy was still *virgo intacta*. Sebright was asked nothing else. In a persuasive closing address the attorney general emphasised Giddy's crumbling 'under the pressure of a moral thumbscrew' applied by Sebright and all but asked Butt to make a precedent to allow the annulment if none already existed.

When the court reconvened two days later for Justice Butt's judgment it was packed with legal professionals as well as spectators. The only person conspicuous by his absence was Sebright. In the course of his speech, Butt noted that whenever a contract was said to have been entered into through fear it was usual practice that the fear must be 'such as would impel a person of ordinary courage or resolution to yield to it' but he did not think this was an accurate reading of the law when from 'natural weakness of intellect or fear either party is in a state of mental incompetence to resist pressure improperly brought to bear'. Citing examples from the evidence he determined that this described Giddy at the time of the wedding, who entered into a contract she would never have done – indeed, had refused to do on numerous occasions – were she in her right mind. In the judge's opinion, the one solitary spark of good feeling Sebright had shown was to enter the box and deny they had slept together, but the judge also expressed the view that 'no man possessed of one particle of self-respect would allow Giddy's evidence to pass uncontradicted if he were able to contradict it'.[31] On these grounds he annulled the marriage and condemned Sebright to costs.

The verdict was met with widespread approval. Said the *Daily News*, 'No court in Christendom could have sent her back to such a husband.' But there was also the distinct impression that facts had been withheld. Why had Count Valhermey not been called when he had been in London? Why not Burr, when he had attended court and asked to be heard? The former had written to the PMG denying he acted as Giddy described and the latter sent them correspondence from her which they printed in full and which, on the surface at least, acknowledged that Burr had never told her she must marry Sebright and read as level-headed pleas for help from Giddy and gratitude for his assistance with the moneylenders Williams and Lee. Why had Sebright not been asked about the threat to Giddy's reputation? What deal had been done to prevent this? And how else had Guedalla been involved in the affair? He clearly knew more that he disclosed. The judge was guided by 'untruth', said the *Standard*, and 'most easily moulded by his petitioner's will', said *Vanity Fair*. Though not a single commentator would have sent her back to Sebright, there were none that felt the verdict was correct in strict legal terms on the evidence produced. 'Society may believe Miss Scott to be an angel, and vote Mr Sebright a perfect brute,' commented the *Belfast Telegraph*. 'Well, so let it be; perhaps it is better so.' If the verdict had not gone Giddy's way, agreed the *Sheffield Independent*, 'the uproar would have been worse'.

In the legal press the verdict was seen as 'a bold endeavour to do justice by straining the law' but there were concerns that Butt had appeared to add a new status to the law – that of 'half-married' if a marriage had not been consummated.[32] It was certainly the case that non-consummation was frequently argued in nullity suits, not just those involving impotency, and it seemed to carry weight. Would these two suits have produced a different verdict if Durham's had not been consummated but Sebright's had? The non-consummation of the Sebright marriage gave Butt sufficient leeway to end a marriage though the *Law Journal* said it was 'difficult to put a finger on the precise ground on which [it] was set aside'. Many white rabbits were pulled out of the hat – a little fraud, a little intimidation, some weakness of mind – but never would they all magically make the black rabbit of a legal verdict.

At the root of their concern was the perpetual fear of opening the floodgates on divorce. The *Solicitors' Journal* saw the verdict as 'something like the judicial sanction of the dissolution of marriage by mutual consent'.[33] Both this and the Durham case highlighted the insufficiency in the law to address the full range of marital disharmony. The Durham case raised ethical questions in the press concerning the role of a spouse. If a wife could not fulfil the function of helpmeet what was the marriage for? Perhaps incurable insanity should be made a ground for divorce (with the obvious difficulty of diagnosing incurability). The point was reinforced only nine days later when the president, in another suit, 'with great pity and commiseration' denied Mr Cannon an annulment after he failed to prove that his wife's insanity, for which she was committed to Bethlehem hospital a month after their wedding, was triggered by exhaustion from nursing his sick mother a month before it – a view that was supported by the testimony of Bethlehem's senior physician.[34] The Sebright case raised practical questions as to what could be done to prevent coercive marriages. Couldn't the law be changed to oblige registrars to get evidence that a family at least knew something of the marriage before a young woman was tied for life? If there was no way marriage could be made harder, then the inevitable solution was that divorce should be easier. It was dangerous ground when the press began seriously to suggest that, whether one thought either verdict right or wrong, 'the conviction, nevertheless, is strong that it is both cruel and immoral to tie men to insane wives or women to felon husbands'.[35]

The consequences of these verdicts reinforces this point. Released from her marriage by the granting of a decree absolute on 25 May 1887, Giddy married stockbroker Richard Russell three days later. A son was born to them the following year. The early years of their marriage, at least, are reasonably well documented by Giddy and her husband being a constant supportive presence in the background of her sister Mabel's subsequent divorce court battles with Earl Russell. The marriage also allowed Giddy to escape the manipulative clutches of her mother – something that Mabel never did. Undoubtedly, Lord Russell had been groomed by Lady Scott as a suitor for Mabel for the security his financial and social status would potentially provide; the suggestion is that she applied the same tactics to Sebright assuming he was equally equipped to provide for Giddy. It was a narrow escape for Giddy. Sebright's non-appearance at court on the last day of their hearing was also felt in the bankruptcy court where he should also have been that day and where it was revealed he had unsecured debts of £12,544 on top of the £3,350 of bills Giddy had accepted. His financial position remained precarious and in 1899 he was imprisoned for six months for obtaining credit without disclosing he was an undischarged bankrupt. In 1903 he was found guilty of inducing the Marquis of Devonshire to accept two bills for £5,750 and sentenced to eighteen months' hard labour.

Regarding the Durham suit, Lord Burghersh's broken engagement sadly had no long-term impact on Ethel's mental state. She remained in one institution or another all her life with sporadic attempts at her removal by the Milners which always failed.

Immediately following the hearing the Milners moved her from Barnwood to Ticehurst, 'the Mecca of private asylums' – a large house in substantial grounds which boasted an aviary, a bowling green, a summer house, a music room and pleasure grounds, and where Ethel had her own attendant as well as her own companion and a carriage and horses and from where there were outings to St Leonards-on-Sea and Eastbourne.[36] Quite a different experience to Mrs Hunter, who ended up in Bethlehem, and the thousands of others housed in public asylums. Records show Ethel remained wilful. She had to be forcibly fed for the first year and 'does not mind it in the least'. She brooded on murder and suicide – her own and her mother's – and 'has lost all decency'.[37] There are only two references to her being conscious of Durham as her husband: once, when she put on her wedding ring and expressed great delight in it, and another when she showed pride in Durham being made Lord Lieutenant. Decisions about her care were made principally by the Milners but Durham paid the bill: £1,500 rising to £1,800 per annum until she left Ticehurst in 1899 and thereafter at other locations until her death in 1931. The fact that Ethel outlived Durham by three years meant he could never marry the woman he was thereafter said to be 'very much in love with' – the actress Letty Lind – or legitimise their son born in 1892.[38] Durham's title passed to his twin brother Frederick and thereafter Frederick's descendants. So absent was Ethel from his life that many obituary writers assumed he died a widower.

10

Issues of Access

'I ha' coom to ask yo, Sir, how am I to be ridded o' this woman...
   I cannot bear 't nommore... I want t' know how?'
'No how,' returned Mr Bounderby.
'If I do her any hurt, Sir, there's a law to punish me?'
'Of course there is.'
'If I flee from her, there's a law to punish me?'
'Of course there is.'
'If I marry t'oother dear lass, there's a law to punish me?'
'Of course there is.'
'If I was to live wi' her an' not marry her... there's a law to punish
   me, in every innocent child belonging to me?'
'Of course there is.'
'Now, a' God's name,' said Stephen Blackpool, 'show me the law
   to help me!' ...
'Now, I tell you what!' said Mr Bounderby, putting his hands in
   his pockets. 'There *is* such a law.'... 'But it's not for you at all.
   It costs money. It costs a mint of money.'
Charles Dickens, *Hard Times* (1854)

One of the conclusions drawn by the 1852 Campbell Commission, charged with investigating the desirability of introducing divorce into the statute books, was that the 'great expense and the long delay' of the old parliamentary system produced 'a grievous hardship and oppression to individuals' that amounted 'in many cases to a denial of justice'. The commission recognised that even under the most favourable circumstances £700 to £800 was necessary for a divorce in England while in Scotland at the time the average cost was £30 and when there was no defence £20 would suffice. In this manner Scottish divorce was 'not a privilege for the rich, but a right for all' and, it was noted, 'almost all' litigants in Scotland were of the lower classes while in England they were of the upper.[1] The injustice contributed to the passing of the 1857 Matrimonial Causes Act but not before the hardships of the old system were laid bare in Dickens's journal *Household Words* through the serialisation of his new novel.

Happiness in marriage (or rather, the lack of it) is a theme that runs throughout *Hard Times*. It contrasts the matrimonial fortunes of Josiah Bounderby, banker, merchant and manufacturer from the northern industrial town of Coketown, with those of his 'steady Hand' Stephen Blackpool, culminating in the scene quoted above. Bounderby is on the cusp of proposing to his best friend's daughter, oblivious to her obvious dislike of him, when the honest, law-abiding Blackpool seeks his advice on how he might escape his drunken, dissolute wife who has, for the previous nineteen years, caused him no end of misery and whose very existence prevents him from finding happiness with the object of his affection, the unremittingly patient Rachel. The irony and pathos of the scene is devastating as Bounderby crushes Blackpool's hopes, leaving the humble weaver to conclude that the law is 'a muddle ... an' the sooner I am dead, the better'.[2] For Blackpool's real-life counterparts the 'muddle' was soon somewhat alleviated by the Matrimonial Causes Act offering the working classes access to divorce for the first time. Increasingly, they took advantage of it: by 1871, 17 per cent of all petitions in England and Wales were filed by manual workers; and for the period 1881–1900 the figure had risen to 28 per cent with a further 31 per cent petitioning from the lower-middle class.[3] Yet this figure was still disproportionate in terms of population and there remained echoes of Stephen Blackpool in many of the letters that flooded into the Barnes Commission from 1910 complaining that despite the changes in the law 'the present system of divorce is not obtainable to poor people'.[4]

On close examination it is not hard to see why many potential litigants from the lower classes felt this way. Not only was the process itself quite daunting, but every interaction with the court was affixed an allowable cost that would eventually have to be settled.[5] It cost £1 to draw up a petition of up to 720 words (that's ten 'folios' in legal jargon, where each folio consists of no more than seventy-two words), 2s 6d to have it filed with the court registry at Somerset House on London's Strand, and another 6s 8d to attend the filing – something the petitioner or his local solicitor must do in person, no matter where in the country they lived. Each petition had to be filed with an affidavit sworn before a commissioner of oaths verifying its statements – that's another 1s per folio for drawing, 6s 8d for swearing, 2s 6d for filing, and so on. The citations then issued by the registry to serve on the respondent and any co-respondents in the suit cost another 7s 6d each. These documents had to be stamped (5s) and sealed (6s 8d) before serving (another 5s). If the respondent's whereabouts were not known – something that court registrars observed happened most often in cases of working-class wives whose husbands had abandoned them – advertisements must be placed in relevant newspapers before the court could grant permission for substituted service on a close relative in a lengthy process that could cost another £2. There were rules as to how and when a suit could progress if the respondent was not discovered (with more accompanying costs), but in all cases in which the respondent was successfully served their appearance marked the start of a second set of costs that might be incurred for, say, a demand for particulars before the filing of an answer, which might in turn require a reply, the costs of which were all comparable.

If the court was asked to intervene in other ways – in an application for alimony for the wife pending the hearing, for example, which as a rule was calculated at one-fifth of the husband's income, or an order for access to the children of the marriage – these all carried yet more costs. Every subsequent summons to attend court that was drawn, issued, attended and ordered carried an additional cost of £2. Finally, when the cause was 'set down' for hearing and notice of the fact sent to the respondent's solicitor, a further £3 5s was required for so doing. Each subpoena for witnesses added another 5s to the bill; in addition to which witnesses could expect an attendance allowance on a sliding scale depending on social status – 5s a day for labourers and journeymen rising to £3 3s for professionals – as well as travelling expenses (up to 1s per mile) and lodging expenses. This could prove costly. In 1896 Arthur Asbury, an electroplater from Birmingham who was divorced by his wife and condemned to pay costs, was alarmed to discover that the five witnesses she brought to London resulted in a bill of some £12 2s 3d. Asbury's weekly wage was then 40s, meaning this alone represented more than six weeks' work to him. But by far the most burdensome single expense was engaging a barrister. His fee could be anything from 5 to 100 guineas depending on status and experience, dwarfing the 13s paid to solicitors for drawing up his brief and his clerk's stipend of anywhere from 5s to more than £2. The nervousness of a working-class petitioner as all these costs accumulated can well be imagined. To top it off, the very drawing up of the bill for approval, which was done by a solicitor's clerk after the hearing and approved by a court registrar, was charged at 2s for the first £4 of costs and 1s for every £2 thereafter.

Mrs Asbury's total costs were a little over £68 – more than thirty times Mr Asbury's weekly wage. There would have been little sympathy for him: he had been found guilty of adultery and cruelty and this was his punishment. But the disparity of costs over earnings seen in his case was by no means unusual for working class litigants and affected petitioners and respondents alike. Data from the 1881–1900 sample makes it clear that at the lower end of the social scale divorce could not be achieved without either a benefactor or savings. The data also shows that though it was repeatedly stated in evidence given to the Barnes Commission that an uncomplicated undefended divorce cost around £50, the Asbury suit, which fits this description, was one of many that cost more. The lowest cost recorded was £34, but the highest was £102 and the average across all fifty-eight of those working-class court files with approved costs recorded was £62 10s. The further one lived from the court the greater was the likelihood that costs would be higher. Ten out of the sixteen calculated at under £50 belonged to London-based petitioners with another four petitioning from the Home Counties. On average, those from the Midlands and the North incurred costs of £70, representing something like a year's wages for workers in the best paid manufacturing industries and nearly three years' worth for those in some of the least: the manufacture of boxes, sugar confectionery and materials such as linen, worsted and jute.[6]

Costs were predictably higher in defended suits and it is interesting to note that, after removing from the sample all petitions that were abandoned immediately following filing, only one in five of the working-class petitions remaining were defended as opposed to two out of every five from the classes above. Defended petitions that progressed beyond filing were also ultimately far more likely to be abandoned before reaching court than undefended suits and it is easy to conclude that lack of means was a significant factor. Mary Jane Duckett's 1888 divorce petition, for example, was abandoned after the court ordered her husband to pay her 7s a week in alimony pending the hearing. Mr Duckett wrote to the court explaining that as he was letting his wife 'have all her own way so that she can get married to the man she has been living with for months' and as his earnings as a freelance reporter for a Durham newspaper never amounted to more than 5s a week and his worldly possessions were stored in a tin trunk in the single room he had been renting for four years, his wife had clearly misrepresented his wealth and he consequently could neither afford nor intended to pay for her upkeep: 'It takes me all my time to live respectably as it is, and as for paying any costs it is an utter impossibility,' he wrote.

Three more husbands in the sample abandoned their petitions after being asked to pay their wife's costs up to the point at which their cause was set down for hearing. A husband was legally obliged to finance his wife's defence and whether or not preliminary costs were requested was entirely at her and her solicitor's discretion. The more they wished to apply pressure on the husband or the more precarious his financial position, the more likely they were to do so. They were also entitled to ask that her husband lodge in court sufficient funds to cover her share of the cost of the hearing – a figure that was estimated by a registrar based on such things as the number of witnesses she intended to bring and the length of her barrister's brief. Once ordered, a husband could not proceed further with his cause until both sums were paid. If he could not raise them then he must find two friends willing to provide bonds of surety – another lengthy and expensive business. The three husbands who abandoned their suits rather than do either of these things – a sergeant, an engine-room artificer and a post-office letter sorter – still faced bills of £23, £33 and £42 respectively in addition to their own expenses. Writers to the Barnes Commission described how quickly costs could spiral. One had spent £200 'gathering evidence' before abandoning his cause for want of money; while another became bitter at what he believed was his 'expensive counsel' spinning out the trial of his defended suit for five days with costs rocketing to £630 before he had to pull out – all his life savings gone – and he a piano tuner earning 30s a week with no divorce to show for it.[7]

Of course, if a husband's petition succeeded the co-respondent was customarily condemned to pay his costs, usually within seven days of their approval. They were paid into court but not paid out until the decree *nisi* was made absolute six months later. This meant, at very least, a husband granted costs still had to find his solicitor's out-of-pocket expenses during proceedings unless their agreement stated otherwise. If he could not do this, access was effectively denied him. One working man writing to the Barnes Commission found himself in such a situation. He earned 16s a week and told the commission that his wife had left him seven years previously for a man who earned twelve times as much. He had been told by a solicitor that he could not expect to divorce for less than £150: 'I did not possess that many pence, and therefore had no redress at law, but have had to live within 400 yards of them' to remain in the vicinity of his employment. Little wonder, then, that he felt he had been stung twice: once by his wife's betrayal and again by the injustice that the lovers seemingly lived happily together while his freedom was denied him. As a consequence his life 'has been and still is Hell upon earth'.[8]

When it came to full access to the law, a working-class man was also disadvantaged in his capacity to claim damages. Suits with damages were nearly seven times more likely to fail than those without and one reason for this was the increased likelihood of a determined defence by the co-respondent. Very few co-respondents could afford to be so cavalier as, for example, the wealthy owner-manager of the Lyric Theatre, Henry John Leslie, who offered absolutely no defence when charged with committing adultery with popular actress Marie Tempest and then more-or-less offered to pay her husband's demand for £5,000 damages on the spot. Leslie had already made an estimated £100,000 from Marie's performance as the eponymous heroine in the stage show *Dorothy* and was portrayed by counsel as an unscrupulous man who had used his position of power to seduce the young actress away from her quiet and unassuming husband, Alfred Izard, a music professor at the

Royal Academy with an annual income of £500 a year. The special jury consequently allowed the full claim. When the judge ordered the sum to be paid within a fortnight and Leslie's barrister tried to bargain for an extension given the size of the award, Leslie piped up that a fortnight would be more than sufficient to pay the full sum. The following Monday his solicitor posted notices in the press stating that he was already in possession of a cheque to hand over to Izard. Had Leslie taken out his chequebook and waved it at the judge, the gesture could not have been grander. But it was also distasteful and deepened the sense of injustice for those of lesser means than either Leslie or Izard for whom the very possibility of a defended suit precluded them claiming for their loss. Only a fifth of working-class husbands in the sample made claims though they filed nearly two-fifths of eligible petitions. They were successful only a third of the time and typically awarded between £50 and £100 – a huge sum for a working man, but nonetheless a real lottery both in terms of the likelihood of the claim resulting in an award and the co-respondent's capacity to pay it.

The working-class petitioner also had to consider a possible intervention by the Queen's Proctor. All petitioners did, of course, but for those with limited means the stakes were arguably higher as the consequences of being found to have broken the rules were greater – particularly after the proctor began targeting adulterous petitioners. One man challenged in 1885 was Arthur Pearman, a farrier from Finsbury. The proctor intervened in his undefended suit after Pearman divorced his wife of twenty-five years by proving her adultery at a hotel in nearby Holborn at least four years after they'd separated. To the proctor it reeked of collusion and after gathering evidence he filed a plea alleging that since 1883 Pearman had cohabited with a widow named Webb and that they'd lived together at three separate addresses in Camden. His local agent discovered that Mrs Webb was known to some of her neighbours as Pearman's sister and to others as his wife. His sister she definitely was not, but ultimately the proctor was unable to prove to the court's satisfaction that she was his mistress either. Pearman was fortunate. The proctor was condemned to pay his £55 costs for defending the intervention – costs that would have doubled his original bill had he been found guilty as well as denying him his divorce that was made absolute in 1887. The 1891 census shows

Mrs Webb still living with him as his 'housekeeper', but whether in any other capacity is uncertain.

Less fortunate was Mrs Sarah Airey, a thirty-eight-year-old shopkeeper from Newcastle who had married Dumfries coachman Francis Airey in November 1889. In March 1890, Airey threatened and assaulted her. He was summoned, but absconded before the hearing. In his absence, he was committed for one month's hard labour and ordered to pay Sarah 7s a week maintenance. He didn't pay and she survived on the meagre 7s she earned after rent from her small grocery business. She didn't see Airey again until 1893; after which, according to her petition, he came and went and they cohabited on and off until October 1898 when she discovered he was living with a Mrs Simpson and had several children by her. In April 1899 her undefended divorce petition was granted on these grounds. During proceedings she stated that Airey also went by the name William Mark. Perhaps it was this that alerted the proctor who made enquiries of a Newcastle solicitor and subsequently filed a plea stating that Mark was *not* Airey and therefore *not* Sarah's husband and his relationship with Mrs Simpson was *not* therefore adultery.

At the trial, Mark recalled how Sarah approached him in 1893 at a railway station while he was working and called him 'Francis'; that he told her his name wasn't Francis but she was so persistent that over time he tired of trying to disabuse her of the fact. Thereafter, others started to call him Francis and he allowed it to continue. When the divorce papers were served on him he did nothing about it because he was poor and because they were not in his name. The proctor produced documentary evidence to prove the separate identities of the men, and witnesses on both sides testified that Mark *was* and *wasn't* Airey. With Sarah's witnesses claiming both that Mark *was* the man she married but that the man in a photo of Mark produced by his sister and shown them in court was *not* Airey, the judge decided, in the balance of probability, Mark was who he said he was and Sarah had perpetrated 'a very deliberate fraud'. Sarah's divorce was rescinded and she was condemned to costs of £288. If she was fortunate at all it was that she was neither prosecuted for the deception nor subsequently pressed for the costs. On hearing that she had to support her invalid mother on her earnings and had no other savings, the Treasury picked up the bill. Doubtless they realised the futility of attempting to recover it.[9]

To many unhappy spouses, then, divorce remained a decadence well beyond the passing of the 1857 Act and recompense for any personal or material loss or the prospect of future happiness in marriage a distant dream. Two solutions of sorts were offered, both with unforeseen consequences.

The first was that a person of very limited means could approach the court *in forma pauperis* – literally, in the form of a pauper. It followed a principle written into law in the time of Henry VII that was automatically applied to divorce in 1857. The 1495 'Act to Admit Such Persons as Are Poor to Sue In Forma Pauperis' allowed every pauper with a cause against another person of the realm to sue with 'nothing paying' for the services of a clerk, attorney and counsel at the relevant court's discretion.[10] For an application to the divorce court this meant appearing in person before a registrar at Somerset House and signing an affidavit stating that their total worth after payment of just debts was less than £25. A wife also had to prove her husband could not finance her cause. It was also necessary to secure the opinion of counsel as to the reasonableness of the grounds for proceeding. In other words, it must be fairly certain that the petition would succeed.

The 1885 application of Ellen Jane Howe, a milliner from Southampton, fulfilled the first criteria because she earned only 10*s* a week, lived in austere lodgings with her child and her husband was a ship's cook of intemperate habits and often out of work. The detailed notes submitted with her application reveal a life of struggle and hardship with a violent man who over time sold all her belongings to feed his habit and whose periodic returns after long absences she perpetually dreaded. After one absence she discovered he had been living in another part of the city with a barmaid who posed as his wife. Ellen had sued for divorce in 1882 but had only been able to prove cruelty and was awarded a judicial separation. Believing that her solicitor had failed in his duty by not procuring evidence of the adultery as instructed, the plucky woman went out and secured it for herself, thereby fulfilling the second criteria required for her application. From this point on, as a pauper petitioner, Ellen had to do all the legwork in her cause. She was obliged to find another solicitor willing to represent her for only the bare minimum of out-of-pocket expenses to draw up her petition, affidavit and citation. She then had to appear in person at the registry on five separate occasions before her case could be heard: to file her papers, to collect the sealed copies, to prove that her husband's non-appearance was not because she had failed to serve him with them, to collect the registrar's certificate stating her documents were all in order and to set down the cause for trial – all tasks which under normal circumstances would have been carried out by a solicitor's clerk. Thereafter, it became her responsibility to keep her eye on the daily list at the Royal Courts to ensure she did not miss her hearing, all this time maintaining herself in London – to say nothing of any witnesses she might need. A registrar's memorandum to the Barnes Commission stated that the procedure was so labour intensive that many pauper petitioners living outside London abandoned their causes or saw them struck out for non-appearance by missing them being called. He suggested that much of what was being done in person could be done by post. Moreover, though court costs were waived, the minimum many solicitors charged for basic expenses was £10 – far beyond the reach of a pauper. Hardly surprising, then, that on average there were only ten to fifteen pauper causes heard each year.

The second solution was altogether a workaround and in many instances a very unsatisfactory one. Realising that access to the court was still beyond the means of the majority and that many wives continued to suffer at the hands of violent husbands and, unable to support themselves, were effectively left unprotected by the state, in 1878 Parliament introduced the concept of separation and maintenance orders. Henceforth, if a husband was convicted of aggravated assault and the court or magistrate convicting him was satisfied that his wife was in peril, they could order that she was no longer bound to live with him and that he should pay her a weekly sum in accordance with his means (and with any means she may have of supporting herself). In 1886 this provision was extended to include wives whose husbands abandoned and neglected them and, following an 1895 rewrite of both these laws, in which their terms were consolidated and further clarified, in 1902 it was extended a third time to include habitually drunken husbands – where habitual drunkards were defined as being dangerous to themselves and to others or incapable of managing themselves or their affairs. The maximum maintenance a wife could expect to receive was £2 a week. An order was enforceable with a prison term if necessary, could be varied on the application of either party and revoked if it was at any point discovered that the wife had committed adultery. By the terms of the 1902 Act, a husband could also separate himself from a drunken wife and apply for custody of their children but was still obliged to pay her maintenance not exceeding the £2 limit.[11]

The 1895 Act was considered 'a major advance' because it allowed magistrates to order a weekly payment when the husband's only offence was the 'wilful neglect to provide reasonable maintenance'.[12] It was designed to deal with marriage breakdowns that had occurred but were not considered irretrievable. Moreover, such an order cost only 4*s* to pursue – a trifle in comparison with divorce – and even this fee was often remitted. It served to protect women without extending the grounds for divorce, thereby simultaneously protecting the sanctity of marriage. Yet in practice it left a wife in a sort of half-existence, lacking the physical protection and support of a husband yet wholly dependent on the man who had ill-treated her. Her only means of enforcing the order was to issue a summons against him if he chose not to pay. The voices of those who were satisfied with the system and subsisted well on it are silent; but many suffered. Historian Stephen Cretney points out that if in response to a summons a husband claimed he *had* paid his wife's maintenance it was difficult for the court to ascertain who was telling the truth; and one of the women who wrote to the Barnes Commission complaining about the scheme said that her husband went to extreme lengths to avoid paying. A joiner by trade, he left his employment every time a summons was issued. He'd 'go into the workhouse and then appear before the magistrate in workhouse clothes'. The writer, by now sixty-seven, had received nothing for ten years and was 'not able to do much'.[13] Yet despite these apparent failings, applications for separation orders were filed at a great rate. Nothing more clearly demonstrates the gulf between rich and poor and the deficiencies of the laws concerning matrimonial causes than the two-tier system that evolved whereby the affluent went to the divorce court and obtained some 600 divorces and 80 judicial separations annually while the poor went to the magistrate to secure 8,700 separation orders.[14]

The sheer number of separation orders necessarily meant that the poor were more likely to form 'irregular unions' and the research of historian Ginger Frost in this area led her to the conclusion that 'working class adulterous cohabitation was widespread' and that in their communities cohabitees were largely treated with tolerance and sympathy, becoming 'regular members of their neighbourhoods'.[15] They saw themselves as married and acted accordingly. The majority would have preferred to have been married and felt forced into an unwanted situation by the inequities of the law. 'How can we be a Loyal Christian [sic] until we get a remedy?' one cohabitee whose wife had deserted him nine years previously asked the Barnes Commission. The man previously mentioned who had spent £200 gathering evidence before abandoning his divorce suit, meanwhile, felt he was forced to live 'an unnatural life' as a consequence. Poor people, Frost concluded, 'did not have the luxury of standing on principle'.[16] What incentive was there for a woman alone to remain moral when faced with the more pressing issue of survival, asked another writer to the commission? If an old friend or lover offered to take care of her 'she would indeed be a strong woman who would see her children want food and clothing when [such an offer was made] to her in all honour but that of the law of the country'.[17]

Yet many did resist temptation despite the hardship. 'Oh the misery,' wrote another man, echoing the sentiments Dickens put into the mouth of Stephen Blackpool nearly sixty years earlier, of being separated from a drunken wife and attempting to maintain a moral standard. This man lived in a small country town where 'everyone knows': 'you are shut out from any society, you dare not form the companionship of an honourable woman, you can have no society of the opposite sexes, I have to live my life lonely and sad simply because I made a mistake in early life…' Similarly, a twenty-three-year-old woman deserted while pregnant spoke of her 'suffering before my child was born and afterwards through being deserted', finding she was 'pointed out to everyone through no fault of my own … As I stand I am neither maid wife or widow.'

Frost found that, on the whole, women were less eager to cohabit than men. She also suspected that rural communities were less tolerant of immorality than urban folk and argued that those who did cohabit did not necessarily have an easier life. One man reflected on the difficulties of being ordered to pay 5s a week to a wife 'who went into bad ways' from his 18s wages, leaving him only 6s 8d after rent, insurance, gas and coal were paid for to support his common-law wife 'who is the best in the world to me' and their three children. Such families found little support beyond their immediate circle. Authorities were unsympathetic towards adulterers; charitable societies had been known to refuse assistance and London creches, for the avoidance of 'rewarding' immorality, rejected illegitimate children.[18] Separation and divorce was hard on children too; and for more than just financial reasons. The autobiography of Jane Walsh, a millworker from Lancashire, recalled the 'dreadful burden' on one of her workmates of having divorced parents due to the fact that in their circle divorce was considered 'a worse disgrace than drink' and the children of such parents were thought liable to have 'bad blood' that would eventually reveal itself.[19] That Walsh was writing about life in the 1920s demonstrates how such attitudes persisted well into the twentieth century.

Small mercy, then, that for the fortunate minority who were able to save enough for a divorce, their suits did not create the same sensation in the press as the spectacle of well-to-do litigants and that when it came to reporting local cases, regional papers were more interested in middle-class people well known in their community. A draper from the small market town of Corsham in Wiltshire discovered this to his cost. The town had only ever seen two divorces since the passing of the Act – both involving gentlemen – and none at all since 1873. George Douglas Crook's 1888 suit therefore caused quite a local sensation. Crook had taken a prominent double-fronted shop on the High Street some seven years earlier, having already met his future wife, Miriam Clark, when he was apprenticed to a draper in the Oxfordshire town of Bicester in 1881. They married at Corsham parish church on 31 August 1885 and Miriam moved in with him above the shop and worked with him. The following year Crook took on his own apprentice, William Gabriel Baker, to enable him to expand his business as a travelling draper. One can only imagine the scandal when it became known in the town that in Crook's absence Miriam and Baker had been seen kissing by the female shop assistant and heard calling each other 'Darling Minnie' and 'Tottie'; and the manner in which it was compounded when Crook then dismissed Baker on 16 November 1886 and sent Miriam back to her father.

Whether gossips then spread other facts that would later come out in court – that Miriam was in the habit of taking Baker breakfast in bed when Crook was at church on Sundays; that their maid had heard laughing and talking in Miriam's bedroom on several occasions after Crook had left the house; and that Miriam was pregnant when she left and Crook denied paternity – is not known. But that the whole of Wiltshire and Somerset knew afterwards is certain given that the story was picked up and reported as 'A Local Divorce Case' by no less than eight papers across the region. Crook stayed in Corsham and brazened it out, remarrying in 1891 and running the business with his second wife until the early 1920s. Miriam's son was born at her father's house, registered as having been fathered by Crook but baptised as Baker's. She remained with her family for the rest of her life, passing as a widow, while Baker moved to Totnes, married and became a railway clerk. Corsham did not have another reported divorce until 1933 when the landlord of 'The Packhorse' public house at the other end of the High Street divorced his wife in similar circumstances.[20]

So much for the fleeting scandals of the lower-middle class. The handful of working-class suits that caused a sensation usually did so for being tragic or amusing or both. The 'Amusing Brighton Nullity Case' of 1901 was so called because of the manner in which its defendant, Henrietta Brinton, delivered her evidence.

The forty-nine-year-old bricklayer's wife was accused of still being married to a railway porter named Luther Trower when she married Joseph Brinton in 1894. Henrietta claimed she thought Trower was dead. This was not implausible: they had separated in 1877. Still, Brinton had no difficulty in tracing Trower working on a farm in Henfield, 7 miles from Brighton, and in court Trower claimed that Henrietta knew he was alive because in January of that year she had visited him to ask that he surrender their marriage certificate and his birth certificate for the unlikely reason that she needed them to claim a £4,000 inheritance that was coming her way. 'Oh, look at him committing perjury,' Henrietta called out from the well of the court (laughter), before entering the box herself and almost immediately declaring she felt faint. On her recovery, President Barnes asked her directly whether Trower was not the man she married. 'I don't hardly recognise him,' she replied; and when Barnes challenged that Trower was certain, she retorted, 'Well, I ain't.' (Laughter.) Subsequently asked whether she was the author of a letter produced she declared, 'I never wrote that. I'll kiss the book. Where is the book?' (more laughter); and when presented with another in which she had supposedly written, 'I have two husbands and one is too self-righteous', she leant down towards a clerk of the court and said, 'Lend us yer specs. I can't see.' (Loud laughter.) She further evaded counsel's questions, saying they must not keep her there too long as she felt faint again, before appealing directly to Barnes for sympathy – an appeal that appeared in the press thus:

> As you are a gentleman, and I am not a lady but a poor woman, I did not write them. It is a cruel thing for a poor woman with only one eye, and one leg, and a diseased heart (laughter). Look at him over there laughing (pointing to Brinton). Don't you call it a cruel thing to get rid of a wife like this?

The judge did, but he was powerless to do anything about it. In passing judgment he said it was very sad but the case was proved: he must annul the marriage and give Brinton custody of their three children, adding that he hoped Brinton would make provision for Henrietta whose life would now be one of hardship. It would indeed, but from the headlines that appeared in regional papers across the length and breadth of the country – and most particularly the evening and weekend papers aimed at middle- and working-class readers – you would never have known it. 'The Woman With Two Husbands' was most popular, with various subheadings including 'The One-Legged Woman's Bad Eyesight' and 'The "Widow" Faints But Fails to Save Her Marriage'. No one asked why Brinton sought an annulment now when Henrietta had declared in court that she had been a good wife to him for fifteen years and he had not contradicted her. In fact, though they had only been legally married for seven years, records show she'd lived with him for at least twenty. And the case would altogether cease to be amusing but instead become 'The Brighton Tragedy' when on 11 August 1901, less than two weeks after the hearing, police were called to a house in Cambridge Street where they found Henrietta lying on the kitchen floor in a pool of blood having slit her own throat.

At the inquest her landlady said Henrietta had been in a terribly depressed state since the verdict and that her talk of suicide and the 5s 6d she already owed in rent had made the landlady nervous about having her in the house. She had asked her to leave and had put her mattress out into the street by way of encouragement. The previous week Henrietta had told her that she would not stand by and watch Brinton marry again. She'd meant it. The *Brighton Gazette* that had recently been so amused by her performance in court led with the sentiment,

> Poor Henrietta Trower! Are there not many Brightonians who will shed a tear of sympathy over her cold grave? ... Had she been a brazen adulteress ... her punishment could have been no worse ... What useful purpose has been served by divorcing her from her love? The Society moralist may scratch his head, and gaze upon her tomb, as he sternly answers, 'It was the law.'[21]

It was, but it was also the will of Joseph Brinton, who remarried within weeks of Henrietta's death.

Suicide being a criminal offence until 1961, had Henrietta failed in her attempt she could have been prosecuted and either fined or imprisoned. How much press attention would this outcome have afforded? Proprietors knew that nothing sold papers so well as violent crime – particularly those papers aimed at working-class readers. As it was, Henrietta's death was picked up by three times as many papers as her annulment and then as quickly forgotten. She was far from being the most notorious working-class heroine of the divorce court in this era. That accolade surely went to thirty-six-year-old Australian-born mother of two Mrs Eleanor Thompson.

By the time Eleanor approached the divorce court in 1892 she was already well known at the Royal Courts, having started her campaign the previous year by successfully petitioning *in forma pauperis* for a writ of Habeas Corpus against commercial traveller Arthur Henry Rourke. Habeas Corpus protects individuals against unlawful detention or imprisonment and in this instance the writ was essentially a summons with the force of a court order against Rourke for unlawfully detaining Eleanor's two children: Arthur, aged twelve, and Alice, aged ten. The parties appeared before Justices Cave and Smith in the Queen's Bench on 6 July 1891. In his defence, Rourke claimed to be Eleanor's husband and the children's father and therefore legally entitled to their custody.

Eleanor argued that he was neither: that their true father was a bank clerk named Arthur Herbert Thompson whom she had married on 3 October 1876 in Melbourne, Australia, and with whom she had travelled to London in 1878, but who had returned to the antipodes in 1882. In response Rourke claimed *he* was Thompson: that he had married Eleanor under a false name to avoid news of their marriage reaching England and exciting the wrath of his father, on whom he was financially dependent. Eleanor had been a seventeen-year-old waitress in a hotel bar when they first met and was not the sort of daughter-in-law his father, who managed a warehousing business in London, aspired to. After nearly three weeks' deliberation the judges found in Rourke's favour, concluding that Arthur Herbert Thompson had never existed. On hearing the verdict Eleanor leapt from her seat and rushed towards the front of the court where her children sat with Rourke, screaming, 'Give me my children! I will have them. I claim my children. He has told you all lies!' Hysterical, she was removed from the court; but not before she had brandished her umbrella at an astonished court reporter whom she accused of unfairly representing her in the press.[22]

Over the course of the next few months, Eleanor was frequently to be found at the Royal Courts, each time dragging the increasingly weary Rourke in her wake. She appealed the Queen's Bench verdict and secured from the appeal judges two hours' supervised weekly access to her children. When Rourke resisted she made multiple appeals for the court to force him to comply and on one occasion made such a scene outside Judges' Chambers where Justice Jeune was sitting that he was forced to hear her. She brought with her the founder and director of the NSPCC, Revd Benjamin Waugh, whom she had interested in her case, and the upshot was that it was agreed Waugh would supervise access. Still Rourke did not comply, prompting Eleanor to complain. In October 1891, Jeune saw the children in private and afterwards said he would not force them to see their mother against their will. The children were quietly removed from court; their mother less so.

For the appeal hearing in November 1891 Eleanor was represented by barrister and editor of *Reynolds's Newspaper* W. M. Thompson (no relation). Rourke represented himself. A statement by Eleanor was read in which she declared she'd had sole custody of the children until 1888 and had endeavoured to bring them up well. Now she feared they lived in one room with Rourke and never went to school. As a poor milliner she had been put to great expense by court costs but Revd Waugh had undertaken to place the children in good homes until she could afford to take care of them. It spoke against her, however, that in her desperate state she had entered the workhouse twice and had once tried to commit suicide. Where would it leave the children if she tried again, the judges wanted to know. For his part, Rourke stated that he earned 30s a week as a traveller on commission and that the reason the children did not go to school was because they had been forced to move lodgings due to Eleanor perpetually making trouble at their previous residence and new school places were yet to be found. He further accused Eleanor, not quite of being mad, but certainly of having a violent temper. She tried to strike him every time they met, he said.

More significantly, Rourke also claimed that before they left Australia a daughter had been born to them whom they'd named Mabel Nellie Thompson. She'd died in infancy and Rourke produced her burial slip. Justice Lopes considered this highly significant: Rourke's possession of the slip strongly suggested he was the father of a child baptised and buried in the name 'Thompson' *before* Eleanor's supposed marriage to the other man. Eleanor's side hit back with Revd Waugh's evidence. Waugh stated that Eleanor had told him Rourke was sexually abusing young Arthur and Alice, and Waugh thought this ought to be investigated. Rourke fervently denied the charge, saying it was not he but Eleanor who was immoral: she had committed adultery with at least two men that he knew of. The judges believed neither attempt at mudslinging, in particular expressing their astonishment that Waugh would believe the 'terrible accusation' that Rourke was 'contaminating his own children' on the ground that he saw 'something' in the children's faces when they heard their mother say it. Waugh was a compassionate man described by that other great late Victorian campaigner W. T. Stead as 'a human sleuth-hound': the 'implacable avenger' of London's brutal parents, child torturers and baby farmers who worked tirelessly for the protection of vulnerable children and had supported the 'Maiden Tribute' campaign.[23] Had he been duped by Eleanor? The judges had spoken with Arthur and Alice and considered them 'nice children, well fed and clothed' and their absolution of Rourke from any imputation was greeted with applause in court. In the judges' view Eleanor's 'abominable' allegation rendered her unfit for custody of her children and they upheld the verdict of the court below, simultaneously removing all access rights until she 'became calmer'. Eleanor screamed, 'Perjury!' – on one side or the other – but the judges preferred to consider the mudslinging a mistake. Eleanor pressed for the case to be sent to the public prosecutor, but the judges were emphatic in their refusal.

The appeal judges may have given no credence to Eleanor's allegation of abuse but neither did they think it proper for ten-year-old Alice to live in a single room with her brother and father. So extensively reported was the case that behind the scenes the Bishop of Bedford had come forward to offer to find Alice appropriate accommodation and schooling. Eleanor's advocate countered it with a similar offer from Cardinal Manning – Eleanor being Catholic. The judges preferred the bishop: it was proper for children to be raised in their father's religion (even if he might not actually be their father) and, for the first time in this whole traumatic business, young Arthur and Alice were separated. On Friday 18 December Alice was delivered into the bishop's hands. Eleanor was not allowed to see her. Distraught, she pestered her way into the appeal judges' presence and received their pity but was told to come back in a month. With difficulty, she was induced to leave the court. A columnist for *The Gentlewoman* wrote that it was the 'last scene' in what the press had been calling the 'Strange Paternity Case': Alice's removal was probably for the best but the mystery was 'by no means cleared up'.[24]

The columnist was right about the mystery but this was far from the last scene. Eleanor returned again and again and was eventually told by Lord Esher of the appeal court that she would 'destroy the girl's happiness – nay, more, that her life would not be safe' if she was granted access. Though this was strong language, Esher perhaps had a point: the children had clearly already stated they did not wish to see Eleanor, though whether for fear of her or Rourke is not known. Either way, the distraught mother was removed from the court protesting that it had all been settled in a private room and was nothing but corruption. The following morning she appeared before the Bow Street magistrate asking to have Rourke prosecuted for perjury. She was sent away to consult a solicitor. This she did; but the solution he came up with was one that probably no one would have predicted.

On 1 April 1892, Eleanor Thompson filed the first petition for 'jactitation' the divorce court had seen in thirty years. Jactitation was an old remedy quite necessary before the Hardwicke Act of 1753 made a marriage ceremony compulsory to determine whether a couple were legally wed, but it had largely fallen out of use thereafter. Its purpose was to prevent one person from 'boasting' that they were married to another when they were not. It enabled a petitioner to obtain a court order restraining the other party from repeating the false claim. Jactitation actions had been used in disputes over titles, inheritances or legitimacy and sometimes even collusively or fraudulently to attempt to validate a second bigamous marriage, most famously by the Duchess of Kingston whose fraud was exposed in a trial by peers in Westminster Hall in 1776.[25]

Eleanor's purpose was to have the divorce court state once and for all that Rourke was not her husband and therefore not entitled to custody of her children. By resurrecting a remedy that even in 1820 Lord Stowell had described as 'not now very familiar' but presumably still in existence, Eleanor added a certain celebrity status to her pre-existing notoriety and made full use of it: on at least one occasion over the next few months she was to be found addressing a crowd in the central hall of the Royal Courts. Soon a new headline appeared – 'Mrs Thompson, Again!' – and beneath it a faithful account of her increasingly wild allegations against Rourke – such as that he was teaching her son to forge bills on the London County Bank! – and of Rourke's growing paranoia that if he sent young Arthur to school Eleanor would arrange for his kidnap. By the time the suit was called on 17 November 1892 Rourke had gained the reputation of being as 'difficult to manage' as Eleanor in his refusal to trust that the authorities would in any way be able to prevent this; such concerns took a toll on his personal circumstances and physical wellbeing, leading him to quip that since 1888, through Eleanor's persistence, he had been unable to work having 'spent more time in these courts than elsewhere'.

With both parties suing *in forma pauperis* and representing themselves to keep unallowable expenses to a minimum, there was, said *The Times*, 'a good deal of irrelevant matter introduced' at the trial notwithstanding Justice Barnes' efforts to prevent it, but no 'scenes' as such: the whole case was laid before the common jury in 'an orderly and decorous manner'. Neither were there any humorous anecdotes to report. Eleanor was described as a fervent respectable-looking woman, sparely built with very dark hair and sharp-cut features. Dressed head to foot in black (but with a splash of colour in a poppy-red sash), she addressed the court for two and a half hours before entering the witness box, sticking to her story about her marriage to Thompson but saying it had taken place in Sydney where Thompson lived and worked. She further explained that before she married him she'd been seduced by Rourke, resulting in the birth of the child that died. Her other two children were definitely Thompson's and their births registered as such. Alice's birth certificate was put in as evidence. She claimed to have met Rourke again by chance in London in 1880 and after Thompson returned to Australia Rourke came to see her to borrow money. They remained friends and in 1884 Rourke took a house in Holloway, Eleanor moving in soon after. They did not cohabit there, but on 10 June 1884 Rourke secured a licence for them to marry, presenting himself as a bachelor. Ultimately, they never married because Eleanor refused him, but they lived in the same house until 1888 with the exception of a short interlude in 1885 when Rourke travelled to America and wrote to Eleanor to say he had married in San Francisco. The letter was also put in as evidence. In 1888, unable to secure employment in London, Eleanor accepted a position as a servant in New York and left the children in the care of Rourke's sister. When she returned from America six months later she found that the children had been taken by Rourke, who refused to surrender them. She spent the next two years trying any and all means to get them back, beginning with personal appeals, followed by fruitless appearances before various magistrates before arriving at the point where we joined her at the Royal Courts.

The dates Eleanor had given were confirmed by Rourke, with the exception of his supposed trip to San Francisco. Rourke swore he had never set foot in America, let alone married there, and the letter was a forgery. There was no explanation for her changing the wedding venue but her suggestion of an earlier affair with Rourke answered the question of how he came by the dead child's burial slip, though not the use of the name 'Thompson'. For everything else Rourke had an alternative explanation. After the wedding and their daughter's death, he said, they had agreed he would return to England ahead of Eleanor to smooth things over with his parents before sending for her. As soon as he left, the impatient (and by then pregnant) Eleanor had got on the very next ship and arrived in London a few days after him. She had always overruled him like this: even their marriage had been hurried and insisted upon by her. On her arrival in London she had defied his wishes and written to his father, who was furious to hear of their secret marriage and chose to pretend it had never happened. He insisted Rourke's mother should certainly never know, she being of fragile health. Thereafter, Rourke continued to reside at his father's house as a single man, seeing Eleanor when he could and fathering Alice. He took the house in Holloway in 1884 – his mother having died by then and there being no further need for secrecy – and introduced Eleanor to his family. He got the marriage licence because the family thought it better that he and Eleanor return to Australia where the government was offering land orders in Queensland to married couples and to qualify they needed to prove they had never lived in Australia before. He had thought a marriage under his real name would be sufficient to prove this. He was aware it was a fraud and he was sorry he had perpetrated it. His brother had offered to pay their fare but in the end they did not go.

Thereafter his life with Eleanor was a nightmare due to her violent temper. She deserted him in 1888, taking the children with her. Three weeks later she brought them back, saying she could not cope. She then attempted suicide at Colney Hatch railway station, for which she was charged at the Westminster police court but received no sentence (the magistrate taking pity on her) and had a spell in Islington workhouse before she went to New York. Her various appeals for her children on her return resulted in many personal assaults on Rourke and another on his brother Robert in April 1889, for which Eleanor was bound over to keep the peace for six months at the Mansion House. Two weeks later she broke a plate-glass window at the warehouse where his brother Francis worked when her demands to see him were frustrated, for which she was again bound over and released on her own recognisances in the sum of £10. Unable to raise this she was sent to Millbank Prison. The family paid her bail bond and after her release she attempted suicide a second time at Charing Cross station and was taken by Rourke to hospital. In all these interactions with the various authorities she had given her name as Eleanor or Ellen Rourke and she had written home from America signing her letters Nellie Rourke. One letter was produced, and a card sent in the name 'Mrs E.G. Rourke'. Rourke concluded his evidence by claiming that it was only after her release from hospital, when she was taken in by the Sisters of Mercy in London's East End, that she invented the story about Thompson; since then she had made his and his family's life a living hell.

It was true that in the course of their dispute Eleanor had dragged the beleaguered Rourke before a total of sixteen different tribunals, but putting aside all moral judgement of her methods and 'madness', the essence of her story was always the same: she was a mother denied access to her children – in part through her own actions, but also through Rourke's determined efforts to keep them apart. Justice Barnes fully admitted that both parties were disadvantaged by having to approach the court as paupers because neither could afford to finance a commission to Australia to ascertain the truth about the Melbourne marriage. He pressed Eleanor to produce any evidence at all as to the existence of Thompson – a letter, a photo – but she claimed such items had all been sent to a private inquiry agent in Australia who was searching for him. She had witnesses to the fact that she was known in Holloway and Camden as Mrs Thompson and Rourke as Rourke, but this was overcome by Rourke's witnesses: a housing agent who testified that they had taken a house together in the name Thompson before 1884; and an official from Islington workhouse who produced her admission statement, which specified not only that her name was Eleanor Rourke but that she was the wife of Arthur Henry Rourke who was the father of her children. Though the marriage itself could not be proved, by the law of jactitation acquiescence in it was sufficient. This Eleanor had obviously done. Indeed, in her appearance at the Guildhall she had gone further. When Francis Rourke expressed doubts about it during the hearing she had clearly stated, 'I was married to him, though.' On 21 November 1892, Eleanor's jactitation petition was dismissed.

Yet neither was this the 'last scene' in the saga. So often did Eleanor flit between the Queen's Bench, the appeal court and Chancery in attempts to gain access to her children; and so often did she make a scene – on one occasion being manhandled out of Central Hall, screaming and shouting as she went that they wanted her to throw herself off Blackfriars' Bridge but she wouldn't: she would buy a gun and shoot Rourke and be hanged for it, but at least her children would be free – that thereafter she appeared in the papers as 'Poor Mrs Thompson'. In February 1894, having exhausted the patience of all courts, the Lord Chief Justice himself, Lord Coleridge, took up the case and he and Justice Day reportedly gave her a whole morning of their time, thinking maybe there was 'something in it'. They found there wasn't; and when Lord Esher told her so Eleanor told him he was 'a wicked old man and ought to be hanged by the neck until he was dead'. Court attendants were ordered to prevent her gaining any further access to the courts, but that didn't prevent her trying and in June she struck an attendant in the face with her umbrella and was summoned before the Bow Street magistrate and once again bound over to keep the peace. Still this did not keep her away: 'I shall come here as often as I like,' she told them when they were forced to expel her yet again. 'Really, Mrs Thompson is Irrepressible,' ran the headline.

It must be noted that as pauper petitioners go Eleanor was the exception to the rule. Her campaign would have been impossible had she not lived in London and had she to work for her subsistence. As it was, she was sustained in the destitution caused by her monomania at various state workhouses and charitable refuges. She was also shown extraordinary latitude by the courts who pitied her, but it behoves us to question her primary motivation when it is taken into account that the thing that finally stopped her was Rourke's sudden death in November 1896. He had been found by a policeman lying in the road and taken to Shoreditch infirmary where he died. The last scene in the saga turned out to be his inquest, where the coroner ruled that he had died as a result of a stroke accelerated by want and exposure. An infirmary attendant testified that Rourke had been in a horrible, filthy condition when admitted – half-starved and with ulcerated legs. His brother Edward stated that Rourke, too, had not worked for twelve years and had been maintained by his family; that he had been destitute for some time and that Edward had been giving him 3s 6d a week. On his person were found a bundle of press cuttings from the case and some letters and pawn tickets for sundry remnants of cloth: the last of his possessions. The letters revealed that the family had latterly thought Edward's charity was doing Rourke more harm than good. They had wanted him to go into the infirmary sooner but he wouldn't, fearful that Eleanor would find the children and take them. It had become as much a monomania with him and he had sacrificed himself in their defence. The children had been at the heart of matter but were they the cause or had this become a personal vendetta on one or both sides? Nothing was heard of Mrs Thompson again. Had she achieved what she set out to do, separating her children from a man she believed to be abusive? Or had she simply run out of money or the will to fight? In the end the law defeated her as convincingly as it had Henrietta Trower. What became of her or Alice is not known, but her son, Arthur, emigrated to Canada where he married and became a photographer and died at age seventy.

The tragic sagas of Henrietta Trower and Eleanor Thompson were the most extreme of those presented by working-class petitioners. Others who managed to raise sufficient funds to escape their unhappy unions and did not excite the fascination of the press quietly went about their business. In recent years historians have expressed astonishment that working-class petitions should account for even a third of all those filed when earlier commentators always regarded divorce as a decadence only available to the affluent. Gail Savage puts this down in part to the 'precariousness and sexual antagonism that characterised [their] marital relationship', which 'could easily erupt into violence and cruelty'.[26] Her point is substantiated by the thousands of applicants for separation and maintenance orders, which were thirty times more numerous than working-class divorce petitions and whose applicants had to be either the victims of marital violence or neglect to qualify. It defies reason to suppose that working-class wives would have chosen a separation order over a divorce had the latter relief been more accessible; and with the odds stacked so highly against them and the numbers of working-class divorce petitioners still significantly disproportionately low, it was inevitable that at a time when the plight of the working class was increasingly taken up by campaigners, eventually the deficiencies of the British system of matrimonial law as compared to the Scottish would be challenged in the name of equality and justice. The only surprise was that when the campaign kicked off in earnest at the start of the twentieth century it was led not as one might suppose, by a group of indignant middle-class reformers, but by a very disgruntled peer of the realm.

11

The Doors Widen

Mr Boom ruminated a while.

'What am I to do?' said the distressed husband.

'I was coming to that. The position is that someone has to commit intimacy for the general good; someone has to behave impurely in order to uphold the Christian ideal of purity; someone has to confess in public to a sinful breach of the marriage vows, in order that the happily married may point at him or her and feel themselves secure and virtuous. The delinquent, you say, is not to be your wife; therefore it must be yourself. You cannot commit intimacy by yourself: there must be A Woman. But it is not, you say, to be the woman you would like to marry. Therefore you must be intimate with some woman whom you do not wish to marry ... Now, is there any other woman you would care to be intimate with?'

A. P. Herbert, *Holy Deadlock* (1934)

The disgruntled peer was, of course, Earl Russell – the grandson and heir of Lord John Russell, the prime minister responsible for calling the 1852 Campbell Commission – whose attempt to introduce divorce by mutual consent this book opened with. The presentation of his bill to amend the laws relating to marriage, divorce and legitimacy delivered on 1 May 1902 was Russell's first major speech in the House of Lords, though he had taken up his seat in 1887. The saga of his life in between – of his being party to one of the most complex, scandalous and sensational divorce suits of the era – would have had a greater presence in this book than the brief references to it had I not already written extensively about it in *Bertrand's Brother*. It culminated in his spectacular trial for bigamy in the House of Lords in July 1901 and his conviction and three-month imprisonment in Holloway. It was a bruising experience for Russell and raised the hackles of his already deeply embedded sense of injustice. Almost his first undertaking on his release was to set his not inconsiderable intellect to the inadequacies of the 'draconian' law that he felt put him there.

As an agnostic rationalist who considered the Church's influence on social policy baleful, it was Russell's opinion that the problem with the existing law stemmed from the insistence of the 1857 lawmakers that the divorce court should operate in accordance with the ecclesiastical courts that went before it. Such deference Russell considered outmoded at the dawn of the modern age and in drawing up his proposal he asked himself what a rational system of divorce would look like if it was freed from what he regarded as ecclesiastical superstitions. The answer was audacious and uncompromising – and not just for being presented to the very people who had sent him down less than a year earlier.

Russell proposed that in addition to adultery (and incest, bigamy, sodomy and rape), cruelty and three years living apart – whether through desertion, imprisonment or certification for incurable insanity – ought to be grounds for divorce for men and women equally. Then, of course, there was the provision for couples who had lived apart for a year or more to be allowed to divorce by mutual consent. Widening the grounds for divorce rendered unnecessary the judicial separations that kept couples in a sort of half-married state, so his bill dispensed with those; and in allowing divorce by mutual consent, all reference to collusion became redundant and with it the proctor's role. No proctor, no need for such a long period before making a decree *nisi* absolute: Russell proposed reducing it to one month from six in all cases where there was no appeal. Mutual consent also conflicted with the whole principle of forcing couples to cohabit, so out went the provision for restitution of conjugal rights. As regards damages, he thought if men were allowed to claim them, so should women be, so his bill made co-respondents of men's lovers and brought equality to the rule. Jactitation he replaced with a simplified petition for declaring a marriage had not been solemnised. And for those with an income of £500 a year or less, he suggested allowing county courts jurisdiction, thereby considerably reducing the cost and inconvenience to the poor. Finally, for good measure, Russell proposed the abolition of the prohibition of marriage with a deceased wife's sister and the legitimising of illegitimate children by their parents' subsequent marriage as was the law in Scotland, thereby leaving, as it were, no matrimonial stone unturned.[1]

Underpinning Russell's proposal were sentiments more at home in radical publishing houses and progressive journals than the Lords – the bastion of establishment – and the effect could not have been greater had Russell taken up a copy of Walter Gallichan's *The Blight of Respectability* (1897) and told their lordships that for Britain to progress in the twentieth century a 'new morality, more reasonable, just, and humane' was needed to replace 'the old which has passed away': the old which viewed divorce as immoral, which professed to adhere to Christian principles but was characterised by an 'intellectual insincerity and social hypocrisy' that allowed Victorian gentlemen to visit prostitutes while considering themselves faithful husbands, and which had given birth to the divorce law's sexual double standard. In his book Gallichan had called for more brave-hearted men and women, more heterodox thinkers and consistent heretics 'to stand together in a great attack on the shams and falsehoods that constitute Respectability'.[2] This Russell was doing, but to the establishment (to reapply the phrase Dickens put into the mouth of Josiah Bounderby of Coketown when his 'steady Hand' claimed a right to divorce) his action was nothing short of an attempt to 'knock Religion over, and floor the Established Church', which must be resisted at all costs.[3] His 'outrageous' and 'insulting' proposal was rejected outright. The press largely agreed with the lord chancellor that Russell had gone too far – the liberal *Daily News* commenting that to treat marriage so lightly was 'to strike a deadly blow at national morals'. But Russell was not a man easily deterred. He returned the following year with the same proposal but without the offending clause. It was rejected. In 1905, there he was again with 'a very considerably modified' bill 'in deference to the feelings of the House' proposing the simple addition of divorce for desertion. Again, it was rejected; as was his final attempt in 1908. But all these were small steps on the road to inevitable reform.[4]

Stephen Cretney's seminal *Family Law in the Twentieth Century* (2003) makes the point that the ultimate success of the reform campaign depended upon particular individuals voicing the right message at the right time, expressed in such a manner as to not antagonise or upset the established order. Russell did not possess such a gift. Though eventually all the major points of his first reform bill would be enacted, it required others with greater diplomacy to further the cause. The first of these was a young solicitor and future man of letters named E. S. P. Haynes who engineered a meeting with Russell in 1905, became his personal secretary and then manoeuvred Russell out of the frontline where he was a target for anti-reformers due to his personal history. Russell had established a society in December 1902, to bolster, give voice and add momentum to his campaign. Haynes convinced him to amalgamate it with another that had popped up independently. Together they became the Divorce Law Reform Union, an organisation in which Russell took a backseat. The DLRU set about demanding a royal commission to investigate the state of the law and proved influential for the next three decades. In the 1910s they boasted 300 to 400 members, including 'some persons of position'.[5] Haynes brought its activities to the attention of one such who would add great weight to the cause.

John Gorell Barnes, appointed president of Probate, Divorce and Admiralty in 1905, had been conscious when he first became a judge in the division that his knowledge of divorce law was wanting. A conscientious man, he'd set himself the task of studying its history as far back as the Reformation and, just as Russell had, came to the conclusion there were fundamental flaws. Barnes was known as a liberal judge; as a man who, wherever possible, didn't allow technicalities or the letter of the law to intervene and inhibit fair play, making full use of his judicial discretion. One example of this was the Coombes suit of 1897 in which he allowed the petitioning carpenter a divorce despite the fact that he had committed adultery and fathered an illegitimate child during a five-year period when the co-respondent had evaded being served with a petition. But when in 1905 Barnes' hands were tied in the case of *Dodd* v. *Dodd*, he took the opportunity to voice his frustration.

It would be difficult to imagine a suit that better demonstrates the muddle the law had become after the introduction of the two-tier system than the Dodd suit. It was brought by Mrs Fanny Dodd, who had married Manchester wholesale provision merchant James Arthur Dodd in 1891. The suit was undefended, but according to Fanny's evidence, by 1896 Dodd had given way to drink and ceased to provide for her and their four-year-old son, choosing instead to allow Fanny to maintain him. As a result, Fanny left him in August 1896 and returned to her mother. In September she applied to a magistrate in Manchester for a separation order which was granted on the grounds of wilful neglect and failure to provide reasonable maintenance. Henceforth, Fanny was no longer bound to live with Dodd and Dodd was ordered to pay her 10s a week. Despite attempts to enforce the order, he never paid. So in 1905, after Fanny discovered he was living with a Mrs Butler, she filed a petition for divorce on the ground of adultery aggravated by desertion.

When the case came before Barnes on 19 December 1905 he immediately saw a legal difficulty and referred it to the proctor in order that counsel could be appointed to argue any questions relating to law. Barnes heard these arguments on 9 March 1906 and on 27 April delivered his verdict. He ruled that Fanny's divorce could not be granted because technically Dodd had not deserted. The very fact that the magistrate's order no longer bound Fanny to live with him precluded this, even though Dodd had never paid a penny towards her upkeep. In her divorce petition Fanny had specifically stated that there had been 'no previous proceedings instituted in the Divorce Division' concerning their suit. Ironically, if there had been the outcome would have been different. If Fanny had not gone to the magistrate but taken the other route open to her (illogical though it may be) and applied to the divorce court for an order for restitution of her conjugal rights in the hope that Dodd would ignore it, she could then have obtained a judicial separation on the ground of his failure to return (an action that *did* amount to desertion) and have it upgraded to a divorce on proof of his adultery.

These 'inconsistencies, anomalies and inequalities' in the law 'almost amounted to absurdities' declared Barnes, going well beyond his province and passing sentence on the law as well as the suit. Though the question of grounds for divorce was 'extremely difficult', he further expressed the opinion that no reform would be 'effective and adequate' that fell short of abolishing permanent separation as distinct from divorce, that did not put the sexes on an equal footing and that did not allow divorce for 'such definite grave causes of offence as render future cohabitation impracticable and frustrate the object of marriage'. He concluded his comments by stating that it would have given Fanny no satisfaction to hear that had her suit been brought in Scotland 'or most other civilized countries' it would have succeeded.[6]

The impact of Barnes' damning indictment has been likened to Justice Maule's 1845 sentencing of working-class bigamist Thomas Hall. On that occasion, Maule had listened to the unfortunate man's mitigating claims – his needing to find a new wife to care for his children after their drunken, dissolute mother had deserted them and of him being too poor to legally divorce – before relaying to Hall the convoluted path he should have taken to avoid falling afoul of the law and sentencing him to what he regarded a fitting punishment for his crime: a single day's imprisonment. Maule's satirical speech was afterwards credited with bringing about the 1852 Campbell Commission: Barnes' comments ultimately saw him lead the commission called in 1910.[7]

Meanwhile in another quarter, within months of the Dodd verdict, another aspect of the system came under attack with the publication of the first novel entirely about divorce: Arnold Bennett's *Whom God Hath Joined*. Its plot follows the respective marriage breakdowns of a provincial solicitor and his clerk and in so doing emphasises the sordid nature of divorce court proceedings and the humiliation experienced by parties having their private lives made public. It was a novel Bennett was commissioned to write by specialist publisher Alfred Nutt and an unusual subject for Nutt, whose list was predominantly devoted to folklore and antiquities. By setting it in the Five Towns amid the Staffordshire Potteries and putting through the wringer characters more relatable to his readers than the decadent affluent classes whose cases filled newspapers, Bennett brought the realities of divorce home. The horrifying realisations of the clerk on entering the court (for which see the epigraph at the beginning of this book) conveyed the foremost message of Bennett's novel: that it is the innocent who suffer the indignity of divorce, not the wrongdoers – a point he drives home by making the solicitor's daughter (aptly named Annunciata) the principle witness for her mother.

On publication, the novel was described as dealing with an 'unpleasant' subject with a 'power and realism' it would be 'hypocritical and ridiculous' to ignore.[8] Retrospectively it has been called a 'moving piece of propaganda for a more humane law' and an appeal for generosity in moral judgements.[9] Alongside other works – like the first instalment of Galsworthy's *Forsyte Saga* published the same year – forward-looking Edwardian novels questioned the morality of patriarchal dominance in the home; asked their readers to consider what the object of 'true marriage' really was; and also to recognise the role of divorce in achieving it. In reiterating sentiments expressed by John Milton three hundred years earlier concerning the 'heinous barbarism' of forcing unsuited spouses to live together, advocates of divorce reform – be they social campaigners or novelists – claimed the moral high ground from late Victorian puritans who condemned divorce as destructive. They revealed the speciousness of the mid-Victorian argument that divorce was immoral and scandals and sensations essential to prevent a social revolution. With plays like Bernard Shaw's satirical *Getting Married* (1908) – the first to treat English divorce farcically – a more pragmatic approach was called for that reflected both Milton's realism – that 'all the ecclesiastical glue will not hold together two people of incongruous natures' – and recognised that the whole question of divorce had ceased to be a scriptural dilemma and become a social problem.[10]

The result was the calling of the Barnes Commission which heard evidence between 25 February 1910 and 17 May 1911 from diverse witnesses from the legal and medical professions, representatives of all religious denominations, the press and various relevant charitable societies and pressure groups. Women also entered the debate for the first time, both as witnesses and through the selection of two well-known women's rights campaigners as commissioners: the suffragist Lady Frances Balfour and May Tennant, sister-in-law by marriage of Prime Minister Asquith. The questions they considered reflected Barnes' critique of the law in the Dodd suit, with provisions for the poor, grounds for divorce and the publication of reports high on the agenda. Barnes worked hard for a consensus, but with such a contentious issue the odds were stacked against him. The majority report dated 2 November 1912 was eventually signed by nine of the twelve commissioners and recommended more-or-less the same as Russell ten years earlier – divorce for adultery, cruelty, desertion, long-term imprisonment and confinement for incurable insanity – but drew the line at abolishing judicial separation or embracing the still very offensive divorce by mutual consent.[11] Differing from Russell, imprisonment had to be under a commuted death sentence to qualify and an insane spouse must have been confined for five years.

There were also recommendations for habitual drunkenness to be added to the grounds for divorce, for 'cruelty' to be more clearly defined, and for concealment of various chronic diseases – epilepsy, recurrent insanity or venereal disease – or a wife's pregnancy by another man at the time of the marriage to be added as grounds for annulment. Such provisions reflected both the limitations of medicine at the time and the popularity of eugenics. Procedural changes included giving structure to Russell's county court proposal as well as abolishing trial by jury and restricting reporting of cases to the end of a hearing at the judge's discretion. The judge's discretion was also extended to clearing the courtroom of reporters and spectators at any point during proceedings.

The three dissenting commissioners did not disagree on all points. They backed the increased provision for nullity, equality of the sexes as regards adultery, the county court provision and restricted reporting, but considered the additional grounds for divorce to be, if not quite accepting the right to divorce on the ground of mutual aversion, then at least paving the way for it. While the majority report claimed their recommendations were necessary in the interests of morality and justice, the minority claimed to uphold the interests of family, church and state and implied that the majority had been excessively influenced by tales of individual hardships when the collective evidence indicated that there was no 'large or widespread demand for change other than changes of procedure'.[12] But neither could the minority claim to speak for the interests of the whole religious community despite them all having strong ties to the Church.[13] There had been no consensus among ecclesiastical witnesses as to the indissolubility of marriage. Liberal clerics tended to consider New Testament scriptures dealing with the subject 'a moral ideal rather than a positive rule' and suggested that the Church ought to be able to acquiesce as to grounds for divorce, allowing 'carefully restricted exceptions', while orthodox Christians took a stricter line.[14] Moreover, the majority commissioners found that lay people based their views 'not upon ecclesiastical tradition or sentiment, but upon general Christian principles, coupled with common sense and experience of the needs of human life'.[15]

Who was right? If it is at all possible to gauge public opinion by press reactions then it seems as if the populace were as divided as the commissioners. Certainly the press were. The minority report made it easy for centre-ground papers to back the county court recommendation and equality of the sexes but the extending of grounds was more contentious. While the *Daily Mirror* reported that the DLRU were cock-a-hoop at the majority report – their president Sir Arthur Conan Doyle calling the result 'a common sense triumph' – both the liberal *Daily News* and *Westminster Gazette* suggested desertion and cruelty should pose no difficulty but were dubious about the other recommendations. The conservative *Evening News* claimed that the 'sense of the nation' would be with the minority who were 'few but influential'; and the *Evening Standard* called the minority's arguments against extending divorce 'weighty'. *The Times* went further still. Applauding the manner in which the minority had kept principles 'steadily before them' while the majority seemed to have forgotten 'that complete and immediate redress of all the evil and all the suffering caused by unhappy marriages would not compensate the community as a whole for any degradation in its conception of marriage or any laxity in its condemnation of dubious divorce', they threw their great weight behind the minority by printing its report in full and taking out a full-page advertisement to the fact in the *Standard*. Radical papers retaliated by calling the minority report 'a piece of interesting mediaeval scholasticism' (*Daily Herald*) and complained that the whole system of appointing commissions was 'designed to still the clamour for real and effective social reform' (*Reynolds's*). The *Westminster Gazette* and *Reynolds's* called for an immediate bill in line with the majority report but *John Bull* cynically suggested the government would probably be 'too busy' to implement it. Perhaps they were right. Despite the Liberal government's large majority and Herbert Asquith's personal support for equality and procedural changes (he drew the line at divorce for permanent insanity, expressing the opinion it would lead to 'an immense increase in the number of people certified'[16]), they had no appetite to confront any challenging ethical questions or relive the heated debates of the 1850s, and after much prevarication – including refusing to countenance several private members bills on 'so important a subject' – the outbreak of war saved them from having to take a stand one way or the other.[17]

After the war, reform was slow in coming. In fact, given where we are today, it may be surprising to learn just how far into the twentieth century Victorian divorce survived. Despite sustained campaigning by the DLRU, who published pamphlets and held meetings to educate the public and saw their membership rise to 1,700 by 1919; despite Russell continuing to make persuasive arguments in reputable journals and more frustrated appeals in *John Bull* ('The divorce laws of this country are absurd!'[18]); and despite new well-placed figures entering the fray, most notably a former Lord Chancellor, Lord Buckmaster, who introduced a bill the day after the Armistice was signed to allow divorce on the ground of five years' desertion or separation under a court order, there was no change to the law until 1920.

When it came it was piecemeal and largely unsatisfactory. In 1920 procedural changes allowed assize judges to hear divorce suits – not quite the county court recommendation, but a step towards it (and necessitated by a backlog of cases that mounted during the war). In 1923, equality of the sexes was introduced for all subsequent acts of adultery. In 1926, much of the scandal and sensation attached to divorce finally came to an end with the Judicial Proceedings (Regulation of Reports) Act which restricted reporting of cases to their basic facts: name, address and occupation of parties and witnesses; a concise statement of charges, defences and counter-charges; any points of law arising, the summing-up and judgment. Any 'indecent' matters or medical details or anything 'calculated to injure public morals' was strictly forbidden. Such an Act, if passed sooner, would have prohibited half the contents of this book! But not until 1937 did the grounds for divorce in England and Wales finally change.

Cretney identified three key reasons for this. First, whatever the diversity of opinions voiced to the commission, the Roman

Catholic and Anglican churches remained doctrinally opposed to increasing the scope of divorce and influential church groups, such as the Mother's Union, seemed to convey to women that divorce was contrary to their best interests. Secondly, divorce reform was a cross-party issue that no single parliamentary party was willing to get behind. In his *John Bull* article Russell blamed lack of reform on the 'cowardice' of the Labour Party, but Cretney points out that they and the Liberals were inhibited by their large number of Catholic supporters in industrial cities. Thirdly, there were disagreements among reformers as to what was achievable. Some thought they should push for nothing less than the recommendations of the majority report while others were more reticent. The reticent point was proved by the failure of a bill introduced in 1921 to enact the recommendations on which the majority and minority reports agreed. Radicals in the House of Lords – Buckmaster and Russell principally – inserted an amendment adding divorce for desertion which the Commons would not countenance. When the 1923 bill was procured from a completely different source – it was backed by the National Union of Societies for Equal Citizenship – it was 'difficult if not impossible' to find plausible grounds to resist it, though it was considered woefully inadequate.[19] The net effect was to rob the campaign of the support of those predominantly concerned with sexual equality and, though campaigners continued to highlight hardships caused by an inadequate divorce provision, in the end it seems to have been the question of morality (or immorality) that eventually won the day. In this, the essential protagonist was author and humourist A. P. Herbert.

It is interesting to note how, on each occasion, widening the doors to the divorce court, even ever so slightly, had unforeseen consequences. The 1884 amendment that made non-compliance with a restitution order within a fortnight equivalent to desertion resulted in a significant increase in parties petitioning for orders they did not want to enable them to circumvent the rule that desertion must be of two years' duration to qualify. When the 1923 Act enabled women to divorce on the single ground of adultery there was a similar increase in what became known as 'hotel divorces', in which couples colluded to get a divorce by the husband agreeing to 'do the right thing' and take an obliging woman to a hotel to commit (or not) the single act of adultery necessary for his wife to divorce him. Brighton – through its proximity to London and its 'anything goes' atmosphere – became a hotspot for such arrangements, which were brilliantly satirised by Herbert in his 1934 novel *Holy Deadlock*. The 'distressed husband' of the novel, under the advice of his solicitor (the Mr Boom quoted at the start of this chapter), goes to a 'secretarial agency' to find the requisite woman for this 'intimacy'. Ultimately, their liaison amounts to nothing more than a dinner in a hotel restaurant, an uncomfortable night's sleep for the husband on a couch in the young lady's hotel bedroom and leaping into her bed at the crucial moment so that the maid bringing their breakfast might witness the 'crime'. The book had wide appeal, selling some 90,000 copies and highlighting, as nothing like wit can, the ludicrousness of the law. The point was made still further when in 1936 a certain Mrs Simpson apparently used Herbert's book as a 'how to' guide, suing her husband for a hotel divorce at the Suffolk assizes so that she might marry King Edward VIII and upset the establishment far more than the government following the recommendations of the majority report in 1912 ever could. The following year cruelty, desertion and incurable insanity were legislated as grounds for divorce and wilful refusal for nullity. As a nod to the Church, except in cases of extreme hardship or depravity, petitioners must have been married for three years before they could approach the court.

Aside from the king's actions, it seems that the element missing on previous occasions that won the day in 1937 was public opinion. The fact that couples must by definition collude over a hotel divorce led to the perception that it had been the immoral who had benefitted most from the 1923 Act (a hotel divorce was divorce by mutual consent in all but name), not the most needful. The 1937 Act was an attempt to address this by finally acknowledging that there were other offenses as bad if not worse than sexual betrayal. But although Victorian restriction of grounds for divorce were lifted in 1937, the fact that fault in divorce survived meant the stigma associated with it did too. Despite divorce becoming more normal, with over 5,000 petitions filed annually in the years between the implementation of the 1937 Act and the outbreak of the Second World War – a figure that increased sevenfold by the early 1950s – my own respectable working-class mother-in-law would still feel the effects of it years later. She was never spoken to again by a cousin she had been close to all her life after she divorced her husband for adultery – and that was in 1969. But to the more liberal minded, the statistics merely represented a truer picture. It was better to acknowledge that spousal mistakes happen; that some marriages do not survive the turmoil of life; that 'true marriage' should not be a life sentence. This was as true in the twentieth century as in Milton's time. Human nature did not change. But attitudes did; and as regards divorce, the next most important attitudinal shift was the one that saw the extension of Milton's claim to the right to rectify a mistake in marriage into the right to change one's mind. The option of divorce by mutual consent – the last and most objectionable of Earl Russell's 1902 recommendations – was finally legislated in 1969 and became law in 1971.

Here we might legitimately mark the end of Victorian divorce. Since then, the nature of society and the manner in which we formalise (or not) our intimate personal relationships has changed beyond recognition, but the fact of human beings aspiring to a helpmeet of one description or another has not. In 1686, legal writer Henry Swinburne defined marriage as 'a present and a perfect Consent'.[20] Strictly speaking, he was making a distinction between two people who either are or who act as if they are married and those affianced to marry at some future time. A hundred years later his words were recalled by the wise High Court judge Lord Stowell in considering the question of whether marriage was a civil or sacred contract. Stowell concluded it was neither, but 'a contract according to the law of nature, antecedent to civil institution, and which may take place to all intents and purposes, wherever two persons of different sexes engage, by mutual consent, to live together'.[21] Nowadays, the sex distinction makes no difference to the principle. The important word then as now is 'consent'. The nature of that consent was questioned in an editorial in *The Guardian* in 1912, following the publication of the majority report. Modern unions, it suggested, were no longer based on the supremacy of the husband but on 'mutual respect and affection'. They still involved a marriage ceremony, which remained a sacrament to parties 'in a new and perhaps deeper sense'.[22] The view was advanced for its time and the vision expressed in the editorial remarkably similar to the next major divorce law reform, legislated in 1996 but ultimately deemed 'unworkable'. The abandoned legislation offered funding for marriage counselling for potential divorcees, made attendance at 'information meetings' compulsory and introduced an enforced period of further reflection before allowing, in all instances, parties to proceed with no-fault divorces.[23]

It is with some irony that the current Act, which took effect in April 2022, was only brought about by another well-timed speech by another president of what is now the Family Division of the High Court. In 2016, Sir James Munby complained that the law he and his colleagues practised was based on 'hypocrisy and lack of intellectual honesty' because those unwilling to wait the requisite two years to divorce by mutual consent obtained a fault-based divorce 'by means of a consensual, collusive, manipulation' of the 1969 Act – in essence, by inventing marital offences former reformers had spent decades trying to abolish, thereby making collusion 'the very foundation of countless petitions and decrees'.[24] It is a double irony that Munby's criticisms found support in *The Times*, which had for so many years fought against reformers and now called for 'urgent reform'.[25] Collectively, the divorce these campaigners and their compatriots brought about is divorce without scandal or sensation, pretension or blame. Its effects remain to be seen.

Notes

Data in this book, unless otherwise specified, is taken from the author's own systematic sample, referred to throughout as 'the 1881–1900 sample' and comprising every twentieth petition filed with the court between those inclusive dates:

Petitions/Petitioners	Husband	Wife	Total
Divorce	340	225	565
Nullity	13	15	28
Judicial Separation	2	108	110
Restitution of conjugal rights	2	13	15
Other			4
Totals	357	361	722

For featured cases, primary sources are divorce court files held at the National Archives, Kew; *The Law Reports* (Probate Division); and contemporary newspapers. In each instance, *The Times* was consulted first, and afterwards the following London papers, chosen to give a cross-spectrum of reporting: *The Daily News* (DN), *Evening News* (EN); *Evening Standard* (ES); *Globe* (GL); *Lloyd's Weekly News* (LWN); *Morning Post* (MP); *Pall Mall Gazette* (PMG); *Reynolds's Newspaper* (RN); *St James's Gazette* (SJG); *The Star*; *The Telegraph*; and *The Westminster Gazette* (WG).

Certain provincial newspapers regularly extensively reported cases and were used often. These include the *Manchester Guardian* (MG); *Western Daily Press* (WDP, Bristol); *Western Mail* (WM, Cardiff); *Edinburgh Evening News* (EEN).

In all cases, provincial papers from regions in which the parties were known were consulted. By this method, some eighty national and provincial papers were used. Other journals and publications consulted include: *The Bat*; *Fortnightly Review*; *The Graphic*; *Hawk*; *John Bull*; *London Gazette*; *Modern Society*; *Review of Reviews*; *Saturday Review*; *Truth*; *Vanity Fair* (VF).

Introduction
1. Coalition For Marriage quoted in Fairbairn, p.22.
2. Peter Hitchens, *Mail online*, 9 Apr 2022, available at https://www.dailymail.co.uk/debate/article-10703147/PETER-HITCHENS-Marriage-binding-car-lease-children-suffer.html (accessed 4 Jan 2023).
3. Milton, p.18, p.21.

1 The Doors Open
1. Inderwick, p. vii.
2. Stone, p. 187-190, p. 432.
3. Cretney, p.163.
4. The Lord Chancellor, Lord Cranworth, voiced this opinion on introducing the Bill into the House of Lords, *Hansard* vol.145, col.490; the rebuff came from Grey, p.784.
5. Sir George Bowyer, *Hansard*, vol.160 c.1746.
6. Fenn, p.88.
7. Facts concerning newspapers from Brake & Demoor unless otherwise specified.
8. Humpherys, p.221.
9. *The Times*, 5 Apr 1884.
10. Burnham, p.86.
11. *ibid*.
12. Fenn, p.291.
13. *Saturday Review*, 27 Apr 1861, p.419.
14. *Friends' Review*, vol. XVI, p.603.
15. Conboy, p.120.
16. Berridge, p.188-9.

17. Matthews & Mellini, p.11.
18. Bourne, p.312.
19. Victoria, p.378.
20. Brake & Demoor, p.172.
21. Weeks, p.86; Fisher, p.5.
22. Juxon, p.15.
23. O'Brien, p.2; LWN, 8 Nov 1896; Lord Bowen, quoted in O'Brien, p.95.
24. O'Brien, p.101.
25. Smalley, p.181; Fenn, p.59.
26. Russell, *Life*, p.165; Fenn, p.63.
27. Walker-Smith, p.9-10.
28. Lord Maugham quoted in Walker-Smith, p.6.
29. Fenn, p.64.
30. Balfour-Browne, p.145-6.
31. Russell's earnings: O'Brien, p.267-8; Clarke's from Clarke, p.259. Estimates of nominal earnings: Williamson, p.48. Refreshers: Balfour Browne p.207; *Hawk* 18 Jun 1889, p.654. Juniors' retainers: TS 29/4, p.348.
32. VF, 31 Jul 1886.
33. Reflections on James Hannen: Annual Register 1894; VF, 31 Jul 1886; criticisms of Charles Butt: VF, 18 Sep 1886.
34. Howard, pp.716-7: in most instances, a Crown case 'more nearly resembles an ordinary lawsuit between complainant and defendant than a proceeding instituted and carried on by a sovereign power. For not only are there no local public officials charged by general law with the duty of superintending the conduct of criminal cases in either the courts of summary jurisdiction or the higher courts of trial, but there is no uniform method obtaining throughout the country by which these cases are conducted.'

2 Marry in Haste... (The Problem of Unsuitable Wives)
1. Himmelfarb, p.22.
2. Frost, p.3.
3. Wells, *Experiment*, p.438.
4. Grey, p.778.
5. Grand, p.387 referencing Elizabeth Rachel Chapman, *Marriage Questions in Modern Fiction* (1897).
6. Quoted in introduction to Virago edition, p. iii.

7. Probert, p.227.
8. The practice of eloping to Gretna Green was made harder after an 1865 law stated that the couple must have been resident in Scotland for more than twenty-one days beforehand for the marriage to be legally binding.
9. *Telegraph*, 27 Jan 1870.
10. 'orse' is legal shorthand for 'otherwise'.
11. *Modern Society*, 12 Jan 1884, p.101.
12. *Life* quoted in EEN, 12 Mar 1884.
13. *Modern Society*, 19 Apr 1884.
14. Sievier, p.125.
15. Bingham, p.12.
16. *Times*, 25 Jul 1890.
17. MP, 29 Jul 1890.
18. *Hawk*, 18 Mar 1890, p.302.
19. WM, 1 Dec 1892.
20. Fenn, p.292.
21. *Hawk*, 5 Aug 1890.
22. Bence-Jones, p.94.
23. *ibid*. Information on Clancarty Estate from Casey, p.174-180.
24. *Telegraph*, 1 Jan 1907; MG, 2 Jan 1907.
25. *Hawk*, 5 Aug 1890.
26. Humpherys, p.228.

3 ... Repent at Leisure (The Problem of Unsuitable Husbands)
1. Or failure to comply with a restitution order after 1884.
2. Lewis, p.649.
3. Black, p.591.
4. Details of the sample summarised above. Data from earlier periods in Wright, p.997 and Stone, p.425. N.B. 19 per cent of wives' petitions for judicial separation alleged adultery which would have been sufficient for a full divorce had the applicants been men; and 14 per cent charged aggravated adultery, for which the wives could have sued for divorce but chose not to. Some such choices had a religious basis but others were interpreted as vindictive – either to prevent their husbands remarrying or to continue to receive lifelong alimony awarded with a judicial separation but not a divorce (Russell, *Divorce* p.41).
5. Biggs, p.131.

6. Stowell's judgment in *Evans* v. *Evans* [1790], Hammerton, p.273; discussed in Biggs, p.24-27, p.41.
7. Biggs, p.19.
8. NA, J 77/493/15032.
9. RC *Evidence* I, p.175, p.179.
10. J 77/553/16900.
11. J 77/484/14736.
12. J 77/537/16401.
13. LWN, 29 Nov 1896.
14. Fenn, pp.27-32.
15. LWN, 29 Nov 1896.
16. DN, 6 Mar 1893.
17. Montmorency, p.57.
18. *ibid*. p.11.
19. Marjoribanks, p.3.
20. *Norwood News*, 27 Jul 1907.
21. *Saffron Walden Weekly*, 29 Oct 1897.
22. Biggs, p.3. Here Biggs paraphrases Lord Penzance's comments in *Scott* v. *Scott* [1863].
23. *Star* and DN, 3 Mar 1893.
24. Lockwood to Joseph Birch, Wontner's clerk, MP 10 Mar 1893.
25. *Truth*, 16 Mar 1893.
26. Seymour, pp.4-7.
27. *Chelmsford Chronicle*, 14 Apr 1911.
28. Nominal earnings: Williamson, p.48; Portland income: Cannadine, p.710.
29. Tozer, p.18.
30. *ibid*, pp.49-61
31. *Tasker* v. *Streeter & Co.* reported in *The Times* 23-26 Feb 1895. Tasker won this battle. Comments on Ally Sloper from Banville, pp.151-158.
32. *Tasker* v. *Tasker* 25 Nov 1894 [1895] P1. Tasker lost this one.
33. Fenn, p.107.
34. Stowell quoted in Biggs, p.25.
35. Shaw, p.184.

4 Sex Crimes

1. Published in *The Bat*, 4 Jan 1887, p.4.
2. Weeks, p.23.

3. Milton, p.25-30.
4. Cretney, pp.169-173; Walton quoting Lord Stowell, p.44.
5. Galsworthy, p.192; p.144.
6. Moore, p.183.
7. Wording of anonymous letters and Virginia's confession: DN, 13 Feb 1886.
8. *Vanity Fair*, 15 Aug 1885.
9. J 77/342/296.
10. *The Bat*, 16 Feb 1886.
11. Asquith, p.91. Both *Bat* and VF suggested it had been 'squared'.
12. VF, 20 Feb 1886.
13. DN, 13 Feb 1886.
14. PMG, 13 Feb 1886.
15. Weeks, p.43.
16. 7 Sep 1886, p.180-3.
17. Brown, p.108; Stead, 'Ananias', p.336.
18. Savage, 'Wilful Communication', p.49.
19. Wilde, p.193.
20. For what it's worth, though medical opinion on this and so many other matters differed, the text *Syphilis and Pseudo-Syphilis* by Dr Alfred Cooper (1884) identifies the tendencies which Campbell had to recurrent infections, poor healing, abscess and fistula, and Gertrude's heavy, painful periods and profuse, excoriating and offensive vaginal discharge, as belonging to secondary syphilis – a condition that sometimes appeared years after the initial infection and *was* still contagious.
21. *The Bat*, 30 Nov 1886.
22. PMG, 21 Dec 1886.
23. *Vanity Fair*, 25 Dec 1886; Lowndes, p.43.
24. Robinson-Scott, p.82, fn.1.
25. Moore, p.184.
26. J 77/461/4047.
27. *Reynolds's*, 21 Apr 1895.

5 Occupational Hazards
1. Wells, *Englishman*, p.273.
2. O'Shea, p.189.
3. Stead, 'Story', p.602.
4. Gwynn & Tuckwell, p.445; Harcourt, p.50.

Notes

5. O'Shea, p.160.
6. See Fisher for evidence of bribes offered O'Shea and origins of the claim that Clarke believed O'Shea would not appear (p.127).
7. Brake & Demoor, p.514.
8. RC *Evidence* II, p.193. Also I, p.331; II, p.71, p.181.
9. Parrish, p.10.
10. Both Harriet and her half-brother Thomas Soloman Reach were registered as being the children of Thomas Barnard Reach, yet both Harriet and Page refer to him as her half-brother. It's not clear from extant material whose parentage was in doubt.
11. In the 1881–1900 sample only six petitions involved husbands older by twenty to twenty-four years and three older by twenty-five years plus (>1.5 per cent of petitions with specified ages). The Criminal Law Amendment Act, 1885, which made it unlawful for a man to have intercourse with a female under sixteen, came about as a direct result of Stead's 'Maiden Tribute' campaign.
12. 1881–1900 sample.
13. Weeks, p.43.
14. Chapman, p.10.
15. J 77/303/9029.
16. Davy, p.3.
17. *Lancet*, 6 Dec 1884, p.1009.
18. Family correspondence between the children's descendants.
19. R v. *Collins*, tried in June 1898. The jury appealed for leniency on the ground that the woman had been 'a willing subject' who wanted to indulge her sexual appetite without taking responsibility for the consequences. The judge, working on the principle that if there were no receivers there would be no thieves, sentenced the abortionist to seven years' penal servitude. He could have given him life.
20. Knight, p.200.
21. *Devon & Exeter Gazette*, 18 Jan 1897.
22. *Exeter Flying Post*, 2 May 1896.
23. *People*, 3 May 1896.
24. *ibid*.
25. Last will and testament of Helena Pyatt, 2 Feb 1923.
26. Lee & Cooper, p.16.
27. Crispe, p.155.
28. Fenn, p.140.

29. Data for years 1887–1893, Parliamentary Papers (PP) vol. LXXI, p.30; Schneider, p.42.
30. PP vol. LXXI, p.34.
31. The Perjury in Divorce Cases Bill was withdrawn after a fortnight (Schneider, p.457); Fenn, p.139.

6 Dodgy Detectives

1. Fenn, p.168.
2. Trollope, p.105, p.329.
3. Smith, p.65.
4. *ibid.*, p.69.
5. One of the conspirators was Mr Froggatt, solicitor to the courtesan countess Kate, Lady Euston, who, immediately after serving two years for the turf fraud, was re-arrested for having embezzled the trust fund bestowed on her by Euston at their marriage!
6. Fenn, p.166-167.
7. PMG, 11 May 1871.
8. Geary, p.308.
9. Juxon, p.163.
10. Fenn, p.168.
11. *Punch*, 11 Jan 1890.
12. Old Bailey Proceedings, t19041017-788. 'If she be of evil fame, this carries a strong presumption that her testimony is false or feigned' (*Archbold's Pleadings and Evidence in Criminal Cases*, 19th ed. (1878), p.764).
13. Marjoribanks, p.316.

7 Scheming Solicitors

1. In 1891 petitioner Edward Taplin and co-respondent Jephunah Owen were sentenced to eighteen and twelve months' hard labour respectively for plotting a staged act of adultery between Owen and Suzannah Taplin; and in 1897 respondent Margaret Williams and co-respondent Thomas Rees were sentenced to fifteen months for conspiracy to pervert the course of justice for giving false evidence.
2. t19030518-490.
3. Solicitor statistics: Incorporated Law Society, LES, 24 Oct 1900; *Morning Advertiser*, 9 Feb 1869; Petitions filed: RC *Appendices* III.

4. Haynes, p.63.
5. DNB, 1912 Supplement.
6. Walton, p.10.
7. *Scotsman*, 3 Aug 1892.
8. Lang's partner got five years – Lang was considered his 'tool' in this instance also (*Times*, 27 Apr 1908) and became an 'ex-solicitor' on the Register of Habitual Criminals, 1911.

8 'Clean Hands', Collusion and the Queen's Proctor

1. Heath, p.188.
2. Matrimonial Causes Act 1860, s.5 and s.7 respectively. Under s.5 the QP could also participate in proceedings as *amicus curiae*, or friend of the court, to discuss a complex point of law during a trial or to argue a question when only one party was represented by counsel.
3. Letter from Stephenson to James, 21 May 1883, NA, T 1/14537.
4. Schneider, p.146.
5. NA, TS 78/9.
6. RC, *Evidence* I, p.51, 53, 58, 74 & 80; II, p.143.
7. Russell, *Life*, p.279.
8. PMG, 8 Feb 1892.
9. *The Era*, 16 Oct 1886.
10. All subsequent information concerning the practices of the proctor from Treasury Solicitor File T 1/14537 unless otherwise specified.
11. *Westminster Gazette*, 23 Nov 1895.
12. Schneider, p.179.
13. J 77/601/18372. In this, as in first Cox suit, the co-respondent absconded and Goode provided his wife with an allowance and limited access to their children. Jeune approved this course just as he had Cox's.
14. Bosanquet, p.453.
15. RC *Evidence* II, p.119-120.
16. J 77/176/4430.
17. See Bruce, chapters 2 and 3.
18. Letter from Francesca to Lady Brougham, August 1870, UCL, BP861.
19. Vignati to Lady Brougham, 14 Oct 1869, BP807.

20. Wilfrid to Lord Brougham, 12 Dec 1875, BP858.
21. Henry to Lord Brougham, relaying details of letter to Wilfrid, 22 Nov 1887, BP858.
22. Lord Brougham to Wilfrid, 13 May 1880, BP863.
23. Savage, 'Proctor', p.216.
24. RC *Evidence* II, p.141.
25. Fenn, p.228.

9 Nullity Suits: The Letter of the Law
1. MacQueen comments that historically the Catholic Church had habitually extended reasons to annul marriages so as not to appear to sanction divorce. At the Reformation the prohibitions were reduced to those supposedly sanctioned by scripture which then passed into law in 1835 (MacQueen, p.73). The controversy over the deceased wife's sister stemmed from the scriptural prohibition of relations between a husband and his wife's sister to *his wife's lifetime* (Leviticus 18:18) but the table of kindred and affinities prepared by Archbishop Parker in 1563 and subsequently included in the Book of Common Prayer did not. Victorian man of letters Abraham Hayward chose to interpret Archbishop Parker's reinterpretation as a 'mistake' in his 1845 'Remarks' on one of the earliest reform bills (p.16-17). In Gilbert and Sullivan's *Iolanthe* the fairy queen enrages the peers by declaring not only that she will put Iolanthe's son into Parliament but that she will give him the power to pass any bill he proposes, not least: 'He shall prick that annual blister, / Marriage with deceased wife's sister.'
2. 1881–1900 sample.
3. Geary, p.203.
4. MacQueen, pp.75-76.
5. Wording of petitions in 1881–1900 sample.
6. Geary, p.209. Though detailed assessment of cases is hampered by lack of reporting and the three-year rule was not set in stone, its practical application is noted in the fact that of the eighteen petitions for nullity due to non-consummation in the 1881–1900 sample, the twelve that were granted a decree all involved marriages of three years or more against only one of those denied a decree. The case denied was against a woman married for thirteen years whose medical examination found

Notes

no defects. The following year she successfully divorced her husband for adultery compounded by cruelty. Of the five other failed cases in the sample, three petitioners denied a decree had been married two years or less and the other two were abandoned.

7. *G. v. M.*, 5 Mar 1885, 10 AC 171, HL.
8. John Reid quoted in Parry-Jones, p.11.
9. McCandless, p.86.
10. *Select Committee on Lunatics*, 1860, quoted in McCandless, p.96.
11. *Hunter v. Edney orse Hunter*, 16 Dec 1881 [1885] P 93.
12. Recorded in the admissions register of Ticehurst asylum where Ethel was sent after the hearing, WL, MS6390, vol.30, p.57.
13. Hamilton, p.685.
14. Letter from Charles George Barrington, officer of the royal household and Durham's second cousin, to Durham, 17 Mar 1885, reveals that the prince ordered that pressure be applied to Barrington by Edward Baring, Viscount Cromer, to convince Durham to halt proceedings for what Barrington considered the most banal of reasons: ' ... Why, because P of W wished it. Why did he wish it? because Mrs G[erard] is a very pretty woman.' (LA).
15. Letter from Edith Milner to Mary Gerard, 3 May 1884, HA, DE/X317/F19.
16. Charles George Barrington wrote to Durham on 17 March 1885 lamenting Herschell's inability to break down Mary's evidence 'though we knew well enough she was lying' (LA).
17. *ibid.*
18. Milton, p.30-31.
19. *The Times*, 11 Mar 1885; Letter to Mary Gerard, 15 Mar 1885, DE/X317/F12.
20. *Vanity Fair*, 14 Mar 1885, p.151.
21. Copy of letter sent to Edith Milner, 30 Dec 1884, LA.
22. Letter from Alice Le Quesne to Durham, 12 Mar 1885, LA.
23. *Times*, 15 Nov 1886.
24. *Belfast Telegraph*, 17 Nov 1886.
25. Sebright, p.28, p.118.
26. *ibid.*, p.39.
27. *Times*, 13 Nov 1886; EEN, 17 Nov 1886.

28. *Times*, 15 Nov 1886.
29. *Times*, 13 Nov 1886.
30. Sebright, p.99.
31. PMG, 16 Nov 1886; *Times*, 17 Nov 1886.
32. *Law Times* and *Law Journal*, 20 Nov 1886.
33. Quoted in *Central Law Journal*, no.25, vol.23, p.578.
34. *Cannon v. Cannon orse Smalley*, 19 Mar 1885 [1885] P 96. Mrs Cannon improved and was well enough to return to her father and work as a music teacher by 1891, but never returned to Cannon. By 1911 she was in London County Lunatic Asylum described as a lunatic since age twenty-five. She died there in 1953 aged eighty-nine.
35. *Sheffield Independent*, 17 Nov 1886.
36. Parry-Jones, p.119-121.
37. MS6390-6397; letter from Alice Le Quesne to Durham, 26 Jan 1885, LA.
38. Hollander, p.11. Hollander documents Durham's relationship with Lind (real name Letitia Elizabeth Rudge, 1862–1923) but not their son, John Reginald Harraton Rudge, born 15 January 1892, 'Harraton' being the name of the house Durham had built in the 1880s as his Newmarket residence and stables.

10 Issues of Access

1. PP, vol.40, p.18.
2. Dickens, pp.67-71.
3. 1871 data from Rowntree, representing all 286 petitions filed that year. 1881–1900 data includes >1 per cent who declared themselves unemployed. In both surveys there were petitions in which occupation was not recorded: 23 per cent in 1871 and 12 per cent in 1881–1900. Rowntree speculates that in 1871 these were more likely to be the petitions of gentry than working class (p.222). In the later period that distinction is less evident.
4. Some of the 'large number' of letters to the commission from 'silent witnesses' were included in RC *Appendices* p.p.171-188 and later published in the *Daily Mail* under the headline 'Cheap Divorce' to highlight the plight of individuals disadvantaged by the system.
5. A bill of costs was drawn up by the solicitor's clerk and approved by a registrar in a process known as 'taxing'. Details of costs from Oakley.

Notes

6. The remaining two undefended suits under £50 were for petitioners from the Midlands and Portsmouth. Average annual earnings per head: Giffen, Table II, p.477-481.
7. RC *Appendices*, p.172, p.176, p.188, p.189.
8. *ibid*, p.175.
9. TS 29/5, p.233-234.
10. Jackson, p.2141; Catz & Guyer, p.655-656.
11. Matrimonial Causes Act, 1878; Married Women (Maintenance in case of Desertion) Act, 1886; Summary Jurisdiction (Married Women) Act, 1895; Licensing Act, 1902, s.5.
12. Law Commission Working Paper No. 53 (HMSO: 1973), p.6.
13. RC *Appendices*, p.181.
14. Observation expressed in McGregor, p.24; data from RC *Evidence* I, p.217.
15. Frost, p.108; p.115.
16. *ibid*, p.111.
17. RC *Appendices*, p.181; p.178.
18. Frost, p.113-114.
19. Walsh, *Not Like This* (1953), p.12 quoted in Rowntree, p.199.
20. The Corsham divorce suits cited are the only ones discovered in a search of local papers available online under the headlines A Local/Corsham/Wiltshire Divorce – headlines under which the Crook case appeared and reflecting variations frequently used by provincial papers.
21. 15 Aug 1901. Headlines quoted appeared in the *Western Times* and *Northern Guardian* respectively.
22. RN, 26 Jul 1891.
23. W. T. Stead, 'In Memoriam: Benjamin Waugh' in *Review of Reviews*, vol.37 (Jan-Jun 1908), p.346.
24. 'Portia's Portion', *The Gentlewoman*, 26 Dec 1891, p.858.
25. The term 'jactitation' derives from the Latin *jactitare*, meaning to boast. See Law Commission Jactitation of Marriage (Consultation Paper), [1971] EWLC C34 (15 Jan 1971).
26. Savage, 'Wilful Communication', p.45.

11 The Doors Widen
1. *Hansard*, HL Deb 1 May 1902, vol.107, c.389.
2. Gallichan, p.126.
3. Dickens, p.175.

4. For more on Russell's reform attempts see *Bertrand's Brother* (Derham, 2021), chapter 20, and *To Be Frank* (Derham, 2022), chapters 4 and 7.
5. The DLRU was finally wound up in 1946. It's influence was noted by Barnes during evidence given to the commission (RC *Evidence* III, p.212).
6. *Times*, 28 Apr 1906.
7. Maule's speech was recalled by Russell in presenting his bill to the Lords and can be read in full at https://hansard.parliament.uk/.
8. *Staffordshire Sentinel*, 8 Nov 1906.
9. Drabble, p.127; Hynes, p.195.
10. Milton, p.268-269. For more on the literature of this period concerning divorce see Hynes, p.194-195.
11. The commission began with fourteen commissioners: the Earl of Derby resigned during proceedings and Sir George White died before the report was compiled.
12. RC *Report* (Minority Report), p.179.
13. Cosmo Gordon Lang was then Archbishop of York; Sir Lewis Dibdin was Dean of the Arches; Sir William Anson had been Chancellor of the Diocese of Oxford before entering Parliament as a Liberal Unionist.
14. RC *Report* (Majority Report), evidence of Revd William Sanday, Canon of Christchurch, p.31; and Revd Emnet, Vicar of West Hendred, p.32.
15. *ibid*, p.36.
16. Lowndes, *Diaries*, p.44.
17. Cretney, p.213, fn.103.
18. *John Bull*, 8 Jul 1922.
19. Cretney, p.221.
20. Swinburne, p.14.
21. *Lindo v. Belisario* (1795) 1 Hag. Con. Rep. 230.
22. *The Guardian*, 12 Nov 1912.
23. Bird & Cretney, p.8-9; Fairbairn, p.4.
24. Fairbairn, p.9.
25. *ibid.*, p.18.

Bibliography

Archival Material

Hertfordshire Archives (HA): Family Papers of the Gerard, Gosselin & Milner Families (DE/X317).

Lambton Archives (LA): Private Papers of John George Lambton, 3rd Earl of Durham.

National Archives, Kew (NA):Divorce and Matrimonial Causes files (series J 77); Divorce Returns, 1858-1887 (J 86/250); HM Procurator General: Register of Divorces Cases (TS 29/1-4); Treasury Solicitor: Divorce interventions: Queen's proctor transmits copy of correspondence with attorney general (T 1/14537).

University College London, Special Collections (UCL): Brougham Papers (BP), boxes 807, 858, 861, 863, 864.

Wellcome Library (WL): Ticehurst House Case Records (MS6390-6397).

Published Material

All texts published in London unless otherwise stated

Anonymous, *The Campbell Divorce Case Copious Report of the Trial* (Henning & Co., 1887).

Anonymous, *The Crawford Divorce Case Verbatim Report of the Trial* (Henning & Co., 1886).

Anonymous, *The O'Shea-Parnell Divorce Case: Full and Complete Proceedings* (Boston: National Publishing Co., 1890).

Balfour-Browne, John Hutton, *Forty Years at the Bar* (Herbert Jenkins, 1916).

Banville, Scott, '"Ally Sloper's Half Holiday": The Geography of Class in Late-Victorian Britain' in *Victorian Periodicals*, vol.41 no.2 (Summer 2008), pp.150-173.

Bence-Jones, Mark, *Twilight of the Ascendancy* (Constable, 1987).

Berridge, Virginia Stewart, *Popular Journalism and Working Class Attitudes 1854-1886: A Study of Reynolds's Newspaper, Lloyd's Weekly Newspapers and the Weekly Times* (unpublished PhD thesis; University of London, 1972).

Bew, Paul, *Gill's Irish Lives: C.S. Parnell* (Dublin: Gill & Macmillan, 1980).

Biggs, John M., *The Concept of Matrimonial Cruelty* (Althone Press, 1962).

Bingham, Madeleine, Baroness Clanmorris, *Earls and Girls: Dramas in High Society* (Hamilton, 1980).

Bird, Roger & Cretney, Stephen, *Divorce: The New Law* (Bristol: Family Law, 1996).

Black, Clementina, 'On Marriage: A Criticism' in *Fortnightly Review*, vol. XLVII (Jan-Jun 1890), pp.586-594.

Bosanquet, Helen, 'English Divorce Law and the Report of the Royal Commission' in *International Journal of Ethics*, vol.23 (July 1913), pp.443-455.

Bourne, H.R. Fox, *English Newspapers: Chapters in the History of Journalism*, vol.2 (Chatto & Windus, 1887).

Brake, Laurel & Demoor Marysa, *Dictionary of Nineteenth-Century Journalism in Great Britain and Ireland* (Academia Press & The British Library, 2009)

Brown, Stewart J., *W.T. Stead: Non-Conformist and Newspaper Prophet* (Oxford: Oxford University Press, 2019).

Bruce, Anthony, *The Purchase System in the British Army, 1660-1871* (Royal Historical Society, 1980).

Burnham, Lord, *Peterborough Court: The Story of the Daily Telegraph* (Cassell, 1955).

Caird, Monica, 'The Morality of Marriage' in *Fortnightly Review*, vol. XLVII (Jan-Jun 1890), pp.310-330.

Cannadine, David, *The Decline and Fall of the British Aristocracy* (New York: Vintage, 1999).

Bibliography

Casey, Brian, 'The Decline and Fall of the Clancarty Estate, 1891-1923' in *Journal of the Galway Archaeological and Historical Society*, vol.67 (2015), pp.171-183.

Catz, Robert & Guyer, Thad, 'Federal In Forma Pauperis Litigation: In Search of Judicial Standards' in Rutgers Law Review, vol.31 (1978), pp.655-656.

Chapman, Edwin Nesbit, *Hysterology: A Treatise, Descriptive and Clinical, on the Diseases and the Displacement of the Uterus* (New York: William Wood, 1872).

Clarke, Sir Edward, *The Story of My Life* (John Murray, 1918).

Conboy, Martin, 'Residual Radicalism as a Popular Commercial Strategy: Beginnings and Endings' in Laurel Brake *et al* (eds.), *The News of the World and the British Press, 1843-2011* (Basingstoke: Palgrave, 2016).

Cretney, Stephen, *Family Law in the Twentieth Century: A History* (Oxford: Oxford University Press, 2003).

Crispe, Thomas Edward, *Reminiscences of a KC* (Methuen, 1909).

Davy, J.P.H., *The Arden Club: The First Eighty-Five Years*, available at https://www.bower.me.uk/ardenclub/Arden%20Club%20History%201880-1980.pdf, accessed 30 May 2022.

Derham, Ruth, *Bertrand's Brother: The Marriages, Morals and Misdemeanours of Frank, 2nd Earl Russell* (Stroud: Amberley Publishing, 2021).

Derham, Ruth, *To Be Frank: Politics and Polemics of a Radical Russell* (Nottingham: Spokesman, 2022).

Dickens, Charles, *Hard Times* (Vintage, 2009).

Donisthorpe, Wordsworth, 'The Future of Marriage' in *Fortnightly Review*, vol. LI (Jan-Jan 1892), pp.258-271.

Drabble, Margaret, *Arnold Bennett* (Omega, 1975).

Fairbairn, Catherine, 'No-Fault Divorce', House of Commons Briefing Paper 01409 (9 Apr 2019), available at https://commonslibrary.parliament.uk/research-briefings/sn01409/, accessed 18 Jan 2023.

Fenn, Henry Edwin, *Thirty-Five Years in the Divorce Court* (Werner Laurie, 1910).

Fisher, Trevor, *Scandal: The Sexual Politics of Late Victorian Britain* (Stroud: Alan Sutton, 1995).

Frost, Ginger, *Living in Sin: Cohabiting as Husband and Wife in Nineteenth-Century England* (Manchester: Manchester University Press, 2008).

Gallichan, Walter (Geoffrey Mortimer [pseud.]), *The Blight of Respectability* (University Press, 1897).

Galsworthy, John, *The Forsyte Saga* (Ware: Wordsworth Classics, 2012).

'G.D.', *The Royal Courts of Justice Illustrated Handbook* (G.D., 1883).

Geary, Nevill, *The Law of Marriage and Family Relations: A Manual of Practical Law* (Adam & Charles Black, 1892).

Giffen, Robert, *General Report on the Wages of the Manual Labour Class in the United Kingdom* (HMSO, 1893).

Gissing, George, *The Odd Women* (Virago, 1893/1982).

Grand, Sarah, 'Marriage Questions in Fiction' in *Fortnightly Review*, vol. LXIII (Jan-Jun 1898), pp.378-389.

Grey, Maria Georgina, 'Men and Women: A Sequel' in *Fortnightly Review*, vol. XXIX (Jan-Jun 1881), pp.776-92.

Guthrie, Charles J., 'The History of Divorce in Scotland' in *The Scottish Historical Review*, vol.8, no.29 (Oct 1910), pp.39-52.

Gwynn, Stephen & Tuckwell, Gertrude, *The Life of the Rt. Hon. Sir Charles W. Dilke* (John Murray, 1917).

Hamilton, Edward Walter, *The Diary of Sir Edward Walter Hamilton, 1880-1885*, vol.2, Dudley Bahlman (ed.) (Oxford: Clarendon Press, 1972).

Hammerton, A. James, 'Victorian Marriage and the Law of Matrimonial Cruelty' in *Victorian Studies*, Vol.33, No.2 (Winter 1990), pp.269-292.

Harcourt, Lewis, *Loulou: Selected Extracts from the Journals of Lewis Harcourt (1880-1895)*, Patrick Jackson (ed.) (Teaneck, NJ: Fairleigh Dickinson University Press, 2006).

Harrison, Henry, *Parnell Vindicated: The Lifting of the Veil* (Constable, 1931).

Haynes, E.S.P., *Concerning Solicitors (by One of Them)* (Chatto & Windus, 1920).

Hayward, Abraham, *Remarks on the Law Regarding Marriage with the Sister of a Deceased Wife* (Benning, 1845).

Heath, Sir Thomas, *The Treasury* (Putnam's, 1927).

Himmelfarb, Gertrude, *Marriage and Morals Among the Victorians and other essays* (Chicago: Ivan Dee, 2001).

Hobbs, Andrew, 'When the Provincial Press Was the National Press, c.1836-1900' (unpublished postdoctoral paper) available at

Bibliography

https://www.academia.edu/187659/When_the_provincial_press_was_the_national_press_c_1836_1900_, accessed 11 Jun 2022.

Hollander, Bertie, *Before I Forget* (Grayson & Grayson, 1935).

Howard, Pendleton, 'Criminal Prosecution in England' in *Columbia Law Review*, vol.29, no.6 (Jun 1929), pp.715-747.

Humpherys, Anne, 'Coming Apart: The British Newspaper Press and the Divorce Court' in Laurel Brake *et al* (eds.), *Nineteenth-Century Media and the Construction of Identities* (Basingstoke: Palgrave, 2000).

Hynes, Samuel, *The Edwardian Turn of Mind* (Pimlico, 1991).

Inderwick, Frederick Andrew, *The King's Peace: A Historical Sketch of the English Law Courts* (Swan Sonnenschein, 1895).

Jackson, Joseph *et al* (eds.), *Butterworth's Matrimonial Law Statutes reprinted from 'Rayden on Divorce'*, 11th ed.(Butterworths, 1971).

Jenkins, Roy, *Victorian Scandal: The Biography of the Right Honourable Gentleman Sir Charles Dilke* (New York: Chilmark Press, 1965).

Juxon, John, *Lewis and Lewis: The Life and Times of a Victorian Solicitor* (Collins, 1983).

Kitchin, S. B., *A History of Divorce* (Chapman & Hall, 1912).

Knight, Frances, *The Nineteenth Century Church and English Society* (Cambridge: Cambridge University Press, 1995).

Lee, Anna & Cooper, Barbara Roisman, *Anna Lee: Memoir of a Career on General Hospital and in Film* (Jefferson, NC: McFarland, 2007).

Levi, Leone, *Wages and Earnings of the Working Classes* (John Murray, 1885).

Lewis, George, 'Marriage and Divorce' in *Fortnightly Review*, vol. XXXVII (Jan-Jun 1885), pp.640-798.

Lowndes, Marie Belloc, *Diaries and Letters of Marie Belloc Lowndes, 1911-1947*, Susan Lowndes (ed.) (Chatto & Windus, 1971).

MacQueen, John Fraser, *A Practical Treatise on Divorce and Matrimonial Jurisdiction under the Act of 1857 and New Orders* (Maxwell *et al*, 1858).

McCandless, Peter, 'Dangerous to Themselves and Others: The Victorian Debate over the Prevention of Wrongful Confinement' in *Journal of British Studies* Vol.23, No.1 (Autumn 1983), pp.84-104.

McGregor, O. R., *Divorce in England* (Heinemann, 1957).
Marjoribanks, Edward, *The Life of Lord Carson, vol.1* (Victor Gollancz, 1932).
Matthews, Roy & Mellini, Peter, *In 'Vanity Fair'* (Quiller Press, 2000).
Milton, John, *The Doctrine and Discipline of Divorce* (Sherwood, Neely & Jones, 1643/1820).
Montmorency, J.E.G., *John Gorell Barnes, First Lord Gorell, 1848-1913* (John Murray, 1920).
Moore, George, 'The Legal Laundry' in *Hawk*, 12 Aug 1890, pp.183-184.
Oakley, T.W.H., *Divorce Practice* (W.P. Griffith, 1885).
O'Brien, R. Barry, *The Life of Lord Russell of Killowen* (Smith Elder, 1901).
O'Shea, Katharine, *Charles Stewart Parnell: His Love Story and Political Life* (Cassell & Co., 1914).
Parrish, Dr Joseph, 'Inebriety, and Homes for Inebriates in England' in *The Quarterly Journal of Inebriety*, Vol.3 No.1 (Jan 1886), p.10.
Parry-Jones, William, *The Trade in Lunacy* (Routledge, 1972).
Payne, Chris, *The Chieftain: Victorian True Crime Through the Eyes of a Scotland Yard Detective* (Stroud: History Press, 2013).
Probert, Rebecca, *Marriage Law and Practice in the Long Eighteenth Century: A Reassessment* (Cambridge: Cambridge University Press, 2009).
Robinson-Scott, J.W., *The Life and Death of a Newspaper* (Methuen, 1952).
Rowntree, Griselda & Carrier, Norman H., 'The Resort to Divorce in England and Wales, 1858-1957 in *Population Studies: A Journal of Demography*, Vol. XI, No.3 (March 1958), pp.188-233.
Royal Commission on Divorce & Matrimonial Causes, *Report of the Royal Commission on Divorce and Matrimonial Causes* (Eyre & Spottiswoode, 1912).
Royal Commission on Divorce & Matrimonial Causes, *Minutes of Evidence Taken Before the Royal Commission on Divorce and Matrimonial Causes*, vols. I-III with *Appendices* (Eyre & Spottiswoode, 1912).
Russell, John Francis Stanley, *Divorce* (William Heinemann, 1912).

Russell, John Francis Stanley, *My Life and Adventures* (Cassell, 1923).

Savage, Gail, 'The Divorce Court and the Queen's/King's Proctor: Legal Patriarchy and the Sanctimony of Marriage in England, 1861-1937' in *Canadian Historical Association, Historical Papers* (1989), pp.210-228.

Savage, Gail, 'Erotic Stories and Public Decency: Newspaper Reporting of Divorce Proceedings in England' in *The Historical Journal*, Vol.41, No.2 (Jun 1998), pp.511-528.

Savage, Gail, '"The Wilful Communication of a Loathsome Disease": Marital Conflict and Venereal Disease in Victorian England' in *Victorian Studies*, Vol.34, No.1 (Autumn 1990), pp.35-54.

Schneider, Wendie Ellen, *Engines of Truth: Producing Veracity in the Victorian Courtroom* (Yale University Press, 2015).

Sebright, Arthur, *A Glance into the Past* (Everleigh Nash & Grayson, 1922).

Seymour, Thomas, *My Grandfather, A Modern Medievalist: The Life of the 8th Lord Howard de Walden* available at https://www.nationaltrust.org.uk/chirk-castle/features/lord-howard-de-walden-patron-of-wales, accessed 14 Mar 2022.

Shaw, George Bernard, *Getting Married* (New York: Brentano's, 1908/1915).

Sievier, Robert Standish, *The Autobiography of Robert Standish Sievier* (Winning Post, 1906).

Smalley, George Washburn, *Society in the New Reign* (Unwin, 1904).

Smith, Phillip Thurmond, *Policing Victorian London: Political Policing, Public Order, and the London Metropolitan Police* (Greenwood Press, 1985).

Stead, W.T., 'The Sin of Ananias and Sapphira' in *Welsh Review*, Vol.1, No.4 (Feb 1892), pp.321-338.

Stead, W.T., 'The Story of An Incident in the Home Rule Cause', *Review of Reviews*, Vol. II, No.12 (Dec 1890), pp.598-608.

Stone, Lawrence, *The Road to Divorce* (Oxford: Oxford University Press, 1995).

Swinburne, Henry, *A Treatise of Spousals*, 2nd ed. (Daniel Brown, 1711).

Tozer, Basil, *Roving Recollections* (Boardman, 1945).

Victoria, *The Letters of Queen Victoria, vol. III, 1854-1861* Arthur Christopher Benson (ed) (John Murray, 1911).
Trollope, Anthony, *He Knew He Was Right* (Strahan, 1870).
Walker-Smith, Derek, *The Life of Sir Edward Clarke* (Thornton Butterworth, 1939).
Walton, Frederick Parker, *A Handbook of Husband and Wife According to the Law of Scotland* (Edinburgh: William Green, 1893).
Weeks, Jeffrey, *Sex, Politics and Society: The Regulation of Sexuality since 1800*, 2nd ed. (Longman, 1989).
Wells. H.G., *An Englishman Looks at the World* (Cassell & Co., 1914).
Wells, H.G., *Experiment in Autobiography* (Victor Gollanz, 1934).
Wilde, Oscar, *The Letters of Oscar Wilde*, Rupert Hart-Davies, ed. (New York, Harcourt, Brace & World, 1962).
Williamson, Jeffrey G. 'The Structure of Pay in Britain, 1710-1911' in *Research in Economic History*, vol.7 (1982) pp.1-54.
Wright, Danaya, 'Untying the Knot: An Analysis of the English Divorce Court and Matrimonial Causes Records, 1858-1866' in *University of Richmond Law Review*, Vol.38 (2004), pp.903-1010.

Reference Works and Online Sources
Ancestry (www.ancestry.co.uk).
The Annual Register (Longmans, Green).
British and Irish Legal Information Institute (www.bailii.org).
Dictionary of National Biography (www.oxforddnb.com).
Family Search (www.familysearch.org).
Hansard (https://hansard.parliament.uk/).
The Law List (Stevens).
Newspaper Archives (www.britishnewspaperarchive.co.uk; www.newspapers.com).
Parliamentary Papers (https://catalog.hathitrust.org/Record/1003-35445).
Proceedings of the Old Bailey (www.oldbaileyonline.org).

Index

abortion 108, 123, 127, 130–131, 265
Airey, Francis and Sarah 227
alimony 19, 23, 75, 101, 150, 153, 154, 222, 224, 262
Acts of Parliament
  Administration of Justice Act (1920) 254
  Clandestine Marriages Act (1753) 38
  Clergy Discipline Act (1892) 131
  Contagious Diseases Acts (1864–69, repealed 1886) 28, 101
  Divorce, Dissolution and Separation Act (2020) 12, 258
  Divorce Law Reform Act (1969) 12, 173, 257, 258
  Judicature Act (1873) 33
  Judicial Proceedings (Regulation of Reports) Act (1926) 254
  Licensing Act (1902) 230, 271
  Marriage Acts (1835) 196, 247, 268; (1836) 39, 196, 268
  Married Women's Property Act (1882) 40
  Matrimonial Causes Acts (1857) 12, 13, 18–19, 21, 22, 24, 25, 60, 63, 68, 171, 221, 228, 246; (1860) 19, 171, 181, 267; (1878) 172, 229, 230, 271; (1884) 19, 154, 174, 255, 262; (1923) 254, 255, 256; (1937) 198, 254, 256
  Obscene Publications Act (1857) 27, 112
  Summary Jurisdiction (Married Women) Act (1895) 229–230
adultery 12–13, 18–19, 21–23, 45, 48, 52, 60–61, 64, 67, 72–75, 78, 79, 86–87, 92, 94, 97, 98, 101, 103, 104–105, 109, 111, 116, 121, 124–125, 127, 128, 129, 131, 132, 133, 139, 145, 146, 149, 150, 151, 153, 154, 155, 158, 162, 165, 166, 168, 169, 171–174, 175, 177, 179, 180, 181–182, 183–184, 186, 187, 188, 189–190, 191, 193, 195, 200, 223, 225, 226, 227, 228, 230, 237, 246, 248, 249, 252, 254, 255, 257, 262, 266, 269

Asbury, Arthur and Florence 222–223
Asquith, Herbert Henry MP 251, 253, 264

Balfour, Lady Frances 251
Barnes, Sir John Gorell (see also *Royal Commissions*) 67–68, 134, 136, 137, 150, 153, 154, 159, 169, 176, 177, 189, 233–234, 239, 242, 248, 249–250, 251, 272
Barrett, John and Gertrude 149–155, 164
Barristers 15, 27, 30–32, 158
Bastard, John and Olivia 189–190, 194
Bat, The 48, 92, 103
Bayford, Robert 32, 34, 145
Beddoes, Dr Thomas Pugh 182–183
Bennett, Arnold 250
Bigamy 18, 29, 34, 41, 174, 246
Biggs, John 68
Bilton, Belle (see *Dunlo*)
Black, Clementina 37, 60, 61
Blood, Neptune 107
Bonaparte, Louis Clavering and Rosalie 165–169, 197
Bosvile, Thomas Bolle and Elizabeth 111
Brinton, Joseph and Henrietta 233–235, 244
Brougham, Henry, 1st Baron 172, 190
Brougham, Henry, 3rd Baron 193, 194
Brougham, Hon. Wilfrid and Francesca 120, 190–194
Brougham, William, 2nd Baron 190, 192–193, 194
Brunton, Spencer 189–190, 194

Buckmaster, Stanley, 1st Viscount 254, 255
Burke, Captain Frederick Molison and Lucy 111
Burghersh, Anthony Fane, Lord 206–207, 209, 210–211
Burr, Arthur 214–215, 216
Butt, Sir Charles Parker 10, 33–34, 67, 91, 92, 100, 117, 124, 128, 129, 145, 146, 147, 200, 211, 212, 215–216, 217

Caird, Monica 37
Campbell, Lord Colin and Lady Gertrude 11, 100–110, 113, 264
Campbell, John, 1st Baron (see also *Royal Commissions*) 22, 27
Carew, Frank Murray Maxwell and Edith 175–180
Carson, Sir Edward QC 32, 68, 76, 77, 78, 82, 155
Chamberlain Joseph MP 90, 116
Chandos-Pole, Samuel and Kathleen 158–159
Chester, Edith (see *Carew*)
Clancarty, 4th Earl of 47–48, 52, 54–55, 56–58
Clarke, Sir Edward QC 31, 32, 72, 73, 108, 117, 176, 184, 185, 265
Clarke, George 52–53, 143
Clarke, Granville 52–53, 144
Clarke, Henry John 52–53, 144, 150, 151, 152, 153–154, 155, 157
Clarke's Detective Agency 52, 143–144, 150
Cleveland Street Scandal 46
cohabitation 36, 63, 79, 162, 164, 175, 193, 226, 227, 230–231, 240, 246, 250
Coleridge, John, 1st Baron 243
Collins, Wilkie 35, 36, 143

Index

Cooke, Kate (see *Euston*)
Corinthian Club 47, 59
courts
  Appeal Court 67, 100, 111, 137, 174, 236, 238, 242
  Bow Street police court 137, 238, 243
  Central Criminal ('Old Bailey') 30, 35, 42, 49, 112, 138, 153, 157
  Chancery 129, 242
  Court of Sessions (Edinburgh) 165, 167
  Divorce court (description) 24, 32–33
  Ecclesiastical 21, 22, 67, 172, 246
  House of Lords 12, 174, 193, 200, 245–246, 255
  Queen's Bench 123–124, 129, 132, 235, 236, 242
  Westminster county court 40–41
  Westminster police court 241
Cox, Harding Edward and Hebe 87, 183–188, 267
Crackanthorpe, Monague Hughes QC 176–178, 179
Craven, Inez 158–160
Crawford, Donald MP and Virginia Mary 10, 88–100, 110, 113, 115, 117, 182
Cretney, Stephen 230, 254, 255
Crocombe, James 73–75, 140
Crook, Lizzie 73–75, 140
Crook, George Douglas and Miriam 232–233, 271
cruelty 13, 18–19, 21, 23, 62–64, 66, 75, 82, 83, 100, 101, 112, 113, 128, 129, 130, 145, 150, 154, 160, 170, 182, 188, 191, 223, 228, 244, 246, 252, 253, 256, 269

Darling, Charles, QC MP 140
Deane, Sir Henry Bargrave QC 32, 159, 160, 163, 173, 174, 176
Desart, Hamilton Cuffe, 5th Earl of 174, 183, 195
detectives: agencies; CID; private 52–53, 124, 125, 142–156, 157, 160–161, 164, 178, 186
Dickens, Charles 118, 143, 220, 231, 247
Dieval, Armand and Elizabeth 196–197
Dilke, Sir Charles Wentworth MP 11, 28, 85, 88–100, 110, 113, 114, 115, 117, 182
Dilke, Maye 88, 89, 91, 97
Director of Public Prosecutions (see *Stephenson, Augustus*)
divorce
  Acts (see *Acts of parliament*)
  Bars 13, 18–19, 171–172, 197
  bills (see *reform bills*)
  Church influence 13, 21, 38, 39, 85, 86, 118, 131, 246, 247, 251, 252–253, 255, 256, 268
  Collusion 19, 116, 117, 166, 168, 171–178, 179, 181, 183, 185, 187–188, 191, 193, 197, 199, 200, 215, 226, 246, 258
  Costs 19, 93, 172, 183, 221–229, 270
  court (see *courts*)
  damages 125, 131, 145, 162, 163–165, 183, 184, 185, 225, 246
  grounds for 13, 18–19, 21, 83, 165–166, 245–258
  history of 12–13, 21–23, 220–221
  double standard 13, 18–19, 23, 60, 61, 101, 247
  intervention in suits 93, 172, 181

laws (marriage and divorce):
American 174; English 12–14, 18–19, 21–23, 38; French 108, 111, 166; Scottish 21, 38, 165–170, 172, 200, 221, 244, 247, 250, 262
mutual consent 12, 171, 173, 217, 245, 246, 252, 256–258
parliamentary ('old system') 21–23, 24, 172, 220, 221
petitions 14, 34, 62, 63–64, 100, 158, 221, 223–224, 226, 244, 256, 258, 262, 265, 270
practice: in camera 100, 111, 191, 198, 205, 208
Registry/registrars 222–223, 228, 270
Reporting/publicity 13, 15, 24–28, 48, 54, 58, 59, 64, 87, 99, 110, 112, 119–120, 130, 135, 180–181, 190, 198, 232–233, 252, 254, 259–260, 268
statistics 22, 23–24, 34, 62, 158, 164, 173, 181, 190, 197–198, 221, 223, 226, 229, 230, 256, 259, 262, 265, 268, 270
Divorce Law Reform Union (DLRU) 248, 253, 254, 272
Dodd, James Arthur and Fanny 248–249
Dodd v. Dodd 248–249, 250, 251
Donisthorpe, Wordsworth 37
Drummond, John Nelson and Marie 160–165
Duckett William Routledge and Mary Jane 224
Dunlo, Viscount William Frederick Le-Poer-Trench and Lady Belle 47–59, 87, 111, 144, 177
Durham, John George Lambton and Lady Ethel 200–219, 269, 270
Dutton, Thomas Duerdin 45
Dyball, John 87, 183–188
Dyke, Francis Hart 172

Earle, Loftus 177–179
Edward VII 29, 203, 269
Edward VIII 256
Edwards, David and Catherine 181–183
Esher, Viscount William Brett 238, 243
Euston, Henry James and Lady Kate 35, 39–47, 51, 58, 110, 197, 266
Evening News 27, 45, 79, 99, 116, 253

Fenn, Henry Edwin 24, 25, 54, 82, 144, 147, 149, 195
Finlay, Sir Robert QC 100, 102, 103, 104–105
Finlayson, Revd Arthur 131
Fisher, Trevor 28
FitzRoy, Augustus, 7th Duke of Grafton 41, 42
FitzRoy, Henry James (see *Euston*)
Forster, Captain Henry 89–90, 91, 95–96, 97, 98
Fortnightly Review 36–37
Fox, Francis Edward 160–165
Froggatt, Edward 39, 42, 266
Frost, Ginger 36, 231

G. v. M. 200
Gallichan, Walter 247
Galsworthy, John 87–88, 251
Gardenia, The 47
George, Henry Fennemore 156, 157
Gerard, Lady Mary 203, 205, 206–207, 209, 210
Gilbert & Sullivan 177, 196, 268
Gilder, Ellen Elizabeth 20, 21, 23–24, 28–30, 32, 34–35, 36, 38–39, 197

Index

Gilder, William 23, 28, 29–30, 34–35, 38
Gill, Charles Frederick 49, 52, 54, 56
Gissing, George 37
Gladstone, William Ewart MP 60, 90, 116, 180
Globe, The 27, 45, 75, 76
Goff, Dr Bruce Edward and Florence 130–131
Goode, Minton and Jane 185, 186, 188, 267
Graphic, The 46
Grand, Sarah 37
Great Turf Swindle 143, 266
Greenwood & Greenwood 153, 184, 185, 186
Grey, Maria Georgina 37, 260

Haldane, Richard, Viscount 109
Halsbury, 1st Earl of 12
Hamilton, Edward Walter 202
Hannen, Sir James ('The President') 10, 33–34, 35, 43, 49, 53, 56, 64, 67, 93, 98, 100, 101, 107, 109, 110, 166, 167, 200, 201, 208–211, 217
Harcourt, Sir William MP 114
Hard Times 220, 221, 231
Harrison, William Lomas and Harriet 119–130
Haughton, George 42, 45
Hawk, The 48, 112
Hawkins, Sir Henry 138
Haynes, E.S.P. 158, 248
He Knew He Was Right 142, 144, 147
Henry, George Philip ('Slater jnr.') 155
Herbert, A.P. 245, 255–256
Hern, William Henry and Rosa 133–138
Hern, Rosa 11, 133–140, 157

Herschell, Sir Farrar QC 201, 206, 208, 269
Holy Deadlock 245, 256
Howard de Walden, Frederick George Ellis and Lady Blanche 10, 61, 64–66, 67–68, 69–76, 83, 140
Howe, Ellen Jane 228–229
Hunter Robert and Emma 201–202, 219

impotency 18, 197–200, 217
Inderwick, Frederick QC 20, 31, 44, 49, 67, 91, 92, 145, 163
insane asylums 219
insanity 18, 200–201, 202, 217, 246, 252, 254, 256
Irish Home Rule 114, 115, 116
Izard, Alfred 225–226

jactitation 239, 242, 246, 271
James, Sir Henry QC 32, 68, 69–71, 72, 73, 83, 91, 145, 180, 181, 183, 188, 205, 206, 208, 210, 211
Jenkins, Roy 99
Jeune, Sir Francis Henry 10, 67–68, 71, 72, 75, 82, 150, 160, 164, 182, 185, 196–197, 236, 267
Jones, Revd Hugh 132–133
journalism 25–27
judicial separation (see *separation*)
judges 15, 18–19, 33, 63, 64, 87, 125, 164, 172, 180, 188–189, 197, 254
juries: common 19, 43; special 19, 43

King's Proctor (see *proctor*)
Kingston, Duchess, Trial of 239
Kisch, Henry 150

Labouchere, Henry 29, 98, 144
Lang, John Stuart 166, 167, 169–170, 267
Law Society 161
Leslie, Henry John 111, 225–226
Lewis, Sir George 10, 28–29, 30, 32, 34–35, 42–43, 45, 48, 51, 52, 53, 61, 97, 100, 101, 104, 109, 114, 144, 158–159, 160, 173, 174
Lloyd George, David MP 181–182
Lloyd's Weekly 25–26, 58
Lockwood, Sir Frank QC 31–32, 49, 52, 53–54, 55, 56, 91, 92, 117, 118, 150, 153, 163, 176–177, 178, 179, 185–186
Lonsdale, Gladys, Lady 204–205, 207
Lopes, Lord Henry 237
Lowndes, Maria Belloc 109
Lyons, Ellen 151–154, 155
Lyric Club 47, 54, 177

'Maiden Tribute of Modern Babylon' 93, 103, 124, 237, 265
Manning, Cardinal Henry Edward 99, 238
Marlborough, 8th Duke of 101, 104, 105–106, 108, 109, 110, 148
marriage 13, 14, 36–39, 40, 41, 58–59, 60–61, 63, 83, 86, 124, 188–189, 190, 196, 199, 217, 239, 245, 247, 257, 262
  illegal (see also *bigamy*) 18, 196–197
  laws (see *Acts*)
  non-consummated 197–199, 201, 217
marriage settlements 41–42, 192–193, 194
Matthews, Sir Henry QC 94, 95, 96, 97, 98, 110
Maule, Sir William Henry 250, 272

medical examinations 120, 122, 126, 199
medical practices: addiction 120–121, 192; general 120–121, 126–127; sexual diseases/symptoms 79, 103, 107, 120, 264
Megone, Norfolk Bernard 166–170
Metropolitan Police Service 49, 52, 142–150
Mill, John Stuart 37
Milton, John 14, 86, 208–209, 251, 257
Modern Society 43
Moneylending/moneylenders 175, 192, 213–214, 215
Moore, Augustus 48–49, 57, 58
Moore, George 48, 85, 87–88, 99–100, 111, 112
Mordaunt divorce scandal 29
Morning Post 25, 93, 116, 149
Munby, Sir James 258
Murphy, John Patrick QC 32, 68, 82, 179

National Union of Societies for Equal Citizenship 255
News of the World 25–26
nullity 18, 29, 30, 34–35, 43, 44, 169, 196–219, 233, 252, 256, 268

Oakley, T. W. H. 158
Ochse, Charles 40–41
O'Shea, Captain William Henry MP and Katharine 113–118, 265
Osborn, Henry Albert 155–156, 157

Page, Edward Sutton 119–130, 265
Pall Mall Gazette ('PMG') 26–27, 28, 47, 54, 56, 58, 91, 93, 103, 109, 110, 115, 143, 144, 147, 175, 197, 216

Index

Parnell, Charles Stewart MP 28, 111, 113–118
pauper cases 154, 228–229, 235, 239, 242, 243
Pearman, Arthur and Hannah 226–227
perjury 69, 75, 98, 114, 137, 140, 147, 164, 238, 266
Phillimore, Sir Walter QC 94, 96, 98
Pollard, Thomas and Kate 148, 155–156, 157
Portland, 6th Duke of 70, 71, 76
Prisons: Holloway 139, 154, 246; Millbank 241; Pentonville 139, 154
private inquiry agents (see *detectives*)
Probate, Divorce and Admiralty Division 33, 67, 248
proctor 19, 93, 117, 140, 171–195, 197, 215, 226, 227, 246, 249
Probert, Rebecca 38
Punch 11, 149
puritanism 15, 26–27, 28, 131, 180, 189, 251

Queen Caroline Affair 172
Queen's Counsel ('silks') 30, 31, 32; fees
Queen's Proctor (see *proctor*)

Referee, The 46
reform bills
 deceased wife's sister 196
 divorce: 1892 (Hunter) 165–166, 170; 1902 (Russell) 12, 245–247; 1921 (Buckmaster) 255
 Perjury in Divorce Cases (1888) 140–141, 266
Rentoul, James Alexander QC 136

restitution of conjugal rights 19, 154, 174, 191, 193, 211, 246, 249, 255, 262
Reynolds's Newspaper 26, 46, 55, 75, 112, 139, 236, 253
Rhodes, Josefa 67, 80, 81–82, 84
Robinson-Scott, J. W. 110
Rogerson, Mrs Christina 90, 91, 92, 95, 96, 97
Rourke, Arthur Henry 235–244
Royal Commissions: Barnes (1910) 173–174, 190, 195, 221, 223, 224–225, 229, 230, 231, 250, 251–253, 254, 270, 272; Campbell (1852) 22, 86, 220–221, 245, 250
Royal Courts of Justice 10, 15, 16, 20, 28, 29, 30, 142, 149, 229, 235, 236, 239, 240
Russell, Sir Charles QC 30–31, 32, 43–44, 45, 50, 51, 53–55, 56, 76, 91–92, 93, 100, 102–103, 106–107, 108
Russell, John, 1st Earl 22, 245
Russell, John Francis Stanley, 2nd Earl 12, 14, 16, 111–112, 174–175, 212, 218, 245–248, 252, 254, 255, 257
Russell, Mabel Edith, Countess 111–112, 174–175, 212, 218

Savage, Gail 101, 194–195, 244
Schneider, Wendie 173, 188
Scott, Lina Mary ('Giddy') 200, 211–218
Scotland Yard 142–143, 152
Sebright, Arthur 200, 211–218
separation 16, 188, 232
 judicial 13, 19, 22, 23–24, 60, 62, 63, 100, 150, 154, 174, 182, 228, 246, 249–250, 252, 262

private arrangements 13, 58, 77–78, 80, 82, 183, 197
separation and maintenance orders 229–230, 244, 249
Shaw, George Bernard 83, 251
Simpson, Wallis 256
Slater's Detective Agency 148, 153, 155–156, 157
Smith, George Manley 39, 42, 43, 44
Smith, Martha Eustace 88
solicitors 32, 143, 157–170, 181, 185, 223, 229
spectators 24, 33, 69, 112, 136, 252
Spencer-Churchill, George Charles (see *Marlborough, 8th Duke*)
St James's Gazette 27, 35, 179
Star, The 27, 51, 55, 184
Stead, W. T. 10, 26, 28, 93, 98, 99, 103, 114, 115, 124, 237, 265
Stephenson, Sir Augustus Keppel 93, 140, 172–195
Stephenson, Guy 176
Stowell, William Scott, 1st Baron 62–63, 83, 199, 239, 257
suicide 81, 150, 202, 206, 219, 234–235, 237, 241
Swinburne, Henry 257

Tasker, Joseph Charles and Martha 61–62, 64, 66–67, 68, 76–84, 87, 263
Telegraph, The 25, 26, 41, 147–148, 149
Tempest, Marie 10, 225–226
Tennant, May 251
Thirkettle, George and Mary Jane 145–147
Thompson, Eleanor 235–244
Thompson, W.M. 112, 236
Times, The 24–25, 26, 35, 45–46, 55, 56, 58, 92, 114, 127, 169, 210, 211, 239, 253, 258

Tozer, Basil 76–77, 83–84
Trial of the Detectives 143, 144
Trocadero 49, 56
Trollope, Anthony 142, 144, 147
Trower, Henrietta (see also *Brinton*) 233–235, 244
Truth 26, 29, 75, 98, 110, 144, 148

Vansittart, Captain Robert Coleraine 190–191, 194
Vanity Fair 10, 26, 30, 91, 92, 109, 110, 210, 217
Vaughan, William and Johanna 64
venereal disease 62, 100, 101, 104, 145, 146, 252
Vernon-Harcourt, Lady Laura 206, 210
Victoria 15, 27, 110

Waller, Rosie 186, 187, 188
Waugh, Revd Benjamin 236–237
Webster, Sir Richard QC 190, 211–212
Weeks, Jeffrey 28, 85–86
Wells, H.G. 36, 113
Wertheimer, Isidor Emanuel 48–51, 53–58
Westminster Hall 23, 142, 239
Weston, Aldon Carter 49
Whom God Hath Joined 171, 250
Wilde, Oscar 28, 29, 43, 112
Willis, William QC 145, 146, 162–163
Winnifrith, Revd Alfred 11, 134, 139
Winnifrith, Revd Alfred Baker 11, 133–140
Winnifrith, Rosa (see *Hern*)
Wontner & Sons 49, 74, 150, 184, 185
Wood, Marmaduke 53–54, 56, 177
Worrall, Henry and Louisa 132–133